## A Letter from Steve Waugh

The Steve Waugh Foundation –
Australia has been set up to provide
opportunities for disadvantaged
children who have exceptional
sporting or artistic abilities but who,
for financial reasons, are unable to
exploit their talents.

I am passionate about helping those
less fortunate than myself and I
know that the foundation will be
grateful for the help received from
proceeds of this book.

SAFE SPEEDING. THERE'S NO SUCH THING.
M. A. NOBLE STAND
Helping business do more business.
Coca-Cola
Coca-Cola
GIO
GIO
Energy Australia
ACB
ACB
BLUES
RTA

# Steve Waugh

## Peter FitzSimons

HarperCollins*Publishers*

# Contents

'He's a walking contradiction, Partly truth and partly fiction'

Kris Kristofferson, *The Pilgrim: Chapter 33*

# Introduction

WHAT THEN WILL WE say of Steve Waugh when the days grow cold and we grow old? Likely, a lot. Most generations throw up a player whose fame endures well beyond his last crusade at the crease, and in this regard Waugh should find his place in the same pantheon of players past as Victor Trumper, Sir Donald Bradman, Keith Miller, Richie Benaud, Dennis Lillee and Allan Border.

In Waugh's case, however, it will not simply be his feats with the bat and ball that will drive the discussion. For at least part of Waugh's appeal is that he is such an enigmatic character. We know him, but don't know him. We like him, but don't know anyone like him. We think him quintessentially Australian, and yet somehow, despite our best efforts, find it difficult to quite pin down exactly what sort of a bloke he is.

For so many of the pointers are actually pointing in opposite directions. Throughout his career Steve Waugh clearly revered the history of the game, yet was always at the prow of forging new ways to play it. He scaled the greatest shining peaks of the game, but always credited the time he had spent in the dark valleys for enabling him to do it. He was born in the same bed, four minutes ahead of his twin, Mark, but as men they always seemed a world, an age and a good few metres apart. Steve was internationally famous and extraordinarily well travelled, but there was always a sense that he remained a Bankstown boy at heart. They whispered that Steve was a tight man with a dollar, yet his overwhelming generosity in helping lepers in India became the stuff of legend. On the field, in the face of the kings of the game, he was a hard man to beat all hard men and everything but polite, yet off the field among the punters, he was almost always affable. The accusation that most dogged him was that he only ever looked after himself and his average, and yet batsman after batsman attested that Waugh was the most nurturing partner and team-mate they'd ever had, constantly encouraging them on the pitch, as well as giving them his time and tips in the nets. He was known as the man for the big occasion, yet was out in the nineties more than any other Test cricketer.

And even though he was the cricketer who defined his era, Steve was always so very different from those around him. In an age where cricketers tended to know more and more about cricket, and less and less about everything else, Waugh was always notable for pushing beyond the closed confines of the cricket pitch, team bus and hotel to experience as much of the world outside as he could. While his years in the baggy green were ones where off-field scandals of all varieties were not uncommon, never did the tiniest whiff of such scandal attach itself to his name, whether it be betting, boozing or blondes. This was not only in the public domain, but also within the tight circumference of the real cricket cognoscenti. Waugh was a man unto himself, and as such in many ways unknowable to all but a very few.

So what then will we say of Steve Waugh when the days grow cold and we grow old? Maybe we'll give our own version of what Sir Winston Churchill once famously said of Russia, and say that he was 'a riddle wrapped in a mystery inside an enigma ...' But, by God, he could bat!

Yet just like the Man from Snowy River, we'll probably 'tell the story of his ride', and I reckon it will go something like this ...

# Rising
# Sons

# Chapter 1

'I know myself
growing up
at Panania in
the back yard
I always wanted
to think I could
play for Australia'
Steve Waugh

# 'Too energetic sometimes. A keen sense of humour. A sensitive type whose behaviour lapses are an over-reaction to embarrassment' STEVE WAUGH'S THIRD-GRADE REPORT CARD

ABOVE Possibly the last time the twins had a cuddle!
OPPOSITE PAGE Serious Steve off to Panania Public School, with Mark.
PREVIOUS PAGES: LEFT Steve, stolen dummy in hand, leaves twin brother Mark wailing in his wake; RIGHT TOP twin cowboys at home in Earlwood with dad Rodger and little brother Dean; RIGHT BOTTOM three Waugh brothers on the concrete driveway that became their makeshift cricket pitch.

WHEN STEVE WAUGH FIRST came to himself he found himself to be one of twins, first-born children of Rodger and Beverly Waugh, living in the suburb of Panania out in the vast expanse of Sydney's western suburbs. Both sets of grandparents lived not too far away, brother Mark lived cheek by jowl by towel, and all around was a stable, loving environment.

The Waugh parents had married when they were only eighteen years old and been blessed with the twins just a year later. All together they lived the simple life of Australian families of that era. Dad worked in a bank, Mum was a mum, and when it came to entertainment for the boys there was sport, sport and more sport. Most importantly of all in those early days, the sport was on tap, right there at home — and that tap was always coming a gusher.

For of all the many things Australia offered its people on its urban coastal rim, green grass was one, plentiful space another, long days of sunshine still one more, and all came together in shining splendour in that place so beloved of so many — the great Australian back yard. This was the field of dreams where game after game was played, imaginations ran wild as one glorious day blurred into the next, and who cared if you didn't have much money as this was so much more important.

From tottering toddlerdom onwards, Rodger would have his twins out there mucking around with balls of all descriptions, and of course when he went to work it wasn't long before the twins could throw the ball to each other and catch, and not long after that before they could swing tiny bats at it … Sometimes Beverly would look at them and, conscious of how coordinated and intent they seemed, find herself fantasising about how wonderful it would be if they could one day play for Australia in a sport.

Certainly their father continued to play with them when he could, but having a twin meant you had a built-in playmate at all times, and play is what they did. Played till they dropped. And loved it. Though both parents had been highly talented tennis players and both boys enjoyed playing tennis as well as soccer, golf and baseball, it was cricket that the boys loved most particularly. For it was in

playing cricket that they could emulate the deeds of the heroes who wore the revered baggy green cap of the Australian cricket team, the ones who were constantly fighting the good fight against the teams from other nations.

It was true that going to school proved to be quite an interruption to the true passion of the twins, but day after day, afternoon after afternoon, Steve and Mark would get back to the cricket, sometimes fighting over who got to be Australia and who got to be England in their imaginary Ashes series. And sometimes, just as their father would join in when he was free, so too would their uncle Dion Bourne, who was the stalwart captain of the Bankstown Cricket Club First XI and something of a local legend.

A popular song of the era was 'I scored a century in the back yard at Mum's', and each twin did that and more, many times over. Then, if one momentarily tired, the other could keep practising by hitting a cricket ball in a nylon stocking on a string, which their father had suspended from a tree.

While in the northern hemisphere at this time, young blokes by the name of Gatting, Gower and Atherton, for example, were obliged to curtail a lot of their physical activity in the long and dreary winter months, the twins had no such constraints and there were barely enough hours in the day, year-round, for them to get through all the sport they wanted. Somehow, though, they just managed and their skills across a broad range of sports — not to mention their physical prowess and confidence — expanded accordingly.

For, truth be told, they weren't just mucking around.

To a certain extent they took their cues off their young parents, both of whom continued to play tennis as well as squash. When their parents went at either game, there were no beg-pardons, no excuses, just a total focus on finding a way to win, albeit while still playing in the right spirit. And the boys were the same, but more so.

While in a game of tennis, their father might ease off just a little on their mother, because it was hardly chivalrous to use his superior strength to overpower her on the court, there was no such constraint when your opponent was your twin. And along with this,

## Hallowed Ground

And if the boys did go on to play for Australia, they'd be doing it right here, at the mighty Sydney Cricket Ground. It was 24 November 1973, and after they'd played for Panania in the morning, their coach had piled the boys into the back of his ute and taken them to see their first Sheffield Shield game, in this case the second day of a match between NSW and South Australia. Both Waugh boys were mesmerised. They sat in the cheapest, best seats of all, of course, which were on the grassy verge of The Hill, and soaked it all up. Out there on the field, there they all were, the stars of the day, parading before them!

South Australia was captained by the mighty Ian Chappell — all moustachioed machismo, atop a swagger that just wouldn't quit — and he was backed by the likes of the great spinners, Ashley Mallet and Terry Jenner. But however great they were, they were no match for the men of NSW, who were led by one of Australia's heroes of the day, Doug Walters, ably supported by such SCG favourites as Rick McCosker and the rotund fast bowler, Gary Gilmour.

Sitting there, sunning himself to the sizzle, Steve Waugh was particularly taken with the sheer *greenness* of it all, the rolling green of the Hill they were sitting on, cascading down onto the impossible green of the field, and all of it against the backdrop green of the roofs of the grandstands.

Just two years later, the two lads were back again for an actual Test match, this time in the company of

LEFT Practising for the future, Steve (left) and Mark don their whites and a baggy green. PREVIOUS PAGES David Moore's iconic photograph of the SCG Hill, 1963.

the soundtrack to a large chunk of their lives together was people constantly comparing them and just about keeping a scorecard as to who was doing better at a variety of activities. If that was the way it was, then so be it.

The brothers played in their first real cricket game when they were seven years old, turning out for the Panania–East Hills under-tens. Mark was out for a golden duck, while the first ball that Steve faced was sent to the boundary for four. And then he was out next ball. Never mind. Both boys went on to score centuries soon enough in their junior years, and as a matter of fact were good enough that by the time they were nine or ten years old their first coach, one Alan Dougherty, was telling everyone who'd listen — and even many of those who wouldn't — that both Waugh boys would go on to play for Australia.

*Play for Australia …*

Since time immemorial, that phrase has had a particular resonance for young Australian males of a sporting bent, and in the dreamtime of the young Waugh boys' lives, the thought of one day pulling on the baggy green cap could put a bolt right through them.

Another who believed that the boys just might be able to go all the way was Rodger Waugh, though he was only prepared to take that belief so far. One friend from London once called him on it, saying that if really did think his boys were as good as he said they were, he should put some money on it with Ladbrokes of London, where he would be sure to get odds of around 10 000 to one. Rodger declined …

FROM THEIR BEGINNINGS IN the game, there really were signs that both of the Waugh twins were more than a cut above the rest, not to mention possessing a blistering array of cover-drives, square cuts, pulls and hook shots that the other kids didn't have either.

An example was when both brothers were selected for their school to play in the New South Wales Primary Schools cricket carnival — and on the back of their performances the team made the 1977 final, held up in Lismore. Mark went into bat first, but was

Hallowed Ground
[ *continued* ]

their father Rodger, who had taken them to see a truly superb Australian team up against a West Indies side led by Clive Lloyd. It was the summer of '75/76, and Clive Lloyd didn't look too happy. And why would he be happy? The imperious Greg Chappell was completely slaying the Windies, going on to make 182 not out on the day, and sending the visitors chasing leather all over the ground. And, always in this series, when they finally got him out, then the Windies would have the charms of Dennis Lillee and Jeff Thomson to look forward to.

Watching closely, Steve Waugh loved it all, and would later write of that all but perfect day: 'The story goes that when the young Don Bradman was taken to the fifth Ashes Test of 1920–21 at the SCG by his father to see Charlie Macartney make 170 as Australia completed a unique 5–0 clean sweep of the series, he said flatly on the way home that he would not rest until he, too, played at the ground. I cannot say I had the same determination after that Windies Test. But I knew that it would be fantastic to be out there, and I was in awe of the great players — how fast were the Windies pacemen, Andy Roberts and Michael Holding, yet Greg Chappell seemed to handle them with ease.'

The lads went home, well content.

ABOVE Cricket wasn't the twins' only passion, or specialty. Both boys were accomplished at many sports, including soccer. Childhood team-mate Robbie Slater, who went on to represent Australia as a Socceroo, once thought he'd never be as good at soccer as Steve.

BELOW The Bankstown Under-12 representative soccer team, one of many childhood sporting teams to feature both Steve (far right, second row) and Mark Waugh (first row, third from left).

OPPOSITE The boys on a tennis trip to Taree with Rodger.

almost immediately felled by a bouncer and was escorted from the field, his face a red mess. Their team-mate Gavin Robertson was watching closely as the twins crossed at the gate, wondering just how Steve would react to seeing his brother hurt like that. Would he be intimidated, as was reasonable to expect under the circumstances?

Not a bit of it. After blocking the first ball Steve started swinging, and didn't stop swinging for some time, sending the persecutors of his brother to play 'fetch' in all parts of the ground. The Waugh boys' team won the carnival, and Robertson would later recount, 'Though he was only a boy, this was a man's innings, a display of determination and responsibility. It showed the qualities of a natural leader.'

Others felt the same, and both Waughs continued to be selected for their age team as they moved up through the ranks, and the captaincy tended to alternate between the two. As well, they were selected in representative teams in other sports, and by the age of eleven both brothers had represented NSW in cricket, soccer and tennis.

In soccer and tennis, as with cricket, the competition between Mark and Steve was keen, and though their two younger brothers, Dean and Danny, were not yet old enough to join in and be competitive, that time would come …

In the meantime, the twins were now advanced enough for there to be plenty of serious cricket competition to get involved in. When they were fourteen years old, they were playing for the Panania lads in the morning and in the lower ranks of grade cricket with nearby Bankstown in the afternoon. And yet despite the fact that it was Steve who had marginally the better of Mark in results — in one summer Steve had knocked out 1500 runs, including four unbeaten centuries out of five in total — it was Mark who was favoured by selectors when the state under-fifteen side was read aloud, while Steve was left out. Now Rodger Waugh was not a man for taking a backward step on such matters, and he got into contact with the coach and selector to see why his boy had been left out. The answer was, and Rodger Waugh would never forget it, 'He scores his runs too quickly.'

'My first emotion upon hearing my selection was panic ... I was also excited and thrilled at the same time, but in reality I was hoping rather than expecting to do well' STEVE WAUGH

See, the reckoning was that anyone who could reel off runs as quickly as the young Waugh boy wasn't quite playing the game as it was *meant* to be played, and though he might go all right at a low level, there was no way known he wouldn't be found out at the higher, representative level. Steve had been exposed to a similar attitude a couple of years earlier at an intense training camp at Sydney's exclusive Cranbrook School for the best and brightest young cricketers of the day, under the tutelage of the great South African batsman Barry Richards. Young Stephen was belting the ball to all parts of the park and terrorising the bowlers to the point that Richards hauled him out of the nets and told him straight: 'Get out of here! If you are going to play like that, you might as well not play!'

Never mind. Steve would get over his omission from the NSW under-fifteen side, and forget it ever happened — in about twenty-five years or so.

At the very least, it wasn't as if cricket was Steve's only avenue of sporting advancement, as he continued to star all across the sporting spectrum, most particularly at soccer, where he was among the first picked in all the representative sides. Steve was so good, as a matter of fact, that one of his team-mates who also came from the Bankstown area — a bloke by the name of Robbie Slater — came to the sad conclusion that despite having his own lofty ambitions to play for Australia, he would never be as good at soccer as that bloke Steve Waugh was.

And he wasn't the only one who thought Steve was unbelievably good. The great Socceroo and commentator Johnny Warren would write in *The Sydney Morning Herald* in 1983: 'I have not seen a better goal this year than the one scored by East Hills High School's Stephen Waugh in the Commonwealth Bank Cup at Mt Druitt Town Soccer Centre last Wednesday evening. It was a goal of which the legendary Franz Beckenbauer would have been proud.'

If Steve had wanted to pursue soccer, it was all laid out there before him — and it wasn't long before the powerhouse Sydney soccer club of Croatia made him a firm professional offer to join them. As it turned out though, it was Robbie Slater who would go on

OPPOSITE Shoeless Steve
celebrates Australia's win
against England in the 1987
World Cup, held in Calcutta,
India, with a beer and ... can
it be? ... a grin!

to a great soccer career, turning out forty-four times for the Socceroos and playing for many years in the European leagues, while Steve's sporting career returned, at the expense of all else, to his original great passion. Cricket.

To be sure, not everyone in the Waughs' neck of the woods was equally into cricket, and among those not so moved was one Lynette Dougherty, who attended the school across the road, East Hills Girls High.

For this attractive, quiet brunette, cricket had always been this unending summer drone coming out of the television at her grandfather's house, and she never really focused on it much. She hadn't even *heard* of the Waugh brothers, who were such a big noise at East Hills Boys, but on the last day of school — 'Muck-up Day' it was known as — she came face to face with this bloke Stephen Waugh, who all but on the spot asked her out to the school formal.

Look, it wasn't as if she did cartwheels or anything, and as a matter of fact she actually seemed a little underwhelmed, but the main thing was she said yes — *she said yes!* — and the two took it from there. (Whatever else, Lynette thought him very attractive. She was most particularly taken with the way he parted his mullet haircut right down the middle, which marked him as a very fashionable kind of bloke.)

Not that Stephen's career prospects were all that good, mind, at least not by conventional measure.

Over lunch one day at Lynette's parents' house not long afterwards, Stephen was asked by Lynette's cousin what he intended to do to make a quid, now that school was over.

'I want to play cricket for Australia,' he announced.

Of course you do, Stephen. We all do. But what do you *really* want to do?

Play cricket for Australia. No joke.

It was at this point that most of the peas on most of the plates seemed to assume an extraordinary fascination for most of the members of Lynette's family, because it seemed a staggering ambition to state out loud for one who was, after all, eighteen years old and no

# Beginner's Nerves

December 1985. This was the big one. This was his debut on the national stage.

This was his big chance to show that he had what it took to make it. For there was no doubt about it — the young bloke had just been given a pretty big gig. As a television reporter for Channel 10, his job was to interview another kid of much the same age who was about to make his own debut, a bloke by the name of ... what was his name again? ... Steve Waugh. Waugh would shortly be wearing the baggy green cap of Australia, in the famed Boxing Day Test at the MCG, and, as it turned out, Waugh's attitude was remarkably similar to his own.

For this was indeed the big one for Steve Waugh. This too was his debut. This was his big chance to show that he had what it took to make it in the big-time. And if a part of that big-time was doing a one-on-one television interview for the first time, for the evening news, then so be it, even though he was nervous. Almost as nervous as the cub reporter, as it turned out.

One way or another though the two debutants, Steve Waugh and the cub reporter, got through it. Both felt they had done well enough, that they were kind of launched, and they were right. Steve Waugh went on to achieve great fame and acclaim in his field. And so did Eddie McGuire ...

'I was scared of the media, very shy and wet behind the ears. Sport was my whole life. I didn't know anything else existed except for sport. I wouldn't say I was very well-rounded ... much different than people these days who are better trained and better equipped to handle pressure situations' STEVE WAUGH, ON HIS TEST DEBUT FOR AUSTRALIA

longer just some kid fantasising. But Lynette didn't see it like that. Her boyfriend, she realised, wasn't like other boyfriends. He had real ambitions. *Different* ambitions. And he had confidence enough to say them out loud.

In the meantime, of course, Steve would have to keep busy doing other things and when — on the basis of getting a solid mark of 300 out of 500 for his Higher School Certificate — he was accepted into Milperra Teachers College, he grabbed the opportunity.

Somehow, though, that opportunity didn't quite grab him.

The other students didn't seem like his sort of people. The lecturers droned on like half-dead blowflies coming to the end of a marathon journey from one cowpat to another. The courses were dull and extremely arty-farty. The whole place seemed drab and uninspiring. So just like that, he upped and left.

Fair dinkum, it was the worst two hours he'd ever spent in a place.

Mark, meantime, if not quite marking time was equally ambivalent about a job outside of cricket, doing just enough to keep body and soul together and make some money working in some sports goods stores, but continuing to focus most of his energies on cricket.

WHAT NOW FOR STEVE, then?

Exactly. What else was he qualified to do, apart from swinging a bat? Pretty much only swinging a pick. So that's what Steve did, on the road gang with the Bankstown Council, alternating it with a few weeks on the dole and some time spent being an indoor cricket umpire. He didn't like any of them. If the blokes on the road gang had been going to a fancy-dress party trying to look like bludgers, then in Steve's view they would have passed muster. The dole was just too damn dull, and didn't seem right. And being an indoor cricket umpire, well, it was just ridiculous how much some blokes carried on when a decision didn't go their way. Just *ridiculous*.

Fortunately, though, cricket really did save him, and really did take him away from all that. For after Steve showed stunning early

season form with the Bankstown Cricket Club, one fine morning in early December 1984, the morning radio blared the news that one *S. Waugh* had been picked to make his first-class debut for NSW against Queensland in Brisbane. In the many phone calls of congratulations that the Waugh family received, one was particularly noted. It came from Alan Dougherty, Steve and Mark's first coach, the bloke who'd been telling everyone for years that they would go on to play for Australia.

'I'm looking pretty good,' he told Steve's mother, Bev. 'People are not laughing at me now.'

Though Steve was of course thrilled at his selection, it was a measure of the man that he gave his first NSW cap to his best friend through high school, Richard Lane, saying he wanted him to have it.

Sure, Lane's mother made Richard march straight over to the Waughs' house to give it back, but it was such a generous gesture that Lane never forgot it.

Steve's performance in the drawn game was middling only, only making 31 runs in his one time at bat, but not picking up a wicket for his 23 overs. The most important thing was that the selectors and his team-mates seemed to like his attitude and they decided to stick with him, which was as well.

Not long afterwards, no less than the great Bill 'Tiger' O'Reilly was immediately impressed upon getting his first good look at Steve one day out at the Sydney Cricket Ground.

'That young fellow Waugh is going to be as good as Stan McCabe one day,' he opined in his extremely influential column in *The Sydney Morning Herald*. From Tiger, who had once said that if he was reincarnated he would like to be a 'batsman like McCabe', this was high praise indeed, and surely something that the Australian selectors took note of. Tiger was always one to pick talent early and young talent was precisely what was most needed in the Australian team at that time. For in the previous year, three greats of the game in Dennis Lillee, Rod Marsh and Greg Chappell had retired, and it was time to rebuild the Australian side around whatever steel they could find. Too, the vacancies in the Test side got all the greater in late 1985,

when several senior Australian players (including Kim Hughes, Terry Alderman, Graham Yallop, Rodney Hogg, Trevor Hohns and Carl Rackemann), departed on a very lucrative rebel tour of South Africa, and were promptly suspended from the national team for their trouble.

With that in mind, and practically on a whim, the selectors picked young Stephen Waugh — who had only played nine Sheffield Shield games at that point, though one was a NSW victory in the Shield final — to make his debut for Australia at the Melbourne Cricket Ground on Boxing Day 1985, for the second Test against the visiting Indian side. At the MCG! For selectors intent on rebuilding the national side, Waugh offered great batting potential, a handy bowling ability and, besides, in a cricket cupboard that was looking extremely bare, they couldn't think of, or find, anyone else.

OPPOSITE **Maybe he can shine the ball on his three-day growth ... In England, July 1989.** BELOW **Brothers Dean, Danny, Steve and Mark Waugh show that cricket really is in their genes.**

# Into the Dreamtime

## Chapter 2

'One of the most uncool people in the world' Greg Matthews on his new Australian team-mate

WAS IT A DREAM? Just a short time before, Stephen Waugh had been anonymously working for Bankstown Council on a road gang, a nameless bloke with a shovel, and yet here he was, walking out on to the hallowed turf of the MCG bedecked in his baggy green cap as one of the focal points of 65 000 roaring fans, making ready to play for Australia …

It was nominally great, but actually extremely difficult. The very nervous Waugh — feeling a little like 'an impostor' who was about to be sprung and exposed — was not at all sure if he was ready for this. Still, as he walked out onto a ground that suddenly felt about as big as the Nullarbor, there was some solace in knowing that among the crowd somewhere as he took strike was Lynette, who had driven down from Sydney to be there with him for the duration. And his dad, Rodger, was on his way. But that was about it in terms of familiarity and friendliness.

As a matter of fact, he'd only briefly met the night before the Australian opener he was walking out there to join, Geoff Marsh, and the 'welcome' from the rest of the team had been perfunctory at best — with the exception of the two NSW blokes, Dave Gilbert and Greg Matthews. As Waugh later described his team-mates: 'They were too worried about saving their own necks. It was almost as if they were thinking, 'I hope that guy fails, so I can keep my position for a bit longer.'

But now it really was time for Steve to play for his neck.

The first run he scored would stay with him ever afterwards. With such legends of the game as Sunil Gavaskar, Dilip Vengsarkar, Mohinder Amarnath, Ravi Shastri and Syed Kirmani crowding his bat, and the equally legendary Kapil Dev charging in to bowl at him, Waugh took a deep breath and made a well-guided nudge through the covers, and he was away. You bloody bewdy. Whatever else happened in his life, in the history of the world *even*, this could never be taken off him. He'd scored a Test run!

Now for a Test ton … a century on debut, which was always the follow-up dream of a young batsman wearing the baggy green for the first time.

But it was not to be. Out for 13, Steve had at least got into double figures, which was something, though he was bitterly disappointed to be out for 5 in the second innings, even if he picked up 2/36 from his tight medium-pace bowling. The batting was the thing though, and while Waugh was feeling out of his depth, as were many of the others in the team, there was one among them who clearly knew exactly what he was doing. Allan Robert Border.

As Waugh watched from the players' balcony in awe, Border put together 163 runs of Australia's total of 308 in the second innings, in extremely difficult conditions. Every fibre of the captain's being seemed focused on every ball, his aura one of complete defiance, his approach so totally professional that as Waugh watched him from close up back in the dressing room on breaks, it was clear that Border's head was clear of every other thing bar staying in and racking up the runs. This was *Test* cricket, sonny Jim, and it was different. It was in such moments that Waugh knew that he had much to learn about the game at this level, and that Border — who had debuted for Australia six years earlier on the same ground — was the man to learn it from.

Despite Border's magnificent effort though, things really were grim. The draw against the Indians in Melbourne meant that Australia had now gone for *fourteen* Tests without putting together a

OPPOSITE Mighty Merv Hughes shows the form that made him a fan favourite, here at the MCG.
PREVIOUS PAGES, LEFT Bowler Dave Gilbert is congratulated by Greg Matthews and Steve Waugh (at right) following his dismissal of Srikkanth during the Australia v India Boxing Day Test in 1985; RIGHT In a shot that looks like it has been dredged out of a box of memorabilia, Steve Waugh is here at full tilt on 15 January 1987.

'There are a lot of players you look up to and take bits and pieces from, and AB was one of those. The thing I took mostly from AB was concentration' STEVE WAUGH

ABOVE **The ever-defiant Allan Border in 1991.**

victory, and their lack of true firepower with bat and ball was now so apparent that it really seemed as if the men of the baggy green were in danger of becoming the jokes of international cricket.

Somehow, and probably only just, Stephen Waugh retained his position in the team for the next Test, in Sydney, perhaps on the grounds that the bottom of the barrel of Test contenders had already been reached, and for the selectors to have dropped him after just one Test would have been an admission that the Australian players weren't the only ones who didn't know what they were doing ...

But *did* they know what they were doing in picking this young fellow Waugh? For at the SCG in the third Test, which was another rather dull draw, Waugh only made eight runs in the first innings, and a duck in the second, giving him a Test batting average after four innings of — *dot three, carry one, subtract two* — 6.5.

Times were tough and getting tougher, and it would ever after be part of the make-up of Steve Waugh that he arrived in the Australian team at a time when it was near to its lowest ebb, seemingly without even the personnel to put things right. When the Australian team went on a tour of New Zealand a short time afterwards, Allan Border had played more Test matches than the rest of the other thirteen players in the squad put together.

Under such circumstances, it continued to be Border himself, his tone and outlook, that the younger ones clung to in the rushing floodwaters of midnight — the Rock that didn't move. What they saw was a man who clearly wanted to win so badly he could taste it, and projected that sense in his every waking minute.

Border felt very keenly the burden upon him to whip his young charges into shape, to make them understand the difference between being *selected* to play a Test and actually playing TEST cricket — where ruthless professionalism was the currency and no quarter was asked for or given. And because of that, and Australia's continued failing to get a win up — the first two Tests against New Zealand were also drawn — the captain's mood in Waugh's early days was akin to that of bear with a sore head, *and* a toothache.

And it was a toothache that was about to get a whole lot worse.

The '86/87 Ashes series in Australia was notable for, among other things, a lot of sledging between the two teams. None engaged in it with more gusto than everyone's favourite fast bowler of the era, Merv Hughes.

Oft cited is the moment when he told a struggling English batsman: 'I'll bowl you a f—ing piano, ya Pommie pooftah. Let's see if you can play that.'

The Englishman's reply to this is sadly not recorded, but fortunately it has been documented what happened when, in a Test in this series, Hughes continually beat the bat of the English batsman Robyn Smith by a bee's whisker.

Finally, Hughes snarled: 'Smith, you can't f—ing well bat to save your life!'

On the next ball, Smith smashed Hughes to the boundary, wandered down the pitch and said to Hughes: 'Make a good pair, don't we? I can't f—ing bat, and you can't f—ing bowl!'

For now came the absolute stone motherless rock bottom of the fortunes of Australian cricket team in the modern age.

At the third Test in Auckland, Australia suffered a humiliating defeat after being bowled out for just 102 in the second innings. Steve's own contribution had been 1 and 0, being out twice after facing a total of only seven balls. The twenty-year-old Bankstown boy sat in the dressing room with all the rest, feeling lower than a snake's bellybutton, and no one daring to meet Border's eye. At this point Waugh wasn't sure if his own flaky game was good enough for Test cricket, and he wasn't the only one.

The disgusted Border — who bled for every run and only ever lost his wicket at the point of a gun — was barely sure *any* of them were good enough.

'I've said everything I can to that bunch,' he said. 'If they don't know how I feel, they never will. The guys should be hurting really bad because Test careers are on the line. You can stick with blokes for so long. I'm basically leaving it to the players. They are going to show whether they really want to play for Australia and whether they really want to play under me. It's reached the point where if we continue to lose, you've got to let someone else come in and see if they can do something different ... The fellas are not responding to me. The enjoyment has gone out of it ...'

And he certainly got that right. The one good innings that Waugh had had on tour, 74 during the second Test in Christchurch, together with the few wickets he had picked up, ensured that he remained in the side, but it was in all likelihood a close-run thing. To this point the Australian public hadn't really warmed to Waugh, noting only that he didn't seem to smile that often, though, to be fair, he hadn't really had a whole lot to smile about ...

At least not on the field. Off the field though, well away from the unending public gaze, the wonderful thing was that his relationship with Lynette Dougherty had continued to expand and deepen over the previous three years, to the point where she now even professed to *enjoy* watching cricket, most particularly if Stephen was at bat. She, and they, had come a long way.

# Courage Under Fire

The other key thing that emerged from Steve Waugh's first tour of India was a crash course in toughness. In the famous first Test at Chidambram Stadium, Madras, the temperature was simmering around the 40-degree Celsius mark, the humidity horrifying, with the barometer perpetually hovering between Oppressive and Depressive.

On the second day, Steve Waugh's team-mate Dean Jones went out to bat, despite suffering from a terrible combination of dysentery and vomiting and feeling like he was going to faint. Seeing him wobble to the wicket, the 30 000 chanting Indians seemed to chant even louder. In an extraordinary effort of will, though — and overcoming terrible leg and stomach cramps along the way — Jones somehow put together a century. And *still* kept going. In the tea break it was Steve Waugh who helped him change his clothes, removing the drenched and disgusting whites, and assisting the Victorian with putting on something fresher. For all that, by the time this singularly tough batsman was on 120 runs, with Australia still struggling to get a dominant total, Jones thought he was going to collapse from heat stroke — and he very well might have. He was already so crook he had been dry-retching at the end of every over, and the Indians had allowed him to have a runner. But by the time he got to an extraordinary 150 runs, he just couldn't go on.

'Mate,' the Victorian croaked to his batting partner and captain, Allan

And just as Steve Waugh the cricketer was growing, so too was Steve Waugh the man. Nowhere more so than when the Australian team toured India in September of 1986 for an eight-week tour. Broadly, there were two ways to deal with a place like India. One was to retreat from it, to seal yourself in as tight a cocoon as possible, moving along a strict axis between the hotel room, the bus and the cricket ground. And the other was to embrace it, get out amongst this entirely different culture and learn from it.

Steve Waugh, more than any other Australian cricketer before or since, chose the latter option. For it was his great friend, the NSW and Australian fast bowler Mike Whitney, who had encouraged him from their first days in the NSW team together to get out there amongst it and *enjoy* the tours and the countries they were going to for more than the cricket alone. Waugh, always fascinated by Whitney's tales of his backpacking adventures to different parts of the world, as well as his cricket tour stories, took him at his word. From a bloke who had few general interests outside the parameters of the cricket pitch on one side and Lynette on the other, broader interests, and involvement, began to grow.

To be sure, India was not easily definable, and there were many things that were totally shocking. One time Steve was in a Bombay restaurant and looked up to see a bloke carrying around a dead baby as he begged for money. Another time he pulled open the curtains of his hotel window and was confronted by the vision scarifying of a beggar cursed with as Waugh later described it, 'elephantiasis or something, he had skin disease and his legs were just massive'.

One thing was for sure, he was a long way from Bankstown. But there was just something about India that kind of got into your blood. Something of a love affair between Steve Waugh and India had just begun. And a very absorbing love affair it would prove to be …

AS TO WAUGH'S OWN performances on that tour, they were modest at best, with a high score of only 39 not out in the Tests, and the best bowling figures of 1/29. Despite that, though, Allan Border for one

felt that he'd seen enough in the youngster to tell him he was made of the right stuff, and he was one voice that spoke up in favour of staying with him in the hope that he would really develop. By now, while by no means a Test 'star,' Steve was attracting so much media and public attention that among NSW team-mates Mark Waugh had become known as 'Afghanistan', as in, 'the forgotten Waugh'. Laugh? *Laugh?* Mark thought he'd never start.

(Never mind, this would prove to be just one of perhaps 400 variations of the play on words provided by war/Waugh. WAUGH DECLARES! AUSTRALIA GOES TO WAUGH! TOTAL WAUGH! etc, etc … Tire? *Tire?* The sub-editors never would.)

The weird thing was that even though Mark was now an established member of the NSW Sheffield Shield side, and had been since 1985, reeling off century after century, as well as beginning to shine in English county cricket in the off-season — which is to say he'd already shown a lot more than Stephen ever had before being given his chance — the Australian selectors didn't give *him* a look-in.

## Courage Under Fire
[ *continued* ]

Border, 'I'm going to have to go off, I just can't go on, I'm too crook.'

You could have hit Border's eyes with a sledgehammer right then, and the hammer would have cracked.

'Sure, *mate*,' Border said in reply, his voice dripping with a particularly acidic kind of sarcasm. 'And when you go back in, can you ask them to send a *Queenslander* back, because that's who we need out here.'

Jones stayed, and went on to score 210 runs, which would prove to be his highest Test score. He savoured it while lying in hospital on a saline drip — and it would take him well over six months to fully recover. For Steve Waugh, as for all Australian cricketers of that generation, it would ever after stand as an object lesson of what could be achieved with enough concentration and application, whatever the conditions.

ABOVE Mike Whitney, who was to prove a stalwart support for Steve Waugh when he first entered the national side.
LEFT Waugh up in lights during an August 1989 game.
OVERLEAF Steve's then fiancée (now his wife) Lynette Dougherty watches Steve and Mark bat together for the first time in a Test, 9 April 1991.

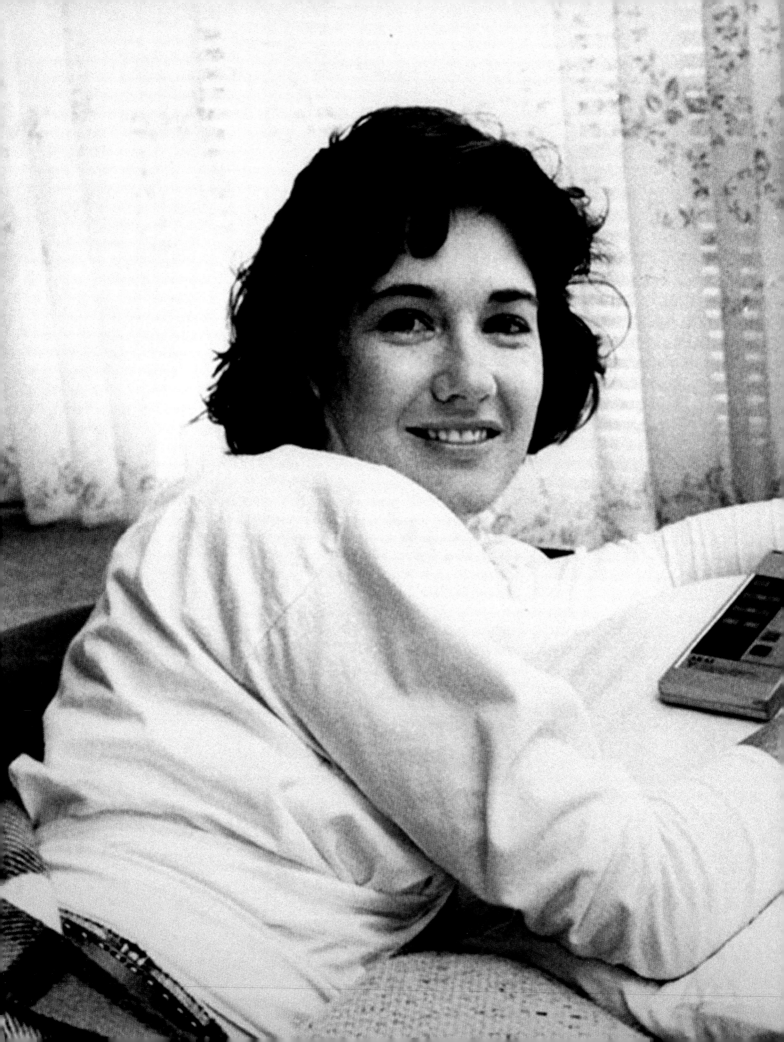

# Enter the Iceman

# Chapter 3

'You'll want a serious face, won't you? They always want the serious face'

Steve Waugh when posing for a *Bulletin* magazine cover

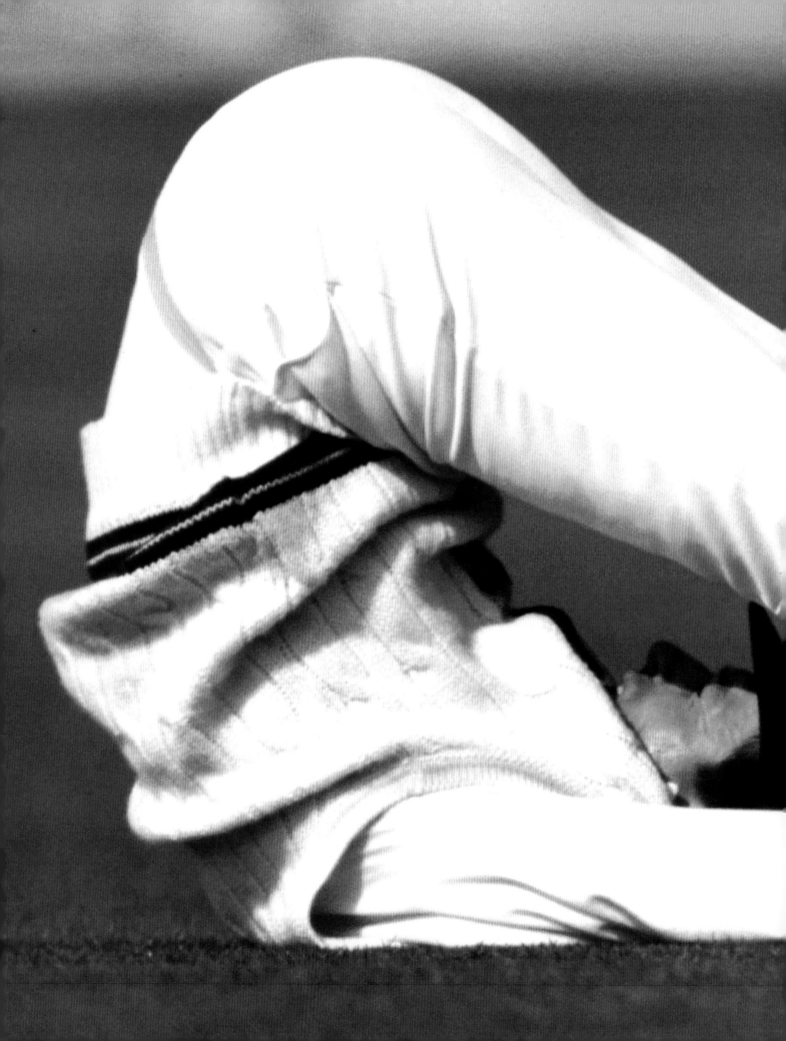

# 'I'm tired of being a good bloke and losing. I'd sooner be a prick and win' ALLAN BORDER, WHEN AUSTRALIAN CRICKET WAS AT ITS LOWEST EBB IN THE MID-1980s

WHILE STEVE WAUGH HAD enjoyed his Test cricket to this point, sort of, he remained frustrated by the team's inability to come up with a win, and his own inability to make the difference to allow them to do it.

And there was never going to be a better time to change it. For in the summer of '86/87 the English side, led by that beer keg on legs, Mike Gatting, arrived to play the Ashes series and Steve Waugh was able to experience the ancient enemy close up ... with yet more mixed results. Despite opening his account with a duck at the Gabba, Steve had his moments with scores of 71 in Perth and 79 in Adelaide, and yet he *still* couldn't arrest yet one more Australian slide to defeat against an English side that by the time of their victory in the fourth Test in MCG — humiliating Australia in under three days — had secured an unbeatable 2–0 lead to again take the Ashes. Finally, though, after one year of Steve playing Test matches, the best of all possible things happened. Australia won a Test! Against *England*!

Waugh contributed too, making 73 runs in Australia's second innings and taking a wicket as well. Having gone through the twelve Tests of his career without a victory, Waugh now felt terrific, as did most of the other Australian players. The euphoria in the dressing room was palpable. An hour after the game though, a few of the young ones were still in the rooms having a drink when Allan Border came up to them.

'Why are you two blokes so bloody happy?' the man sometimes known as Captain Grumpy said to Dean Jones and the fast bowler Bruce Reid.

'Allan,' Dean Jones replied, 'this was my ninth Test match and up till now I hadn't been on the winning side. This was my first win.'

'Yeah, but we've lost the Ashes,' Border growled. 'Don't you know what that means?'

That was Border all right. Rounding up a stray Test match was fine, but that was not what the game was about. Border wanted nothing less than for Australia to be the best team in the world and he only wanted guys around him who wanted that too.

At least, under Border, the fortunes of the Australian team were

# 'Steve Waugh carried the Australian side during the 1987 World Cup. The resurgence of the team as a one-day side dates back to him' GREG MATTHEWS

soon to rise when, in the 1987 World Cup — held in India — the previously unfancied Australian side was able to go very well indeed. Though they had arrived on the subcontinent so derided by the experts that they were considered 20/1 long shots and the famed Pakistani batsman Zaheer Abbass had opined that the local schoolboys would be a good chance of beating Australia, Border's blokes showed they were actually made of sterner stuff — and none more so than Steve Waugh. Throughout the tournament, when the time came for tight bowling, Waugh became the 'go-to man'. Though Steve Waugh's deliveries were neither fast, nor particularly dynamic, they were tight and different — as over the years he had developed such things as a devastating slower ball which emerged from the back of his hand and to the untutored eye looked like a wrong'un, 'cept it *wasn't*. Whatever it was, Allan Border had noticed that the tighter the game became, so too did Steve's bowling. So it was that time and again the skipper would throw the ball to the young'un to have him bowl the final, crucial overs, and Waugh *always delivered*.

Against India, for example, the ball came to Waugh to send down the final six balls with the entire game in the balance. In front of their own cricket-crazy crowd, the Indians, with one wicket in hand, needed just six runs for victory, but with his fifth ball of the over, Waugh nailed tail-ender Maninder Singh, and Australia won the game by a single run. In the semi-final against Pakistan, Waugh contributed most notably with the bat, blasting an extraordinary 18 runs from the last over. Australia won by … 18 runs. Against England in the final, in front of 80 000 spectators at Eden Gardens in Kolkata, it was Waugh again who seemed to be everywhere, most notably hurling in a splendid throw to run out Bill Athey, and in the 47th over famously sending Allan Lamb's off stump cartwheeling end over end. Then, given the penultimate over to bowl, with England needing 19 runs off the last two overs, Waugh conceded only *two* runs, taking the wicket of De Freitas as well, and the game was effectively over. Craig McDermott did the honours in the next over and Australia — in what would always be considered a major turning point for a team that had been doing it tough — had won the 1987 World Cup!

It had been a good tournament for Waugh, as he'd scored 167

runs at an average of 55.66, and taken no fewer than 11 wickets at a very economical strike rate of 4.53 runs an over. Most importantly, he'd shown he was the Minister for Tight Spots.

On the strength of such feats, the early foundation stones for his later legend were laid. Now, for some serious brickwork …

LOOK NOW, FOR EXAMPLE. Here comes *Da Man*, Viv Richards, not only the West Indies captain, not only the finest batsman of his generation, but also around the cricketing world a byword for sheer *class*. There is such an aura about him now, as he makes his way to the Gabba pitch in his 100th Test, in a curious combination of swagger and glide, that you just can't take your eyes off him. The hottest batsman in the world, and yet somehow cooler than Bob Marley. Some might say he appears to own any cricket ground he sets foot upon.

But Steve Waugh is not of their number. As a matter of fact, he doesn't give a bugger for any of that kind of talk. When Border tosses him the ball, to have a go at the Master, Waugh has a clear choice. He can either meekly submit to the Richards aura, and bowl in a tight, defensive fashion, or he can *have a go*, and serve up some notice that things are going to change around here. And there, you see how he takes another step back in his run-up?

A short stuttering run later and Waugh has sent a *bouncer* whistling past Richards's nose. The insolence of it! The sheer gall! Around the ground there is a sudden stunned shiver at what has just occurred, followed by thunderous cheers when Waugh does it twice more in succession!

*Attaboy, Steve! At him! Give it to him!*

Waugh is not a fast enough bowler for the bouncers to actually be dangerous to the great man, but that is not the point. The point is that Waugh is serving notice that he has had a gutful of falling back to the Windies' attack, and maybe their captain can have a small whiff of the grape for a change, and see how *he* likes it.

Despite himself, Richards was impressed, as he later confided to Allan Border. Of course, the next time Waugh was at the crease he

ABOVE 'Da Man', Viv Richards. OPPOSITE Dean Jones and Allan Border celebrate the Australian team's victory in the 1987 World Cup.

'If you concentrate at the right times — just when the bowler's about to bowl the ball — and you stop concentrating after you've played it, it's amazing how much easier it gets throughout the day' STEVE WAUGH

received it in kind from the West Indies pacemen — with Richards telling the massive Curtly Ambrose, 'He thinks he's tough, this one, thinks he can bowl a bouncer. Let's see how he *takes* it.' The short answer was not too badly, as the Bankstown boy responded to that kind of challenge and went on to score 90 runs — the closest he'd got to a Test century to this point.

For all that, the Windies' fearsome bouncing barrage from a seeming endless array of fast bowlers didn't fall away, and it seemed extraordinary that they had so many of them who were so very, *very* fast. Where did they all come from? How was it that the Windies were suddenly awash with guys who had lightning and thunder coming out of their arms? Where did they all come from?

Therein lay something of a story with a certain symmetry for Steve Waugh. For, back in legendary summer of '75/76 when Steve and Mark had visited the SCG for the first time and Dennis Lillee and Jeff Thomson were at their absolute height, it wasn't only the Waugh boys who were impressed.

The West Indies' captain, Clive Lloyd, too, had come to the conclusion in that series that it was fast bowlers who held the key to Test domination. After all, why go fly-fishing, with all the skill and patience that that required, *à la* spin bowling, if you could just throw in a couple of sticks of dynamite with some fast bowlers and quickly bring lots of dead fish to the surface?

Something like that, anyway …

The point was that from that summer on, it was Clive Lloyd who pushed West Indian cricket to encourage, nurture and select fast bowlers ahead of everyone else, and the results of that policy were right in Waugh's face right now. And whistling past his chin.

And they weren't mucking around, either. The legendary Windies fast bowler Malcolm Marshall had on a previous tour snarled at the pugnacious David Boon, 'I know this is your first Test match, but are you going to get out or do I have to come around the wicket and kill you?' And clearly none of the West Indies bowlers had lost any ferocity since.

OPPOSITE The long and the short of it: the hardly diminutive Steve Waugh in the shadow of West Indian fast bowler Curtly Ambrose, in Trinidad, 21 April 1995.

## 100 Years On

LEFT In a delicate move that could be mistaken for a pirouette, Steve gives it all he's got during a one-day match with South Africa in Melbourne, 9 December 1993. ABOVE A selection of cartoons from throughout Steve Waugh's career.

# The Ecstasy and the Agony

## Chapter 4

'I got sick of watching the other guys scoring runs and I was there, looking a million bucks for 20 runs. Something had to change'

Steve Waugh

# Never Enough

With Steve's failing form at Test level beginning to cause him concern, he was more than usually keen to show his worth to the selectors by performing brilliantly at NSW level. An opportunity came in December 1990, when at the WACA against a Western Australian bowling attack that included the likes of Bruce Reid and Terry Alderman, Steve was able to combine with his brother Mark to knock out a world-record, unbeaten fifth-wicket partnership of 464.

Mike Whitney — a long-time team-mate of both Waugh brothers — was there in the dressing room when, after NSW captain Geoff Lawson's declaration, the twins came in from this extraordinary innings, providing a classic mental snapshot that he would take out many times over the years to examine again. All of the NSW players crowded around the twins, whooping it up, slapping them on the back, and celebrating their extraordinary feat. In response, the brothers reacted differently, with entirely different priorities. Mark, who had scored 229 runs, somehow still looking impeccable in a perfectly creased shirt and trousers despite having been out there for seven hours, took his helmet off to display not a single bead of sweat on his forehead, and went straight over to the mirror to make sure there was not a hair out of place. Steve though — dishevelled and looking like a Christian who had just triumphed after a tight fifteen-rounder with a lion — had other priorities. Mightily annoyed, despite his own

BY 1989, WHEN STEVE Waugh arrived in England for his second Ashes series, and his first on English soil, he was an established and respected member of the team, who had only one slight question mark next to his name, and it went like this:

Steve Waugh?

Yeah, he's good, but can he go on to make the really big innings, without losing concentration somewhere in the mid-range? After all, he'd been in the Australian team since the last days of 1985 and — *goodness, can that be the time?* — this was the middle of 1989, and 26 Tests and 41 innings into his baggy green career he still hadn't racked up a century, despite having nailed down ten half-centuries!

Yes, it was only a question mark, as opposed to the dreaded *questions-are-being-asked*, but it was a fact that, together with Waugh's relatively modest average at this stage of only 30.53, was noted by successive commentators as the Australian team moved through its warm-up matches and made ready for the first Test.

Waugh's response, certainly not for the last time in his career, was reminiscent of the famous report from Marshal Ferdinand Foch in a sticky situation in WWI: 'My centre is giving way, my right is in retreat; situation excellent, I will attack!'

For in that first Test, at Headingley, Waugh did exactly that, as the Australian team put the English to the sword, and — wearing his baggy green cap, instead of the regulation helmet — he racked up a blistering array of square- and cover-drives, hit imperiously off the back foot to score 177 unbeaten runs when Allan Border declared the first innings closed at 601.

And there was plenty more where that came from as, in the next Test at Lords, Waugh knocked out another superb innings and England in the process, with a superb 152 not out. As a matter of fact, it was the third Test before Waugh would be dismissed for the first time in the series, by which time he was 393 runs to the good.

On the strength of it, no less than the great Ian Botham said of him: 'Steve Waugh is a batting genius. He can be anything as a batsman. I think he might just be a freak.' Still, Waugh could always count on his own team-mates to keep his feet on the ground. When,

'There's a lot more tough times than good times in Test match cricket. It's a matter of overcoming those tough times. Not getting too down and when you're going well, not getting too up. You've got to stay on a level plane all the time' STEVE WAUGH

for example, after arriving at the crease in the fifth Test with the score at 4/454, the Bankstown boy scored a duck, it was good ol' Dean Jones who called out to him as arrived back in the dressing room … 'Only as good as your last innings!' Never mind. Even with that duck, Waugh finished the series with an average of 126.5 and many — most notably in the Australian press — inevitably began to compare him with Sir Donald Bradman, who was the only other Australian batsman to have ever finished a full series against England with a century average.

Traditionally, the Bradman comparison is the kiss of death to batting careers, and while that was not the case with Waugh, he certainly ran it close.

For from the heights of 1989, the depths of 1990 were only a step away …

With only rare exceptions, all great careers need to have valleys as well as peaks, valleys to make the subsequent ascension of the peaks all the more gripping a story and impressive a feat, and Steve Waugh certainly had his Death Valley.

The track down towards it began in the Australian summer of '89/90, after he had fairly ordinary series against New Zealand, Sri Lanka and Pakistan, with a distinctly mortal average of 40.11 over that time. The following summer, in his third Ashes campaign against England — with Graham Gooch's men touring Australia from October 1990 onwards — Steve could barely *buy* a run and had a series of humiliating failures.

He had just one run to his name to show for the first Test, and 19 for the second, and by the time of the third Test, the same man who had been the man of the series on the previous Ashes campaign just sixteen months before could manage scores of only 48 and 14. He wasn't at all sure it was going to be enough to hold his spot, as it seemed like a shadow had fallen across his land …

IT IS A COMMON enough occurrence in sport of course, for a sportsman on his way down the stairs to pass directly by the sportsman on his way

PREVIOUS PAGES, LEFT Steve Waugh strikes a pose at Arundel in England, in a match against the Duchess XI in 1989.
RIGHT An early shot of Mark Taylor with team-mates Peter Taylor and Steve Waugh, following Mark's 1989 selection in the Australian Test team. One day Mark would rise above the more experienced Steve Waugh to captain the national side.

216 runs and the fact they had become the first brothers to score double centuries in the same first-class match, Steve threw his helmet angrily down and marched right up to Lawson and said outright, 'F—, why did you declare? We could have got 600!'

And that was Steve all over. When you had the opposition at your mercy, there was to be none — just as Border had taught him. For all that, Mike Whitney tried to remonstrate with his close friend, and calm him down, but Steve Waugh would have none of it.

'You probably wanted to declare as well,' Steve hissed back at him, 'so you could have a bloody bowl.'

That was Steve: when 216 runs was still not enough!

And while that knock did do Steve a little bit of good, on the other hand it did Mark a *power* of good. For, by any measure, Mark was having an extraordinary summer, piling up century after century to go with the eight centuries (including two double centuries) he'd scored for the English county of Essex in the northern summer of 1990. Mark was a bloke who was starting to look like an idea whose time has come, a force that could no longer be denied ...

up — and for the two to have a brief chat along the way — but it is something of a rarity when the two sportsmen concerned are brothers and the meeting takes place at their parents' house.

But such was the case for Steve and Mark, on the afternoon of 21 January 1991.

After getting the crushing phone call from the chairman of selectors that he had been dropped after playing forty-two consecutive Tests for Australia, Steve made his way to his parents' home for solace, and the first family member he came across was Mark.

'Congratulations, you're in the team,' Waugh the Elder said to Waugh the Younger.

'Oh, what, the Test team?' Mark replied.

'Yes, the Test team.'

'Who got dropped?'

'Me.'

'Oh, bad luck.'

'Don't worry about it.'

Nothing much was said for a little while, and Bev Waugh for one found it a bit difficult. On balance though, she decided that between the twin demands of celebration and commiseration, it was celebration that should win out, on the grounds that while Mark was in the Test team, it surely wouldn't take Stephen long to work out what he needed to do to get back in there, and then they could *both* be in the team!

Hopefully, anyway.

That the one spot in the Test team was not going to be open to Stephen any time in the near future became obvious from the moment that Mark made his debut and scorched a stunning century on the first day of the Test in Adelaide, going on to notch up 138 runs and be warmly acclaimed by all. Allan Border was photographed, *beaming*, reaching out to pat Mark on the back as he came from the field to a standing ovation.

'Why didn't you pick me earlier?!' Mark jocularly wanted to know of the gathered selectors, though under the circumstances it

was a fair enough question. He had already scored 7000 first-class runs by the time he had been given his chance, but it was clear that he had now seized that chance with both hands and was not going to be letting go for some time to come.

So who was 'Afghanistan' now?

Though pleased for Mark in his own quiet way, the backing track of a film of this period of Steve Waugh's life — when his brother was the toast of Australian cricket, and he, Steve, was just plain *toast* — could well have been the famous song originally penned and put out by Australian rock band Moving Pictures.

> *What about me?*
> *It isn't fair.*
> *I've had enough,*
> *now I want my share.*
> *Can't you see?*

Indeed. What *about* him? Where to from here?

There! In Trinidad, in April, Allan Border has just been superbly run out by Carl Hooper, leaving Mark Waugh safe at the other end. And who is the new batsman walking out now towards Mark? None other than twin brother Steve, who has been given another chance and selected at fifth drop in the batting line-up ahead of Greg Matthews. As he takes his place at the crease, it is the first time that twin brothers have played in a Test cricket match together. Both brothers, mind, manage to hide superbly their deep emotions at the feat — though the same could not be said for the rest of the Waugh family gathered around their television set in the middle of the night in Panania — and if they were remembering all those years ago when they were two little boys with two little toys, dreaming of this very moment, it certainly doesn't show.

What does show is a business-like approach to the job at hand, and over the next ninety minutes they score 58 runs, until ... ... ... Steve-is-out-and-it's-over-just-like-that. Just like that! A momentary lapse in concentration is all it takes for him to misjudge a ball from

Courtney Walsh, and when wicket-keeper Jeffrey Dujon takes the catch he is gone for just 26 runs. In some ways that Test with Mark against the Windies in Trinidad proved only that the doubts about Steve had been well-founded, and even though Steve was selected for the next Test, he could only harvest 2 and 4 not out and he was dropped again for the fifth Test — maybe forever. This time it really had a feeling of *permanence* about it.

Some commentators were saying openly that he really should give it away, and at least one of the most influential cricket writers in the country was saying privately that Waugh would never play for Australia again, as his technique had been definitively proved unsound, and it was unlikely he would ever be able to change it this far into his career.

*Should* he give it away? After all, some might have thought that, given he was already over forty Tests to the good, had knocked out centuries and experienced a lot of the best that Test cricket had to offer, it might be time to go out and get a real job. At a much later point Waugh acknowledged this, saying that upon being dropped he had two choices:

'You can say "I don't want to make it back" or, "I can try to prove people wrong, do myself justice and get back in there and play to my ability".

'I chose that path. Twenty years down the track, I wouldn't have been happy sitting in a chair, watching cricket, knowing that I could have done better. I wouldn't say [getting dropped] is a necessity, but if it happens, it will make you a tougher cricketer if you do come back.'

Tough it was, and *toughening*.

In re-forming himself and his whole approach to cricket, Waugh was, typically, ruthless. The great cricket writer Peter Roebuck once said of Steve Waugh that he usually looked like 'a bloke whose lawnmower had broken down again ...' but now — while Mark continued to flourish and grow in the baggy green — Steve was actually more like a gardener with shears and a demonic look in his eye. Day and night, night and day, the older twin was pruning,

'Unless you're the best hooker in the world it's going to get you out regularly. I saw blokes getting out all the time and thought, "that's not for me". So I cut it out and it's hard to restore it because it's not in your way of thinking' STEVE WAUGH

pruning, pruning, cutting away every flowery part of his game, every exotic growth that was there just for show but which, when he looked at it, was always going to be more trouble than it was worth. He focused on his batting practice as never before, dedicating himself to working out precisely what the best, most effective style of game he could play was — and then perfecting it from there.

His steering star, in his own words, was: 'It doesn't matter how pretty you look, it's how many runs you get.'

This process of looking at his own technique, however, did not come naturally to Waugh. To this point he'd never really had formal batting coaching, and had lived by his instincts, trying to score off any loose ball that came his way, and plenty of good balls besides. And those instincts had been so good that the former Test batsman Ian Davis had once said that he felt it was *he* who could learn from the young Waugh twins, not the other way round.

Which was fine and flattering. But what had now become clear to Steve Waugh, from the outside of the Test team looking in, was that following his instincts was no longer good enough.

The first part of his game to be pruned away was his hook shot. Whenever he might have felt tempted to play it, he kept harking back to his first series against a West Indies team seemingly built around eleven fast bowlers, a twelfth man who was a fast bowler and a manager, Wes Hall, who was a former fast bowler. In a particular innings of that series, Waugh had been caught hooking for 91, and the more he thought about it now, the more he was firm in his conclusion that because there was no way you could hook a fast bowler unless it was premeditated, and because premeditation was dangerous, and because he had simply seen too many good innings come to a shuddering halt because of the hook shot, he just wasn't going to do it any more. Period.

Generally, he came to acknowledge that playing defensive strokes was not, as he had thought, for losers. There had been a time in his youth when he had thought that the only thrill for a batsmen was to hit huge shots, but now he realised — and it had come courtesy of watching team-mates like Mark Taylor, David Boon

OPPOSITE The loneliness of the long-distance cricketer: Steve during practice at the Allan Border Oval in Brisbane.

'You wish sometimes the articles were a little different. It always seems Mark is the elegant one and I am tough and gritty and hanging in there. That wears on us a bit both ways. I'd like people to see the aggressive, positive stuff when I bat and Mark would like people to see the gritty stuff when he bats' STEVE WAUGH

and Allan Border — that playing defensive strokes was not only a good way of not getting out, it was practically an *investment*. For the more of them you played, the more the bowler would become frustrated and the more likely some easy, loose deliveries would be coming your way.

If this was generally a tough time for Steve Waugh as far as cricket went, it was still the happiest of all possible times when, on 16 August 1991, he married Lynette Dougherty. His best man was his NSW team-mate Brad McNamara, and an indication of just how much cricket was the dominant feature in the young couple's lives was that Lynette's matron of honour was David Boon's wife, Pip — who had become very close to Lynette on recent tours — while David and Pip's daughter Georgina filled the role of flower girl.

As it turned out, the newly married couple's honeymoon would go for some time, at least in the sense that Steve was not called away to Test duty, as he had hoped, and forevermore the '91/92 cricket season could be marked down as the summer of his discontent. Runs flowed, all right, but no more than that, and in some ways it was only the comfort of his new bride that kept his spirits up. Lynette might not know a lot about cricket, but she had come to know a lot about Steve and somehow, whenever he talked to her, he felt better and stronger.

Which was as well, because although he did make his way back into the Australian side for the first two Tests of the Windies tour to Australia in '92/93 — yah-boo sucks to the critics who said he'd never do it — by the time of the third Test, Steve was once again standing on the edge of the abyss, gazing at the cruel rocks below. After failures in the first two Tests, he knew if he didn't deliver now he would be gone a million.

Would the real Steve Waugh please stand up? Are you the man who tore England apart in the 1989 Ashes series, or are you the sometime bunny of previous years who is constantly losing your wicket just when it seems you might have at last lost the yips?

The short answer was 'neither'. The Steve Waugh who took to the crease at the SCG that early January day in 1993 was a bloke who

had re-made himself, who knew he was playing for his career who had learnt his lessons before about how to play the Windies and who was bloody-well going to *punish them*!

And so he did. Sure, the Windians tried to tempt him to play the hook shot, but Waugh the Elder simply refused to do so. The ball would whistle impotently past his ear, he would leave it, and sooner or later the bowlers would get frustrated into trying something different and send down balls that he *could* hit at with a lot less danger to his wicket, which suited the Australian a whole lot better.

In just under 300 minutes, using his now very careful game, Steve Waugh crafted a superb century to move Australia into a handy position — and bolt down his own spot in the side. It was true that within three days, acclaim for Steve Waugh's century was entirely swamped by the extraordinary 277 that Brian Lara then dashed off with almost insolent ease, but Waugh no longer had any interest in playing like that. He knew what he was doing, had done it bloody well and intended to keep doing so for many years to come.

The cruellest thing for Waugh, as for all the Australians, was that despite feeling they had the Windies' measure in this campaign — the mighty Lara notwithstanding — they still were not able to wrest the coveted Frank Worrell Trophy from them for the first time in seventeen years. In the next Test in Adelaide, the Australians got to within *two* stinking runs of securing the victory that would have secured the trophy, but it was not to be and that particular challenge would have to wait …

ABOVE Bev Waugh had lots of reasons to be proud: here with her victorious twins following a tickertape parade for the Australian team celebrating their victory in the 1999 World Cup.
OVERLEAF Mark (left) and Steve not seeing eye to eye during an ING Cup match between the NSW Blues and the Tasmanian Tigers, Sydney, 22 February 2004. Maybe Steve was worried that Mark's wristband signalled a return to tennis …

# Cricket's New Kings

## Chapter 5

'It is as if Steve decided to trade flamboyance and flashiness for runs'
Mark Taylor

NOW THAT STEVE WAS back in the team on a full-time basis and Australia and the wider cricket world were getting their first long look at the Waugh twins on the same international stage for the first time, there was much comment on the seeming lack of warmth and enormous differences between the twins.

When batting together they barely seemed to acknowledge each other, let alone have mid-wicket conferences or share a laugh during a light moment. Their explanation, that after having shared a room for the first eighteen years of their life they really had nothing left to say to each other … appeased no one.

Team-mates reported that they were no different in the dressing room and on the team bus. Far from being two peas in a pod, it was like one was a pea while the other was a walnut. Somehow, though there was only four minutes between them, there really was a lot of the 'older brother' about Steve, and the initially ironic 'Junior' appellation for Mark was also richly appropriate. There was something about the insouciance of Mark dashing off extraordinary centuries and seeming careless ducks that meant he always had the air of the boy genius about him — with the emphasis on 'boy' as much as 'genius' — while Steve's unremitting intensity and evenness of approach always made him appear ten years older. And whereas it would later be written of the younger twin that 'one of the few things Mark Waugh disliked more than getting out was getting out of bed', Steve Waugh always seemed serious and hard-working.

Mark was known, for example, to love punting on horses and dogs, while if Steve had any such passion it never made it into the public domain. After every day's play, while Mark might go to the bar for a drink with 'the boys', Steve never really was one of the boys and often retired to his room to work into the night, doing such things as writing the latest in his series of tour diaries. While Steve, thus, wrote a book a year, the public would have been surprised if Mark *read* a book a year, and staggered if it had been Steve's. Between games Mark didn't mind the odd excursion into nightclubs and the like, while Steve just wasn't the nightclub type. While Steve was popular enough within the team, there was ever and always just the slightest

PREVIOUS PAGES While they often seemed to be moving in opposite directions, the Waugh combination turned out to be good for their country. Here the twins chase runs in a World Cup Super Six match against Zimbabwe at Lord's, 9 June 1999.
OPPOSITE Mark and Steve sharing a warm embrace. In response to allegations of a lack of fraternal affection between them, Mark said that they'd spent the first 17 years together in everything, so they weren't obliged to spend the rest of their lives that way. In this game on 30 April 1995, the second day of the fourth Test against the Windies, they both made centuries.

ABOVE The 1995 Australian
team for the Tests against the
Windies, in the West Indies,
beat the heat en masse.
Steve Waugh is fourth from
right, with Shane Warne
dipping down below him.
OPPOSITE The Waugh twins
celebrate their 231-run
partnership against the
Windies in 1995.

'apartness' about him, which had him at least one step removed from the dead centre of the team — a position that Shane Warne had gravitated to almost the moment he'd made his debut in the national side in 1992, and equally a spot that Mark Waugh was never too far from.

IT HAD BEEN SAID of Allan Robert Border that 'had Australia ever been invaded by the Killer Cricket Balls, then Border is the man we would have put on Bondi Beach with bat in hand to beat the beggars back'. And it was true. For throughout most of Border's career, particularly through the dimmest, darkest era of the mid-1980s and beyond, whenever Australia found itself in any trouble, at 2/12 or 3/43 or 4/not much, then it was the sight of Border which gave confidence, and in those grim situations he very rarely failed.

And if by the encroaching mid-1990s those legendary powers of Border in his 39th year were getting a little scratchy, still he was able to turn it on when required. Such was the case most notably in the 1993 Ashes campaign in England. After Australia's victory in two of the first three Tests, the Ashes were up for grabs and both Border and Steve Waugh rose to the occasion in the fourth Test at Headingley. By the end of an extraordinary second day's play, Border had reached a phenomenal 175 runs, with Waugh on 144, and England were clearly on the ropes and wilting fast. Surely, Steve thought, it was time for the *coup de grâce*, to declare overnight and get stuck into the Poms first thing the following morning? Not a bit of it. To Steve's surprise, Australia batted on for an *hour* the next day, taking the score to a phenomenal 4/653, with Border explaining to him that in that way they could 'cause further mental and physical disintegration' to the English side.

Mental and physical disintegration. It was an interesting concept, and one that Waugh tucked away for further thought, even amid the wild celebrations as Australia won that Test and with it another Ashes series — with Steve Waugh topping the Australian averages with 83.20.

'Batting with Border always makes you concentrate that little bit extra, because you can see how much it means to him not to give his wicket away' STEVE WAUGH

The same two Australian batsmen famously combined again six months later in the third Test against South Africa in Adelaide in January of 1994 — Steve's first against the South Africans after missing the first two with a hamstring strain. Australia was four wickets down in their first innings for a moderate total — and the South Africans just starting to get on top in the good bowling conditions — when Steve Waugh came to join Border at the wicket. Together they proceeded to take both the visitors and the game by the scruff of the neck. They put on 207 runs before Border was out for 84, while Waugh kept powering on until he reached 164.

For many seasoned cricket observers, it was in this match-winning partnership of 207 runs when the chips were down against South Africa that Border effectively handed the 'Bondi Beach bat' to Waugh, as the captain's own massive strength started to wane in his twilight time with the baggy green.

Generally, from that point on, the more dire the occasion, the higher Waugh rose to it, and time and again it was the older of the Bankstown boys who looked to be the point man standing between Australia and Armageddon. It was one thing for opponents to rip through the top order, as they managed to do on occasion, but then, then they would have to deal with *him*.

For all of Steve's new-found strength, however, Allan Border probably retired just a little too soon, in March of 1994, for Steve to have a good chance of succeeding him in the captaincy. Though the selectors in fact interviewed Waugh — along with other candidates Mark Taylor, David Boon and Ian Healy — Waugh was not judged to be the one who should be anointed. After all, could the selectors really install as captain a guy like Waugh who, only eighteen months earlier, had been unable to hold down a spot in the side?

The selectors, and the board, went instead with the solid, stolid Taylor — who'd been vice-captain to Border for 24 of the previous 26 Tests — to all but universal applause, bar just a little private hand-wringing for Waugh. Except that Taylor didn't prove to be solid and stolid at all. As a captain, the opening batsman was suddenly expansive, at least by comparison with Allan Border.

ABOVE Steve Waugh provided encouragement to the young Glenn McGrath from Narromine, seen together here on 21 March 1994 in Capetown, following their victory in the second Test against South Africa.
OPPOSITE Steve Waugh attempts to create a vacancy in the Australian team as Glenn McGrath perches near a waterfall in Barbados, 26 April 1999.

Whereas Border — who had forged his hard captaincy model in the furnace of so many bitter losses — had always been notable for first killing off all possibility of defeat, and *then* going for victory, Taylor went for the victory first. He set supremely attacking fields, he insisted that his own men push the scoring rate along and he instructed his own bowlers to go after wickets first and foremost, with the need to keep the opposition's run rate down a secondary consideration. Declarations came as much as half a day earlier than when Allan Border might have been expected to make them, and all put together it meant that the pressure on opponents to crumple was almost a palpable force.

Off the field Taylor also had an immediate impact, banning Walkmans in the dressing room, as well as mobile phones, books and even playing cards. The point was that such things were distractions from the main game, which was cricket, *winning* the cricket game, and that was what they were to be about from this point on.

So it was Mark Taylor as captain, Ian Healy his deputy — a worthy appointment that among other things helped to balance the NSW domination of the team — and Steve Waugh was simply one of the senior players. Though a little disappointed that he was not in the prime position, it wasn't as if Waugh didn't have a fair measure of input into the way the team was run, and he was particularly notable for looking after the new blokes in the team, ever mindful of how tough it had been for him when he had first arrived.

Young Glenn McGrath, for example, the tearaway quick from Narromine in western NSW. When Steve noticed that the young'un was often fielding wearing his floppy white, he took him aside and gently pointed out that there was no more honoured hat to wear than the baggy green. Glenn had earnt that coveted right and the right thing to do was to wear it, at least on the field. McGrath did precisely that and was equally appreciative when Steve started to spend some time with him in the nets, teaching him some of the mysteries of batting.

In the meantime, out on the field, Steve settled down to do what he did best, which was scoring runs. Lots and lots of Test runs.

PLAYER'S CIGARETTES

S. J. McCABE (N S WALES)

NOWHERE DID STEVE WAUGH'S new-found toughness and powers of concentration find fuller flower than on the 1995 Australian tour of the West Indies. As Australia headed into the third Test in Port-of-Spain, they had gone to a 1–0 lead — meaning they were on the edge of winning their first series in the Windies for two decades. None of the West Indians was feeling grimmer about it than big Curtly Ambrose, the fearsome fast bowler who had shown up in batsmen's worst nightmares from London to Lahore, Sydney to Sri Lanka. Ambrose was an enormous man who always looked a little aggrieved, and as if *someone* was going to pay for it. He had been treated rather cavalierly by the Australian batsmen in the series to date, and some were even whispering insultingly that maybe it was time for him to retire.

Here at Port-of-Spain though, by God, Curtly's view was that things were going to be different. Here the slippery and treacherous green-top pitch was perfect for the likes of him, and hell on earth for the wretched Australians who had been so uppity of late. After just a few overs the tourists were reeling at 3/14, when that punk Steve Waugh comes in. You have to imagine the scene …

As the Australian makes his way to the centre, amid all the searing heat and West Indian whistling and so forth, Curtly stands at the bowler's mark, *glowering*, waiting for Waugh to come and get his medicine. The ground settles down, focusing on the two principal combatants. By an uncanny coincidence, Waugh's physical dimensions are almost a dead ringer for the dimensions of Curtly's left leg, and it hardly seems fair as the enormous West Indian powers in and begins peppering Waugh with an extraordinary array of bouncers.

But Waugh isn't playing that game any more. He just isn't interested in swatting at bouncers and is quite happy to simply fiercely defend his wicket and wait for the loose balls, which he knows must inevitably come. Many times the ball crashes into Waugh's body, onto his torso, arms and hands, but he neither winces nor whinges. All of his body language is making a very clear statement — Ambrose and his mates can do whatever they bloody-

well please, hit him with their bouncers however many times they like, but he is Steve Waugh and he isn't shifting. Got it, Curtly? You'd want to be a damn sight better bowler than you are to get *me* out.

Nothing could have infuriated the mighty Ambrose more. After such a good beginning for the Windies, it was outrageous that Waugh just shut up shop like that, and before long Big Curtly has simply had *enough*.

After one particular ball, Ambrose follows through on his run-up and finishes up well down the pitch, just 2 metres from Waugh, glaring at him. Some men might feel intimidated receiving such a look from a man who was then engaged in hurling a small leather-clad missile at his head at 150 km/h, but not Waugh.

'What the f— are you looking at?' the Australian asks the West Indian.

Ambrose, stunned, moves even closer and gives the punk fair warning.

'Don't cuss me, mon.'

At which point, of course, Waugh cusses him some more, with two rifle-shot words that go straight to the heart of the matter. Ambrose, eyeballs rolling, moves even closer, at which point …

'Fortunately,' Waugh later recounted in his tour diary, 'Richie Richardson moved in swiftly to avert what could have been my death by strangulation, and the game continued.'

In fact, Richardson has to all but physically drag Ambrose away from what could have been a dreadful conflagration in international cricket, but the photo of that moment says it all. There is Steve Waugh, in an open stance, not betraying a flicker of fear as the carpet-biting mad Ambrose towers over him, just barely restrained by Richardson. The sheer *insolence* of that Waugh!

But Curtly Ambrose would have to learn to get used to it, because Waugh was not going to change his approach, and refused to be bowed for the rest of his innings.

That afternoon, not long before stumps, the rain came and play was abandoned for the day, with Australia having moved to the meagre position of 7/112, with Waugh rock-steady on 54. After

## Waugh's a Mess

Steve Waugh's favourite cricketers from the pantheon of the Australian greats were Victor Trumper, Stan McCabe and Doug Walters. It has been said that this was 'presumably because they expressed everything which he eliminated from his own game — spontaneity, inspiration and a gambler's instinct'. But in the case of Trumper these two batsmen from opposite ends of the century actually had one very notable thing in common. For just as Trumper was known among contemporaries as the untidiest man they ever toured with, so too — as surprising as it might sound — was Steve Waugh. And we have it on no less an authority than Glenn McGrath …

'I had to room with Steve Waugh a few times and he was just a nightmare,' McGrath later wrote of this time. 'He wasn't the cleanest guy going round. There was stuff everywhere. He would lose something at least four or five times a day and end up throwing his clothes from one side of the room to the other trying to find it …'

Another to affirm that it was a very short straw indeed to be roomed with Steve was Gavin Robertson: 'Having roomed with him I have learnt that cockroach baits can be of great benefit, because he has a tendency to dislike the colour of hotel carpets and will proceed to spread every article of clothing he has around the floor.' All the rest of his team-mates noted how he would have to often stand on his cricket coffin to get it to close up properly, and Allan Border once opined that you could probably leave a sandwich in there and it would be two years before it was found!

OPPOSITE A reflective Steve
Waugh in Colombo, Sri
Lanka, looking like a
cricketing gent from an
earlier era.

getting ice on to his severely bruised elbow and swollen finger —
Curtly had at least had some satisfaction — and getting a good night's
sleep, he was ready to resume the following day.

Waugh went on to make 63 oh-so-crucial runs, and even
though Australia finally lost the Test match, it was regarded as one of
his best innings and a seminal moment in the changing dynamic
between the two teams.

In the fourth and final Test at Sabina Park in Kingston — with
the Frank Worrell Trophy again within Australia's grasp if they could
just put the Windies away in this one — Curtly was soon feeling even
worse, as Steve Waugh played another extraordinary innings. On yet
one more treacherous wicket, Waugh again focused when the team
needed him as never before, coming to the crease when the score was
3/73. Here indeed was the spirit of Border at his best, where every
ball was treated on its merits, each stroke a new beginning. Up in the
commentary box, as it happened, Border commented that in all his
born days he had never seen such a barrage of bouncers as the
Windies were now unleashing at Steve Waugh. But, just as had
happened the week before, Waugh never flinched.

Though an increasingly frustrated Curtly Ambrose from one
end and Courtney Walsh from the other were trying to *blast* Waugh
from the crease, *he would not / he would not / he would not be moved.*
Time and again the searing ball would thud sickeningly into Waugh's
body, but somehow it only served to put further steel in him. Finally,
after a 425-ball marathon lasting just over nine hours, Waugh had
made 200 runs — forming the heart of a 231-run partnership with
Mark — and on the strength of the first innings total of 531, Australia
went on to win that deciding Test by an innings, thus ending the
Windies' fifteen-year reign over world cricket!

Of the many satisfactions Waugh had in reaching his double
century, one was that the bloke who was holding up the other end,
who allowed him the crucial time at the crease to get there, was the
same Glenn McGrath who Steve had spent so much time with in the
nets in the last three years, encouraging him to take his batting
seriously and squeeze whatever ability he had till the pips squeaked.

'It's still the ultimate test, Test cricket. If you're weak, you get gobbled up in Test cricket. The strong prey on you. That's why it's a great game. If you're not up to it, you get found out in Test cricket. There's nowhere to hide' STEVE WAUGH

OPPOSITE Curtly Ambrose expresses his emotions following a polite conversation with Steve waugh, 21 April 1995.
BELOW AND OVERLEAF Steve Waugh mobbed by fans after scoring a double century against the West Indies in the fourth Test at Sabina Park, Jamaica, 1 May 1995.

Now, McGrath was the first to congratulate him and the congratulations continued the following evening, once the victory was secured …

Late on the night after victory was secured, nearing 4 a.m., Ian Healy was watching closely as Steve Waugh, *still* wearing his whites, his baggy green and his spikes, stumbled down the hotel corridor, trying his key in the lock of every door, just in case one of them happened to lead into his own room. *One* of these bastards had to work. Finally, though, the double centurion, who had also just been voted man of the match *and* man of the series — on the strength of 429 runs at 107.25 and best bowling average with eight wickets at 12.50 — found what he thought to be his room.

Is that it? Yes, that's it. The key worked and he opened the door … to Room 200.

# Leading Questions

## Chapter 6

'They'll be picking completely different sides for Test and one-day cricket' Steve Waugh makes a prediction

# Lost and Found

Of all the things in all the world that cricket had to offer, the very worst of them was losing. Always, Steve Waugh could barely *think straight* after a loss, as he turned over and over in his mind all the what-ifs and if-onlys even as he tried to work out what went wrong so he and the team could improve on it next time.

But being beaten was one thing. Being thrashed was quite another. And that is what happened to the Australian team in March 1998 when they suffered their fourth worst Test defeat ever, losing to India in Kolkata in four days by an innings and 219 runs. Waugh arrived back in his hotel room in the middle of the afternoon, feeling lower than a snake's bellybutton — although at least he personally had scored 80 and 33 — to find an envelope under his door.

Inside was a letter from a man who ran a home called Udayan, which was for 250 sons of leprosy sufferers, most of whom had leprosy themselves. In heartfelt and touching prose, he wanted to know if Steve would like to come for a visit, to have a look at the home and possibly see if he could lend his name and fame to some fund-raising.

*Lepers.* For some reason Waugh had always been interested in them since watching the famous movie *The African Queen*, and already the Australian batsman had become enough of an Indio-phile to know that there were about four million people in the country who suffered from the dreaded disease. Also, he had seen lots of them on the streets, generally begging and

ON THE STRENGTH OF such extraordinary performances, something rather special was in the process of crystallising deep within the Australian psyche in regard to Steve Waugh. For it was around this time that the very name 'Steve Waugh' came to connote toughness, certitude and a certain-something-particularly-Australian. As a matter of fact, to be said properly, it had to have the delivery of a rifleman at Tobruk: short, sharp and clean.

It had to come out as 'Steve*Waugh*', with just a slight emphasis on the last name.

There were many precedents in this name game of Australian cricket. In days of yore, for example, the half-strangled cry of '*BOONIE!*' was, if not quite the mating call of the Australian male, at the very least an affirmation that you were a true-blue, baggy-green-loving, red-blooded beer-guzzling bastard from way back, and you were keen to spend your time among others of similar ilk.

'*BOOOOOONIE!*'

But 'Steve*Waugh*' wasn't like that. For a start you didn't shout it, and if you said it properly, with just the tiniest trace of irony, it affirmed that you admired the leanness of his lines, the toughness of his teak, the purity of his performance. This bloke was a throwback to the way things were, and if you were a Waugh admirer, and knew the code of saying his name right, it was a statement that you were too. Shane Warne could peroxide his hair and put ten earrings on the side of his melon for all we cared, but that kind of thing wasn't Steve*Waugh*'s go and that was good enough for us.

See, there was a timelessness about Waugh that you just didn't get with the other blokes in the team. If you had to superimpose the face of one of the modern Australian cricketers over the left shoulder of Don Bradman — in that famous photo where The Don is walking out to bat at the SCG while everyone is applauding — then no other face but Waugh's fits. McGrath? Way too tall for a player of the 1940s. Warne? Please. Mark Waugh? Nobody had a haircut like that back then. But you could have put Steve Waugh right there in Bradman's wake, right then, and everyone would have said he *looks* like an Australian cricketer should.

The Australian team itself, of course, didn't refer to him as

Steve*Waugh*, because that would be conduct unbecoming for a cricketer in regard to someone who was their nominal peer, but on the other hand, nor did they call him 'Steve'.

To them he was always 'Stephen', a slightly more respectful moniker.

STEVE*WAUGH* IT WAS THEN, who was ranked the number-one batsman in the world throughout 1995 and 1996, and who now, in 1997, was on the prow, if not the bridge, of the good ship *Australia* as it manoeuvred so successfully against first the South Africans — in Australia's first tour of the Republic in twenty-four years, where among other things Steve Waugh and Greg Blewett put on an extraordinary 385-run partnership to set up a comprehensive win — and then the English side in that year's Ashes series. For the latter campaign, Steve Waugh had suddenly been elevated to the position of vice-captain at the expense of Ian Healy, a move which was quietly said to have been done to ensure that if Mark Taylor had to be dropped, a long-term captain in Waugh would be ready to take over.

The high point for Waugh in this series came in the third Test at Old Trafford when, despite having a broken thumb that caused him agonising pain every time he struck the ball — and notwithstanding he had to come to the wicket both times in extreme situations with the score at 3/42 and 3/39 — he was able to score a century in each innings. It was on the strength of this performance that Australia was able to even the series 1–1 and go on to retain the Ashes 3–2.

If there was a significant difference in this performance from Steve Waugh to others in his now long career, it was that he not only had Lynette with him for much of the tour, but someone equally important. His baby daughter, Rosalie, who had been born in August of 1996, somehow helped keep everything in perspective. Many other Test batsmen when offered the chance by their wife — as Lynette did — to take the baby into another room, so he could sleep without interruption, would have leaped upon it, but Steve refused outright. They were his family and they were staying, and that was that. His consecutive

ABOVE That's 'Captain' to you! Mark Taylor in October 1994.
OPPOSITE Steve outside the Udayan Resurrection Home in Kolkata, India.
PREVIOUS PAGES The Australian team at the ready at nine slips in a one-day international against Zimbabwe in Harare, 23 October 1999.

## Lost and Found
[ *continued* ]

leading truly horrible existences. So anyone who was doing something for them had his vote, and besides … after the dreadful loss Australia had suffered that day, he really had nothing better to do.

It was a visit that would in many ways change his life, an entirely different experience to any that had gone before …

For the cliché, of course, is the same the world over. The visiting celebrity, with cameras in tow, makes a quick visit to see some sick children and plays with them for twenty minutes as the air fills with the sweet sound of camera shutters falling, recording the celebrity's kindness. A few quick words to the reporters then, about what a delight it is to meet the children, and how much we can all learn from them, and the streamers on the sidewalk outside the hospital are soon eddying with the celebrity's rapid departure.

With Steve Waugh, it was not like that.

From the moment he arrived, to the time he left, the place gripped him, altered him, almost shaped him with the power of its pathos. Some of the manifestations of the disease were grotesque in the extreme, but he was stunned by both the courage of the residents of the home, and the sheer goodness of the people who ran the home, doing so much with so little to improve the lot of these people who so desperately needed help.

Practically on the spot, Steve Waugh made a commitment to the bloke, that he would become

OPPOSITE **Gori Rao, a resident of the Udayan Resurrection Home. Steve Waugh is the patron of the girls wing of the home, which cares for the children of leprosy sufferers.** PREVIOUS PAGES **Steve and Lynette Waugh relax with their first child, Rosalie.**

centuries were proof positive that his family strengthened him, not that he personally needed any convincing.

While Waugh was flourishing with the bat however, his captain, Mark Taylor, had been severely struggling. Dating from the West Indies tour of Australia through '96/97 a successive run of low scores in both Test and one-day cricket — his average in the series for both forms of the game down to around 17 runs — suddenly put Taylor's position in question. It came to a head just a week before the first Ashes Test. In a game against Derbyshire in Derby, Taylor — just holding on to his position by the hairs of his chinny-chin-chin — had scored just one run when he snicked a ball to former Australian player Dean Jones, who was captaining the home side. Jones dropped what was one of the easiest catches of his life, but Taylor was shattered. He walked down the pitch to his opening partner Justin Langer and said, 'That's it. I can't play. I'm gone. I can't bat. I've lost it.'

Langer looked his captain in the eye and said with some force: 'That's bloody rubbish. Just watch the bloody ball and play the bloody ball.'

Taylor did just that, for 63 runs. And though *in extremis* he was able to salvage his position as Test player and captain with a century in that first Test, it wasn't enough to preserve his position totally. In late October of 1997, the news broke that Taylor was dropped from the one-day side, as the selectors pursued a new policy of having notably different one-day and Test teams. Steve Waugh was announced as the new Australian captain of the truncated version of the game.

From the beginning, Waugh introduced a harder edge to the one-day team's approach. It was immediately notable that the Australians had become a much more aggressive side than ever before in terms of their demeanour, the way batsmen went after bowlers and the way bowlers went after batsmen. Against that, it was clear that Waugh's own form was hitting an extremely rough patch as he notched up — and 'notch' was certainly the operative word — humble scores of just 1, 7, 0, 0, 4 and 0 in the innings just after taking over the captaincy from Mark Taylor.

Waugh was so shocked by these scores and his seeming inability to turn himself around that he went to see chairman of selectors Trevor

THE FOUNDATION STONE
OF
NIVEDITA BHAVAN
(UDAYAN GIRLS WING)
WAS LAID BY
STEVE WAUGH
AUSTRALIAN CRICKET CAPTAIN
AND
PATRON, UDAYAN
ON
JULY 21ST 1998

patron of the home, speak at dinners, make appearances and generally do all he could to raise awareness about what the home was doing and to get the message out that leprosy was only contagious with long, sustained contact and *could be controlled* with the right care and treatment.

And he followed through, too. Not only would Steve Waugh become a constant visitor to the Udayan home, and lend his massive fame to the cause in India, but at home in Australia he quickly became involved in such fund-raising ventures as staging an art show featuring the works of Pro Hart and selling signed photographs that he'd taken on his trips overseas.

Waugh was also instrumental in getting the home to expand to build a wing exclusively devoted to young girls of the families — many of whom, he came to understand, would be forced to prostitute themselves from as young as the age of ten unless resources were put towards housing, educating and saving them.

It was done. All because Australia had badly lost a game against India. There really were more important things in life than sport.

Hohns and offered his head. Hohns refused on the grounds that it was way too early to think Stephen wouldn't be able to turn his scores around and, besides which, it would not be for the good of the team to make another change in the captaincy so quickly. So stay with it, and let's see what happens …

FINALLY, IT WAS ALL over for Mark Taylor. After going into one more fearsome batting slump on the Australians' tour of Pakistan in the northern autumn of 1998, the Australian batting captain had entered the realms of the legends in the second Test in Peshawar. After nearly losing his wicket with an inside edge off his first scoring shot, Taylor had gone on to carve out 334 runs, not out, before declaring overnight — as Australia consolidated their first series victory in Pakistan in thirty-nine years. And it was not far in the descent from that career peak that Taylor took the opportunity to bail out entirely. Just one of many factors was the realisation that in the life of his four-year-old son Jack, he had been away on tour for no fewer than fifty-eight weeks. So it was that — after an admittedly poor home Ashes series where his own performance once again began to look suspiciously like 'a slump', but at least the Ashes had been secured once more — on Tuesday, 2 February 1999, Taylor announced his retirement to extraordinary fanfare. One newspaper trumpeted the headline: 'THE KING IS DEAD, LONG LIVE THE KING!'

But who would be that king?

After earnest discussion, the members of the Australian Cricket Board came up with the right answer …

On Friday, 12 February 1999, the news broke. Stephen Rodger Waugh had become Australia's 40th Test captain and his dearest dream of all was realised.

For all that, the ascension of Steve Waugh to the captaincy was not greeted with universal acclaim. Ian Chappell, for example, came right out and said it on Sydney radio station Triple M.

'I think he's been a selfish cricketer,' Chappell declared. 'I've always felt that the things you do as a player leading up to getting the captaincy do have an effect on how players perceive you. I've had the

'If your instincts tells you the ball's going to go to a place, I'll put a man there rather than holding back and saying that's not quite the right position. I think you've just got to go with it. I've played enough cricket to know that it's probably not orthodox. I think from now on I'll go more with gut instinct' STEVE WAUGH

feeling that a selfish player when he becomes captain ... gets a little less out of his players than someone who is not selfish.'

This was typical take-no-prisoners expression from Chappell and also very much in keeping with what he had been saying publicly and privately: that the person who most deserved to get the captaincy was his own quasi-protégé, Shane Warne.

On the subject of the spinner, Chappell also said that 'a glorious opportunity was missed when Shane Warne wasn't given the captaincy'.

Waugh — who, unlike Warne, never really had a mentor like Chappell, and preferred to fly solo — gave the esteemed former Australian captain a quick return of serve, saying that Chappell's remarks were 'disappointing, but not surprising'.

'As a cricketer,' Waugh continued, 'to be described as "selfish" is the worst thing you can be called. I don't know why he feels that way. I give 100 per cent every time I play for Australia.'

Privately though, he thought it was weird. He had barely even met Chappell — not being particularly disposed to spending any time in the hotel bars in far-flung destinations around the world where the Australian cricket team was playing and Chappell often held court — and yet for some reason the esteemed former Australian captain seemed to have a set against him.

Whatever. Effectively, the only real answer for Steve Waugh from this point was to comprehensively demonstrate that he *could* get the best out of his players and lead a successful Australian side.

Not that it was easy for all that, and by any measure Waugh's first steps along the path to captaining acclaim were tentative at best.

After all, Taylor had retired in a blaze of glory, so what could Waugh do for an encore? What could he possibly achieve that Taylor had not? What do you play on the piano when Mozart has just got up and taken a bow to thunderous applause? The answer could only be more of the same, but more so ...

ABOVE Just after the announcement that Steve has been named Captain of the Australian cricket team. OVERLEAF While Steve was busy being Captain, he was also writing his diaries. Here, though, he's signing autographs in 2002.

# Marks of
# Greatness

# Chapter 7

'Our ambition is to keep improving, to the point that we have an aura of invincibility about us'
Steve Waugh

'When you've got to drop a player as a captain you become emotional. You don't cry, but you feel like crying. It's hard to hold back. You're very ... different in your emotions. It's hard to get out what you're trying to say' STEVE WAUGH

IT WAS, HOWEVER, EITHER Steve's misfortune or his misguided leadership that Australia came up against a Windies side in the West Indies that was suddenly rampant with — that man again! — Brian Lara scoring runs at will to guide his team to a 2–1 series lead after three Tests, with one still to play.

Much of the byplay of the series to that point had been the batting duel between Steve Waugh and Brian Lara.

After Australia's victory in the first Test, Steve had followed up with a century in the second Test in Jamaica to have Australia well on its way to retaining the trophy, when Lara had made a stunning 213 to change the course of the match and guide the Windies to victory. In the third Test in Barbados, Waugh had continued his fine form to post 199 runs in the first innings, but it was Lara's 153 not out in the second innings which just, just managed to get the Windies over the line for a one-wicket victory. At this point, while commendations of Steve Waugh's batting were suitably glowing, the reviews of his captaincy were lukewarm at best. The general view seemed to be that after the thrill-a-minute captaincy of Taylor there had now been a reversion to safety-first, steady-as-she-goes guidance by Waugh, reminiscent of the Border era.

And it bloody-well wasn't working in this day and age! After everything that had been achieved in 1995, when Tubby Taylor had been at the helm to finally wrest the Frank Worrell Trophy off the long-time strutting and haughty West Indians, could it be that after just seven weeks of Steve Waugh's command, the symbol of supremacy between the world's two strongest teams of the last two decades was going to be handed back? The stakes were indeed high ...

While it may not have been immediately obvious to those in the press box, within the team Waugh had by this time started to find his feet as captain and was demonstrating a progressively stronger feel for the role. One thing that helped was a quiet chat with Allan Border, who was over there doing commentating duties and who encouraged Waugh to go with his finely honed cricket instincts and to not worry too much about what the textbook said. After all, this had worked before, when it was Waugh who had pushed for wicket-keeper Adam

Gilchrist to become an opening batsman in the Australian one-day team — a stunningly successful move — and Waugh who, in his first time as NSW captain, had opened the bowling with his off-spinner to gain an entirely unexpected victory.

And there had been other changes the new captain had made in approach that were gradual, but pure Waugh, and were now starting to bear fruit. Always a big believer in the power of one-on-one, he was often having meetings with players, going through what he wanted from them and how he thought they could improve their input to the team. Steve was also fond of memos, which usually included inspirational quotes, and encouraged an ever more aggressive approach: 'If we get a sniff, we must go in for the kill ...'

Speaking of which ...

The crunch now came with the lead-up to the fourth Test, in Antigua, when Waugh, with coach Geoff Marsh, had an extremely hard decision to make. In the series to date the Australian team-member who was clearly out of form was also the team's most famous player, the vice-captain of the whole shebang and Waugh's comrade in arms for nigh on the last decade — Shane Warne. Since coming back from a bad injury earlier in the year, Warne had taken only 4 wickets in his last four Tests. On the last day of the third Test, when they had most needed him to make a breakthrough, Warne had not taken a single wicket. Now, Waugh had reluctantly come to the view that Stuart MacGill — who had earlier in the tour taken 13 wickets in a game against the West Indies Board President's XI in Trinidad, was to be preferred as the one spinner they had decided they would take into the coming Test. Geoff Marsh agreed. In short, they were going to have to drop Shane.

They were going to have to drop Shane, the vice-captain of the tour. To many it was unthinkable, but in Waugh's mind it simply had to be done.

It wasn't pretty. They called Warne into the team room at the Rex Halcyon Hotel in Antigua for what Marsh would later describe as 'a horrible hour ... one of the toughest things I've ever been part of'. The shocked and outraged Warne mounted a sterling case to the

ABOVE Shane Warne in Antigua just after Steve Waugh made the decision to drop him from the side for the fourth Test against the Windies, 3 April 1999.
OPPOSITE Steve appears to be asking for divine assistance after his appeal against Brian Lara was turned down in the first Test against the Windies, 12 April 2003.
PREVIOUS PAGES So near, and yet so far: Shane Warne takes a snooze on close mate Steve Waugh's shoulder as the team poses for a World Cup photo in Melbourne on 23 June 1999.

'You're always learning as a captain. I felt today was probably the best I've captained. I went more with my gut instincts' WAUGH AT THE CONCLUSION OF THE FOURTH TEST AGAINST THE WINDIES, WHERE THE AUSTRALIANS EVENED THE '99 SERIES

skipper and coach as to why he should be included and why the last thing on earth that he needed right now was to suffer the humiliation of being dropped. In short: Were they $%^&* kidding?

No, they weren't.

Waugh did not relent, and neither did Marsh. Warne was dropped, and Waugh did not take the soft option by putting the responsibility for it on Marsh. He told the press that it was every bit as much his decision as the coach's, and that was that.

Not only did MacGill then play the match but, on a roll now, Waugh threw him the new ball in the second innings of the match! To some it might have seemed the most unheard of thing anyone had ever heard of, but after reflection Waugh had decided to follow Border's advice and go with his gut.

It worked. MacGill took three superb wickets, including the crucial one of the opener Adrian Griffith. Another move made by Waugh that had stunned the critics was to throw Greg Blewett into the bowling maelstrom, against perhaps the finest batting side in the world, even though in his whole career Blewett had taken just nine Test wickets. Never mind, Waugh had a hunch that Blewett could do the job for them, and so it proved when he picked up Carl Hooper's wicket. Australia won the Test by 176 runs, meaning that the empire was saved and the Frank Worrell Trophy stayed in Australian hands.

It was with that background that Waugh took the Australian team to England for the 1999 World Cup, where from the start things were tough and getting tougher.

For after a first-up win over Scotland — against whom they could have practically phoned in their game and still won — the Australian team then lost to a strong New Zealand side and an even stronger Pakistan team. Things were now so grim that the only way for Australia to go on and win the tournament was to put together seven wins straight. It was a situation where, just as Banjo Paterson had once famously written in *The Man from Snowy River*: 'And any slip meant death ...'

And that was dinkum.

Against South Africa at Headingley, the entire Australian

campaign suddenly lurched right to the point of no return as they tumbled to 3/48 before a side that had scored an impressive 271. Now as Waugh walked to the centre of the ground that had hosted his first Test century, he was thinking, as he later wrote: 'You've played one-day cricket for fourteen years and this is not the time to end it. There's some unfinished business to be done ...'

And there was that. As a matter of fact, the South Africans were feeling so cocky about it that Herschelle Gibbs, standing at short mid-wicket, dared recall Waugh's words the previous year in Australia, when he had opined that the South Africans were chokers. Now Gibbs called out: 'Let's see how *he* takes the pressure now.'

And funny he should say that. For at the very least, Steve and Ricky Ponting made a go of it, chancing their hand swinging hard at the loose balls and doing what they could with the rest, but sometimes it really was touch and go.

Never more so, as a matter of fact, than when Herschelle himself — who had scored a stunning 101 runs in the Proteas' innings — momentarily caught Steve Waugh when he was on 56 runs, but alas, alas ...

Alas! When Gibbs instantaneously started 'hot-dogging' in celebrations, intending to throw the ball skywards ... it dropped to the ground. Could anything be worse? Yes, the voice of Steve Waugh, crisply noting, 'I hope you realise you've just lost the game for your team ...'

But maybe Herschelle had done no such thing after all. For when Ricky Ponting fell only a short time later for 69 runs, Australia still needed just under a hundred runs with the same number of balls to make it. The South Africans, playing for their lives, mounted the pressure, tightened their field, lifted their work-rate, knowing they only had to crack Waugh and the game was gone and Australia with it.

But this was no lamb to the slaughter, meekly awaiting his end. This was Steve*Waugh*, suddenly verbally attacking all of the infield, the slips cordon, the wicket-keeper and the bowlers. According to the suddenly mouthy Australian, the South Africans couldn't catch, couldn't bowl, couldn't play, and for that matter he was happy to share

OPPOSITE **My protégé vl:** Steve Waugh makes sure Adam Gilchrist's baggy green is on firmly in Adelaide, 13 December 2000.
ABOVE **My protégé v2:** Steve encourages son Austin in a different ball game.
OVERLEAF **Brett Lee** avoids his captain's lens as the Aussies arrive at Georgetown Airport in Guyana for the start of their West Indies tour, 2 April 2003.

# 'I'd rate that as high as any innings I've played' STEVE WAUGH ON HIS 120 AT HEADINGLEY,

TO KEEP AUSTRALIA ALIVE IN THE 1999 WORLD CUP

ABOVE Justin Langer talks to Steve Waugh after being dropped from the team for the first Test against England, at Edgbaston in July 2001.
OPPOSITE Later in the tour, the team celebrates their third Test win.

with them the deep reservations he had about their parentage.

Whether or not such sledging put the South Africans off their game is uncertain, but at the very least it didn't put Waugh off his as he went on to score 120 runs — his highest score in the one-day game and only second century — in the precise match where he needed it most. It was Steve Waugh, appropriately enough, who hit the winning runs off Pollock with three balls to go and Australia lived to fight another day.

Four days later, in the World Cup semi-final at Edgbaston, Australia repeated the dose against South Africa in an extraordinary game, where with three balls remaining in the game, and with just one run to get, South African tail-ender Allan Donald was halfway up the pitch for the winning run when he realised that he'd forgotten his bat … and was run out. When Australia thrashed Pakistan in the final three days later, achieving Pakistan's paltry total of 132 with eight wickets to spare, Steve Waugh's troops had pulled off the extraordinary feat of winning seven sudden-death World Cup games in a row, to win the 1999 World Cup. After a shaky beginning, Steve Waugh and his style of captaincy were now the toast of the Australian sporting world. If there was a difference at this point with the way Waugh had approached the captaincy to the way Taylor had, it was perhaps in the way he nurtured and then trusted his players. Not only was he leading by example, he was also backing them.

Generally, if a player in his side was struggling, Waugh was notable for seeking them out, talking them through it and letting them know they had his full confidence. At different times such team-mates as Ricky Ponting, Matt Hayden, Justin Langer, Andy Bichel, Brett Lee, Michael Kasprowiscz and Shane Warne all benefited from this approach and inevitably responded — often with match-winning performances. Waugh was also a believer in setting goals for the team to reach, both on a daily basis and in designating a position that the team could realistically hope to be at a given point in the season. He then kept the team's attention focused on achieving that goal, no matter if the particular match they were playing in was a dead rubber or whatever. Yet another Waugh initiative was to break down the

# Affirmative Action

This loyalty that Steve Waugh had to his players was no lightly held matter. And it wasn't simply a matter of nurturing team members through difficult times and perhaps speaking up for them to be allowed a little longer than the selectors might otherwise want in the hope that they could soon return to form.

Waugh was even inclined to take matters into his own hands when one of his players was under attack from outside forces. The best example was in South Africa, at a time when a scandalous and completely untrue rumour was circulating about a member of Adam Gilchrist's family and someone in the South African crowd was holding up a banner broadcasting it to the world, while Gilchrist was batting.

Within one minute of spying the banner Waugh had gathered two of his more burly team-mates together with two security guards. As a kind of posse, they walked around the oval, up to the perpetrator and strongly encouraged him to take down the sign. It was done.

OPPOSITE 17 June 1999: Australia ties with South Africa to go through to the final of the World Cup in England. OVERLEAF, FIRST Team-mates Warney and Steve kiss their treasured World Cup. OVERLEAF, SECOND Steve Waugh and Jason Gillespie take adjacent hospital beds in Colombo, Sri Lanka, after their on-field collision in September 1999 left the captain with a broken nose.

barriers between the team and their families. In Steve's first tour of England, the wives and girlfriends had not been allowed to be with the team until the last two weeks of the tour — a code endorsed and enforced by Allan Border himself — and in the meantime you had to make do with meeting them in coffee shops and the like, or their hotel, so long as you were soon after back in your own. Under Taylor that had been softened to a certain degree, but Waugh wanted to take it still further.

As he put it to the press most starkly: 'You can't go on five overseas tours a year and not have family. What's the point of having a family?'

So under Waugh's leadership it became purely a matter for the players to decide. If their wives turned up on tour, with or without kids in tow, then that was their right. Ditto after Test matches. There was to be no more of this nonsense about the inner sanctum being denied to everyone who hadn't worn the baggy green. No more segregation; the families were to be part of it. Waugh invited Lynette and daughter Rosie to come in, and the other players took their cue from that.

And speaking of the baggy green, from now on, Waugh ensured, the moment a new player received his would be an occasion honoured by the whole team. He organised for each debutant to be given his cap by a former baggy green great to make them aware of just what a rich vein of tradition they were now a part of.

RIGHT **Allan Border, the Waughs, Glenn McGrath and Shane Warne backstage with Australian rock band INXS.**

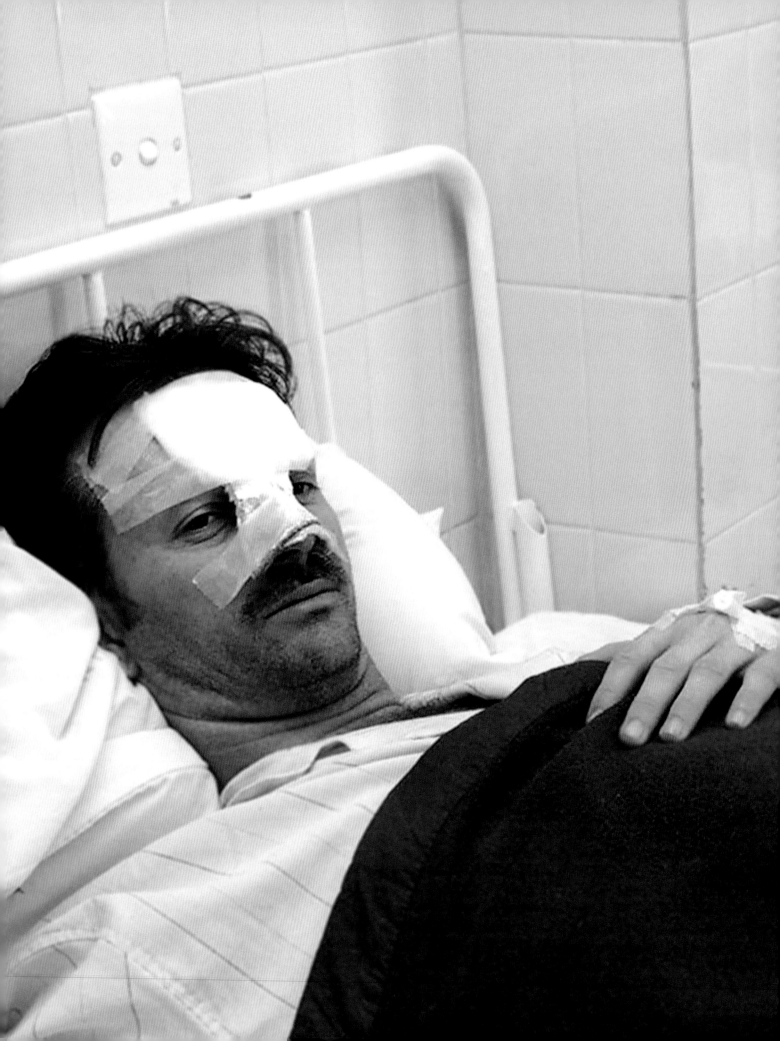

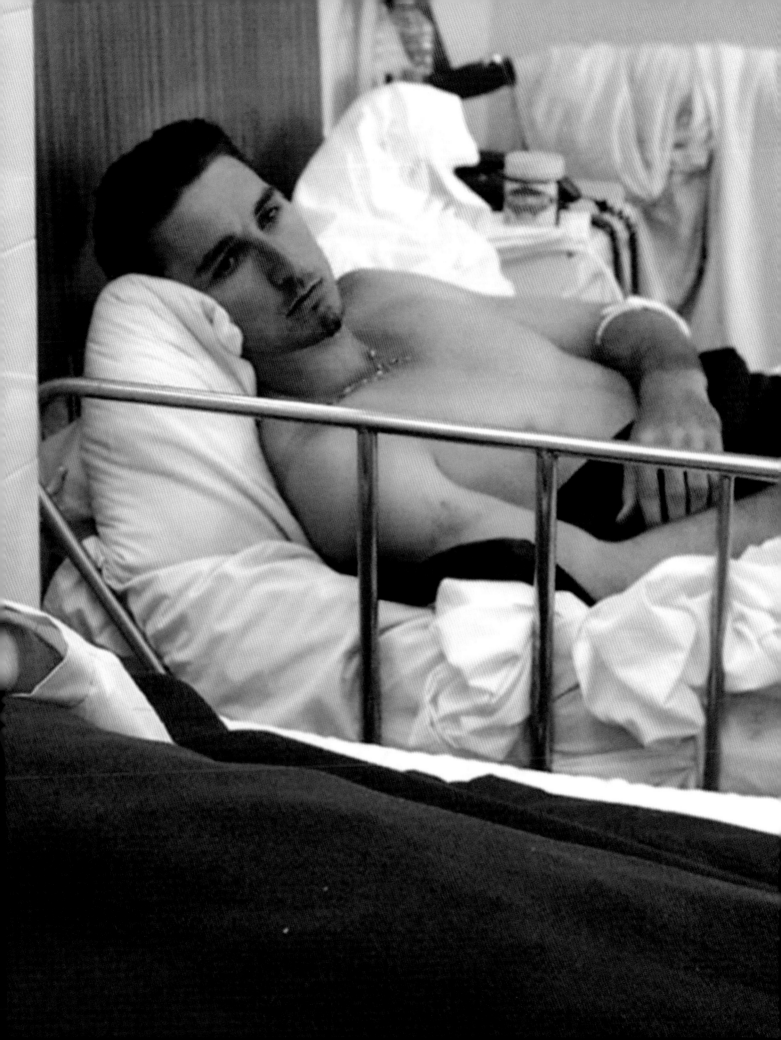

# Waugh
of Words

## Chapter 8

'There is far too much talk about sledging'
Steve Waugh

# 'Sledging, I think, is ... that word is long gone, I think, in cricket. I've always played hard and fair, I've considered it that way' STEVE WAUGH

FOR ALL THE EXTRAORDINARY success the Australians were experiencing, there remained one troubling aspect to Steve Waugh's stewardship. Sledging. As an issue it had been around a long time with the Australian cricket team, and accusations had been levelled many times that the men of the baggy green used it as a naked policy to unsettle the concentration of their opponents.

The word 'sledging' had its origins in the mid-1960s, after a NSW player swore in the presence of a lady and was said to be 'as subtle as a sledgehammer'. Other team-mates put this together with a famous soul singer of the time Percy Sledge, to call such talk a 'Percy', which became 'sledge' and so a whole new word was born. Though sledging was certainly a part of the Ian Chappell era — as it was under Greg Chappell and Kim Hughes — it was said to have become a stronger part of the Australian game under Allan Border's leadership. Under Mark Taylor, there was no doubt that it went on, but without any sense that it was an institutionalised tactic.

But under Waugh, the general impression — backed by a series of ugly incidents — was that it had been allowed to grow to a point where it seemed that the Australian team had turned sledging from mere edgy fun and raised it to a black art. For, traditionally, it wasn't as if sledging didn't sometimes have a certain fun part, most particularly when the 'sledgee' replied in kind, only with a more rapier-like thrust.

The classic and most oft-cited example was when an English county bowler had said to the great Viv Richards after he had played and missed several times: 'It's round, it's red and it's got six stitches in it.' After Richards hit the next ball over the fence and into the far pavilions, the West Indian said: 'Hey mon, you know what it looks like — go fetch it.'

Then there was the time that the great English fast bowler Fred Trueman knocked over the stumps of an ordinary county batsman and was told by the dear departing: 'Good ball, Fred.'

'Aye,' the great Yorkshireman replied, 'and wasted on the likes of thee.'

A closer-to-home example was when Ian Healy called out to

## Cracking Shot

It is the most famous sledging story of the Waugh era, and whether true or not, is the one most often recounted. In 1999, the Australian team was playing Zimbabwe, when one of the Australian bowlers was kept narrowly missing getting the portly Zimbabwean tail-ender Eddo Brandes out. Finally, it was more than flesh and blood and spirit could stand and when Brandes missed the ball completely one more time, still without giving up his wicket, the Australian bowler finished just a couple of metres from the Zimbabwe batsman.

'Why are you so fat?' the bowler snarled, glaring at Brandes.

The reply came back in an instant.

'Because every time I #&$! your wife she gives me a biscuit.'

The upshot?

It was three minutes before the Australian slips cordon could again compose themselves well enough for the bowler to deliver his next ball.

the fieldsman tight around the bat of the English captain, Nasser Hussain — a man with a silhouette that most closely resembled Bill Lawrie's — 'Come in fellas, I want you right up under Nasser's nose' ... before putting them in what could fairly described as a rather broad circle.

Too, it was Healy who in Australia's 1993–94 tour of South Africa had famously called out to Shane Warne when the well-proportioned South African batsman Kosie Venter was struggling, 'Send a Mars Bar down on a length and you'll get him out of his crease!' In response, Venter had pointed to the equally well proportioned close-in fieldsman David Boon, and said: 'No, Boonie will get to it before me.'

And a jolly good time was had by all.

But the accusation against Steve Waugh was that under his command such jesting play got entirely out of hand and turned into virulent abuse. The classic example came just three weeks after the Australian Cricket Board had launched an initiative entitled the 'Spirit of Cricket', a kind of conduct code designed to ensure that all Australian players knew their obligations to behave with good sportsmanship. That was when Glenn McGrath had exploded at the 21-year-old West Indian batsman Ramnaresh Sarwan in a homophobic slur, to which Sarwan had responded in kind — causing McGrath to wildly gesticulate and threaten physical violence, all while the cameras rolled. In the face of it — and just as had happened a couple of years earlier when Michael Slater was abusing an Indian umpire over a decision he disagreed with — Steve Waugh was seen to do nothing. The impression gained, fairly or unfairly, was that the captain had no problem with such behaviour.

And indeed, Waugh made it clear that he really had no problem with the basic concept of fielders and bowlers disturbing a batsman's concentration by talk.

When asked about it at the NRL Grand Final breakfast, in August 2000, Waugh was unequivocal, and used a phrase that would all but instantly become famous.

'I don't think we sledge,' he said. 'I would prefer to call it

Just how did you stop a player like Stephen Rodger Waugh? It was something that was much discussed among opposition teams, and clearly no particular team ever came up with an answer.

From former England captain Michael Atherton's autobiography, *Opening Up*: 'We also decided at the Old Trafford [during the 1997 Ashes series] not to sledge [Steve] Waugh or engage him in any way. We felt he revelled in a hostile atmosphere and sledging merely fuelled his adrenalin. He arrived at the crease and soon realised this: "OK, you're not talking to me, are you? Well, I'll talk to myself then." And he did, for 240 minutes in the first innings, and 382 minutes in the second.'

"mental disintegration". It's all part of the game. Test cricket is about not only testing your skill but testing your mind powers in certain situations, how you handle it.'

Mental disintegration. In all likelihood the genesis of the phrase was Allan Border's remark to Waugh back in 1994, when he was justifying grinding England right down into the dirt to cause their 'mental and physical disintegration', but it would undoubtedly become Waugh's most oft-cited quote.

Where Waugh and we critics parted company, however, was firstly in his assertion that that kind of sledging had always been around. 'People say it didn't happen, but it did,' he maintained. 'I've spoken to cricketers who have been around for a while and there has always been that element of talk out there.'

Secondly, Waugh insisted that contrary to popular belief, sledging was rarely straight at a player, but more in fieldsmen discussing among themselves something that might put them off and change their concentrated approach.

'If we can get them thinking about something other than what they're supposed to be thinking about,' he said, 'then that's what Test cricket is all about.'

In short, no apologies and no quarter asked for or given.

'I think we play in the right spirit 95 per cent of the time, at least,' he told Andrew Denton on his show *Enough Rope*. 'Automatically when you're the top side, people say, "Oh, it's Australia and it's their fault." But that's wrong. We play the game in the right spirit, I believe, and we've made a conscious effort to correct that over the last couple of years.'

Ultimately, it was an area of Steve Waugh's career where he and many of his supporters agreed to differ. He thought it part of the game. We thought the game should be well above that, and that men who wore the baggy green should be doubly so.

OPPOSITE **England's Nasser Hussain (left) watches Steve's back while they await the third umpire's decision, 26 December 2002 at the MCG.**
ABOVE **England captain Mike Atherton at Old Trafford in July 1997.**

# From Dominator to Discard

## Chapter 9

'I'm quite normal. I go down the street and people look at me and I think, "Why do they want to talk to me?" I still don't get that'
Steve Waugh

# The Spirit of
# Shell Green

It was Australia's foremost military man, Lieutenant-General Peter Cosgrove, who told Steve Waugh the story over dinner one night, and the Australian captain was immediately smitten with the romance of it all, and determined to do something to honour it in some way …

It was at Gallipoli, in December 1915. The battle had been lost, the struggle foregone. Britain's General Kitchener gave the orders to pull the ANZACs out and send them on to the Western Front in France.

Under cover of darkness, the evacuation began on December 8, and as the ranks began to noticeably thin over the next few days, it was decided something should be done to alleviate whatever suspicions Johnny Turk might be harbouring about the decreased activity.

Some men from NSW's 4th Battalion thought a game of cricket might do the trick! The relationship between the Turks and the Anzacs had evolved by this time to the point where taking pot-shots at distant figures was not absolutely automatic, but on the other hand, the departing hospital ships were full of diggers who had trusted this line of reasoning too far. It was a tentative group therefore, who, on the afternoon of December 17, set foot on the pockmarked patch of ground known as Shell Green (so named because it was under permanent Turkish artillery fire). The Turks in the trenches above must have wondered what on earth was going on as the game started. Was this grenade-throwing practice? Or perhaps a method of whacking

WITH THEIR SUCCESS IN the 1999 World Cup as their launching pad, the Australian team now moved into a period where victory succeeded victory to the point that records tumbled with their every outing. Prior to Steve Waugh taking over command of the Australian Test team, the record number of successive victories for an Australian Test team was nine, under Warwick Armstrong in 1920/21, while the great West Indies side under Clive Lloyd in the 1980s had shattered that to put eleven straight wins together …

This extraordinary stretch began with a 10-wicket win over Zimbabwe in Harare in October 1999, continued through six hard-fought triumphs over Pakistan and India as they toured Australia over the summer of '99/00 (during which time Steve was able to fly from the first crushing victory over Pakistan in Brisbane to be present for the birth of his second child, Austin), before New Zealand lost three in a row at Australia's hands.

Then the once-mighty West Indies were at last brought to their knees by losing five successive Tests as they toured Australia in the summer of '00/01, and Australia followed it all with very handy chaser of a wonderful 10-wicket victory over India in just three days in Mumbai to make it sixteen wins and allow Mr Guinness Record to at last take pause.

Through it all, there was Steve Waugh, marshalling his charges, pushing them, cajoling, nurturing and showing the way himself with the bat. Dorothy Parker had once famously said, 'I've been rich, and I've been poor — rich is better', but Steve could just about top her. He had known what it was to go for fourteen Test matches without a win, as he had started his career, and now he had known what it was to go for sixteen matches without defeat — and he, too, certainly knew which was better. Always the Waugh way was to pile the pressure on their opponents from the first moment, forcing the scoring rate if the Australians were batting — on the firm belief that even if the first few Australian batsman didn't fire, the middle-order would do the job and they always had the most fiercely wagging tail in world cricket to fall back upon if all else failed. In both bowling and fielding, the emphasis was on attack above all else. While the

likes of Glenn McGrath, Jason Gillespie and Shane Warne blasted, bounced and wove, always searching for a way through the opposition's defences, they were able to do so in the confidence that the best and most highly trained fielding side in the world was right on the case to turn what might have been boundaries into singles, and what were really only half-chances into wickets.

Of course, it had to end sometime, and an end to the run came in the second Test in Kolkata. Just when Australia seemed to have India at its mercy, VVS Laxman delivered India's greatest innings through the ages with a 281, providing the basis for an improbable Indian victory … but what a ride it had been!

IT WAS FROM THIS point on, however, that things began to severely tighten up on Waugh in terms of runs scored. In the summer of 2001–02, consisting of six Tests against New Zealand and then South Africa, Waugh only managed to string together a very humble — and notably scratchy at that — 219 runs at an average of 27.38. In the one-day version of the game things were even grimmer as, for the first time, the Australian team failed to be one of the two finalists in the three-team World Series competition, and Waugh's own form was seen as part of the problem.

People began to talk, commentators to carefully wring their hands. Waugh was, after all, a man in his 37th year, and what does it say when in the summer of his 24th year he had been able to average 126 runs in one Test campaign against the English, and yet his average over that summer was now down in the twenties. What did it say when he was incapable of leading a team to beat even the likes of New Zealand in a World Series?

What it said to a lot of people was that it was time for him to go.

Possibly, just part of the problem — in terms of the captain's lack of Test form — was that as soon as Matthew Hayden and Justin Langer had came together as an opening partnership in the 2001 Ashes campaign, runs had flowed for them as never before, and instead of Steve Waugh walking out to the wicket with the score at

The Spirit of Shell Green
[ *continued* ]

incoming grenades back to the trenches whence they came?

Who knows what they thought, but for the first two hours of the game the Turks held their fire and watched. But after a couple of hours the Turks had had enough and start to lob a few mortars in the cricketers' direction.

Did the mortar fire stop the cricket cold? Not bloody likely. According to the diary of one Granville Ryrie, the game continued anyway, 'just to let them see we were quite unconcerned … and when shells whistled by we pretended to field them. The men were wonderfully cheerful and seemed to take the whole thing as a huge joke.'

When the Australians still didn't retire, the Turks unleashed doubly heavy salvos of mortar fire and, to use historian Bill Gammage's phrase, 'the Australians reluctantly called it a draw and retired to tea'.

Happily, there is no record of any player having to 'retire hurt', or worse, during the game.

Two days later, all players were safely evacuated to either be killed on the fields of France or to survive and make it home, home to Australia …

It was, therefore, at Steve Waugh's instigation that on the way to the Ashes tour of England in May 2001, the Australian team stopped off at Gallipoli for a day. All of the Australian team members were stunned to see up close what they had long heard about, and to realise just what it was that their forebears had faced all those years ago.

Steve, particularly — when looking

3/not much as it had so often been, over that summer it had frequently been 3/HEAPS.

And just as, over the years, Waugh's abilities and determination had always grown in proportion to the grimness of the situation, so too did it now seem that his capacity to put together a huge innings diminished the more that all was right with the world. Though for ten years after his recall to the Australian team in '91/92 he was averaging no fewer than 60 runs every innings, and knocked over twenty-three centuries along the way, things suddenly changed. As Langer and Hayden — the two men in the team whose cause he had most championed over the years and put time towards — continued to break opening partnership records, over that summer Waugh's own flow of runs simply dried up …

Finally, things came to a head.

In mid-February, just five days after South Africa had beaten New Zealand in the one-day finals, a final selection discussion was held over the phone between Trevor Hohns, Andrew Hilditch and David Boon and Allan Border, and among other things a firm decision was taken on Steve Waugh. It had been a bruising, gut-wrenching decision, so much so that Allan Border later recounted: 'I remember putting the phone down and feeling physically ill.'

He was not the only one who felt crook about it. For it was down in Melbourne two days later that chairman of selectors Trevor Hohns visited Steve Waugh in his hotel room, ostensibly to discuss the team that would be playing the forthcoming Tests in South Africa. Delicately then, carefully, carefully, Hohns steered the discussion to the one-day tournament that would be also played. Finally there was nothing for it, and even though he was fully aware of just what effect his words would have, Hohns did what he had to do and came out and said it:

'We have decided to go in a different direction,' he told the Australian captain, 'and you are not part of that plan.'

For a moment, Steve Waugh was convinced he must have heard his old team-mate wrong.

Say, what?

at the narrow shore suddenly giving way to cruel steep hills that looked near impossible to climb unburdened, let alone with 30 kilos on your back and blanket machine gun-fire swarming all around — was deeply moved. Were they, mere cricketers, really often referred to as heroes, for what they did? It really put it all into perspective.

For an afternoon, they wandered all over, sticking tightly together and not talking a lot, soaking up the atmosphere at what all felt to be a sacred site of their tribe. At Anzac Cove, Steve and Mark laid a wreath in memory of the fallen. At Lone Pine, they were shown the spot where 6000 men had died for land that did not total more than two tennis courts. At a spot called Nek, they climbed down into the trenches, where a famous Australian charge had taken place right into the teeth of the Turks, with devastating results. When the first two waves of Australians had been cut to ribbons, still the third wave came on …

'Mate having said goodbye to mate,' the official historian CWE Bean recounted, 'the third line took up its position on the fire-step.'

The whistle blew and they charged. And were wiped out.

'With that regiment went the flower of the youth of Western Australia, sons of the old pioneering families, youngsters — in some cases two or three from the same home — who had flocked to Perth at the outbreak of the war with their own horses and saddlery … Men known and popular, the best loved leaders in sport and work in the West, then rushed straight to their death.'

## The Spirit of Shell Green
[ *continued* ]

Waugh, hearing the story, while standing right there in the very trenches those men had charged from to their all-but-certain deaths felt deeply emotional.

'It was a humbling time,' he wrote in his diary, 'and also a proud moment to think these Australians stayed as one as they went over the top despite knowing they weren't coming back. They believed they were helping the Allies by sacrificing themselves in order for a bigger plan to work.'

While posing for photographs in the trenches, all members of the Australian team wore slouch hats, with more than one accompanying journalist noting that while most of the modern men looked faintly ridiculous, Waugh really looked the part. There was just something about him, where it was easy to imagine him in that place, at that time, making ready to go with all the rest, and just maybe leading the charge.

The climax of the afternoon was when the team visited Shell Green, to recreate the cricket game that had been played so many years before.

The area was all overgrown with thick grass now, but Steve Waugh took up position in much the same spot as the batsman of all those years ago, while Adam Gilchrist squatted behind, Glenn McGrath moved into bowl, and the others fielded. It was odd, weird, but you could just about swear that the spirit of those very diggers were with them right there and then, and were pleased that the men who wore the same baggy green cap that they themselves would have

You're not in. You won't be part of the one-day campaign in South Africa. You're out.

Bloody hell. After politely ushering Hohns to the door, Steve Waugh did what he always did when under the most pressure. He called Lynette.

She encouraged him to take it calmly.

'Things happen for a reason,' she said. 'It mightn't be clear right now but it will work out in the end.'

Then he phoned his manager, who pointed out that people got dropped all the time and were still able to fight their way back into the side. Yes, this was a blow, but it didn't have to knock him down for good in the one-day game.

So it was that in a dignified press conference, on the afternoon of 11 February 2002, Waugh himself affirmed his disappointment, but added a rider.

'I'm a determined sort of a person,' he said, 'and I'll do everything in my power to get back into the one-day side. My campaign begins today.'

It was brave, but few in the room believed he could do it. For the troubled mood among the gathering at the time was a little like what it must have been when Sir Donald Bradman famously got a duck in his last Test innings. It simply seemed out of kilter that such a one-day career as Waugh's — 325 appearances, a stunning win in 1987, countless winning campaigns, holding the 1999 World Cup aloft as the victorious captain — could end thus.

No matter. Waugh's eyes were on the prize, and the prize was clear — to get back into the side before the 2003 World Cup campaign.

So Waugh simply got on with it, confident that he could turn things around by simple dint of the force of his bat, and the runs that could flow from it with such force all obstacles would cede.

Others close to him, however, were less sanguine, and one of these was his maternal grandmother, Dorothea Bourne of Panania, who he heard was most upset indeed.

Landing in South Africa then, one of the first things he did was

to ring her, and tell her.

'Don't worry about me, Nan, I'm all right. I'm looking forward to the future ...'

And sure enough, within a week he had nailed a century against the South African A side, giving encouragement to a groundswell of public support — very close to a campaign — to restore him to his position.

In all the hullabaloo, there were very few voices of real cricketing credibility who spoke up for the selectors, but one of them was Ian Chappell, who wrote in *The Bulletin*:

'It took courage to chop down one of the four pillars supporting the Australian cricket team, rather than let them crumble in unison and bring the whole structure crashing down. One of the few upsides to Waugh's sacking was that it illustrated the selectors aren't constrained by the ludicrous thought that only one person is capable of captaining Australia. The panel made this mistake when Mark Taylor struggled for runs in 1996–97.'

What was sure was that the team didn't struggle without Waugh. His replacement as captain, Ricky Ponting, guided the one-day Australian team to a 5–1 victory over South Africa, well on his way to a 12–4 record from his first sixteen matches as skipper ...

ULTIMATELY THOUGH, NOTHING WAUGH did could change the selectors' minds, and on 2 December 2002, Waugh was officially left out of the Australian Cricket Board's preliminary thirty-man 'shadow squad' for the 2003 World Cup.

It was a bitter blow when it fell, no matter how semi-expected it must have been.

How the mighty had fallen. Waugh had started the year as captain of the one-day team, by definition the primary player in the joint, and finished it as only 31st-ranked player, at best.

In response to his omission, Waugh, while he took it gracefully enough, announced that he would still do everything in his power to make the selectors change their minds, and he was heartened by a

The Spirit of Shell Green
[ *continued* ]

recognised and revered, were doing them the honour of paying them a visit, eighty years later.

'Everyone talks about the Anzac spirit,' Waugh wrote. 'To me, it means being together, fighting together and looking after your mates. These are Australian values, which I want the Australian cricket team to always carry ...'

And so they did. For although going into that Ashes series it had been noted that things had been so bad for England of late that Saddam Hussein had had more victories ... and that the English batting was so ordinary that the selectors were thinking of moving 'Extras' up the order ... Waugh would not have anyone in the Australian Test team laughing about it, least of all him. For of all the blokes in the team he was the only one who knew what it was like to lose an Ashes series, and he was absolutely determined that it wasn't going to happen on his watch. For one of the key Australian values of course, is that on any sporting field you always had to put England to the sword, no matter what, and that is precisely what Waugh's side did, going on to win the series 4–1.

Waugh personally had a few difficult moments — none more so than when he had to break the news to his friend, the opening batsman Michael Slater, that he had been dropped for Justin Langer for the fifth Test — but generally came through it well. Still, even though the runs did not quite flow for him the way they had in previous Ashes campaigns — and even though on his birthday in early June the team,

The Spirit of Shell Green
[ *continued* ]

RIGHT **Steve Waugh at the press conference that announced his removal from the one-day team.**

in high hilarity, had given him a walking stick — the fact that he was able to score a century in the final Test, despite carrying a quite severe calf injury, showed that there was still a lot of fight left in him, and that he was still Steve*Waugh*.

## Shock of the New

It took many people some time to wrap their heads around the fact that the seeming Uluru of both national cricket sides was no more.

At the conclusion of the third Ashes Test in the 2002/2003 season, Steve Waugh was being interviewed by Tony Greig, and their conversation went like this.

Tony Greig: 'So there is now a break from Test matches for the English, which I am sure they will be looking forward to, with one-dayers to be played over the next few weeks. Are you looking forward to the one-dayers, Steve?'

Steve Waugh: 'Well, not really, Tony. I'm not in the one-day team ...'

massive outpouring of anger from the public towards the selectors — 'The selectors couldn't pick Bill Lawrie's nose!' ran the general theme — and an equal outpouring of support for him.

In Sydney, the *Daily Telegraph* ran what was effectively a public campaign to have him restored to the side, with front and back page headlines, editorials, petitions, fax numbers, the lot. Waugh thought there might be a glimmer of a chance if he could just get enough runs, and four days after his omission, playing for NSW against the touring English side in a day/night game at the SCG, Waugh promoted himself in the order above Michael Clarke to blast 24 unbeaten runs off just 12 balls to finish the English off in an 8-wicket victory and remind the selectors, and the public, that he could still do it.

Eighteen of the runs came from three massive sixes of medium pacer Ronnie Irani, and the third of those came when just one run was required to win. As Waugh sent the ball hurtling to the far pavilions, he walked back the dressing room with seemingly the entire SCG chanting his name. The people were with him. But the selectors were not. On December 31, the selectors announced the fifteen-man squad to compete in the 2003 World Cup, and SR Waugh was not among them.

It had been a tough year. The runs had not come easily, and highlighting the fact that his time to finish all cricket must surely be drawing near was Mark being dropped from the Test team in October 2002. The younger Waugh immediately announced his retirement from international cricket.

The case for Steve Waugh himself to be dropped had been put with increasing frequency throughout the year, and never more cogently than by David Hookes, the former dashing Test player turned media commentator of great renown.

'Which player on 700 grand a year is going to retire?' he said. 'The more money in the game, the more responsibility is on the selectors.'

Much of the comment focused on Waugh's age, and the fact that all of the Australian cricket team was getting on — nine players in the Test XI were thirty-something. It had to be obvious even to

Blind Freddie that some rejuvenation of the ranks was called for, and there could be no better place to start than with the 37-year-old captain who was clearly not playing anywhere as near as well as he used to.

To some extent, too, Waugh was hoist on his petard when, as *Sydney Morning Herald* reader Bev Miles pointed out, a passage from Steve Waugh's own *South African Tour Diary* from June 1994 went: 'On May 11, Allan Border announced he had decided to retire from international cricket. Not long after, Mark Taylor was confirmed as his successor with Ian Healy his deputy. The period that led up to AB's decision must have been an agonising one for him, especially as he was still playing to a level that would have seen him continue to be successful for many years to come. Without doubt, there would have been many reasons behind his decision but, in the end, I believe he made the right choice because he went out with his form sky-high, like every champion should.' The pressure on Waugh to stand down, at least from the one-day version of the game, and call it a day, grew by the day.

On *The Back Page*, a pay-television show for talking heads, Peter FitzSimons, a former Wallaby of little note, said that it should be all over for Waugh, that while he really had been a great player over the years, it was clearly time to give it away. As if FitzSimons had any bloody idea at all …

Sometimes it must have seemed to Waugh that just about everyone was agin him, though there was certainly never any doubt where his family stood. On one occasion, as a matter of fact, when a couple of sports commentators on Sydney radio station 2UE were discussing the Steve Waugh situation, and one commentator was advocating that it was time for Waugh to go, they got an interesting talkback call. It was from Rodger Waugh, in a mood to give them a bit of what-for, and he did exactly that. His son, he said, was the best man for the job, and would bloody-well prove it to the lot of them, don't you worry about that …

Steve Waugh himself, not surprisingly, also felt he still had it in him. He felt good. He had done this before, and knew that he could

## Buried Alive

Though stripped of the one-day captaincy, Waugh lost none of his presence because of it. When, for example, the following June he was playing for Kent against Worcestershire in English county cricket, an interesting episode occurred. He was making his way onto the field, bat in hand, when the man on the public address system announced that the 'former Australian captain' was about to take strike. In a split second our Steve had stopped. Turned. Glared. Then, and only then, did he make his way to the pitch …

The story is only spoiled by the fact that Waugh then went on to get only 3 runs, playing on to the English bowler David Leatherdale who, Waugh once said, 'wouldn't get a bowl in a Chinese restaurant'.

On another occasion, when playing Yorkshire, their fast bowler Steve Kirby greeted Waugh with a barrage of abuse as soon as the Australian made his way onto the ground with bat in hand.

'We don't want you here! Get out of my ground!' Kirby shouted to Waugh.

'No, I won't. This is my favourite pitch,' Waugh replied. 'And who are you? The *#@%&+- mayor?'

## Hard Core, Hard Calls

In the era in which Steve Waugh played, there were three notable Hard Men to beat all Hard Men to play for Australia: Allan Border, David Boon and Stephen Waugh. In a way, it was Waugh's misfortune that the first two were on Australia's four-man selection panel, because neither Border nor Boon would likely have been swayed by the Old Mates Act and the fact that both men had played for many years with Waugh. Instead, as Hard Men, they did what had to be done and brought the curtain down on his one-day career.

How do we know that Stephen Rodger Waugh would have done the same, for the good of the team? We don't. But at the very least we know that it was Waugh himself who tapped Michael Slater on the shoulder just before the fifth Ashes Test in 2001 and told him it was over. It was a brutal decision at the time, but was ultimately vindicated by the form of the man who replaced Slater, Justin Langer. Ditto Waugh's move to drop Shane Warne from the crucial fourth Test against the Windies in 1999. Warne had hated it, but it had proved to be the right decision when Australia emerged with a victory and was able to retain the Frank Worrell Trophy.

do it again. In the previous decade, since making his way back to the Australian side, the foundation stone of his extraordinary success had been his immovable self-belief, and that self-belief was every bit as intact now as it had ever been, whatever the bloody critics might have to say about it.

And this self-belief persisted even when, in the second innings of the fourth Test against England, in Melbourne, Waugh came perilously close to humiliating himself, making 14 runs from 25 balls, but effectively losing his wicket on three occasions. On the first occasion, extraordinarily, no one had appealed because they didn't realise the Australian captain had snicked the ball; on the second occasion he was caught on a no-ball, and on the third occasion he was — *Gone! Got him, yes!* — dead to rights, caught at second slip. No matter that, as it turned out, Waugh had a migraine that would have killed a brown dog. It was clear that the Iceman had long ago melted and was now a mere watery version of what he once had been, and we in the media said so with alacrity ... said it was time for him to call it a day.

Reporter: 'There are those who are suggesting it's time for you to retire — how do you react to that?'

Steve Waugh: 'I know myself what my form is like and what I can achieve. I know I can still go on and score Test match hundreds ...'

Much of the international cricket community: 'Yeah, right ...'

# The Century

# Chapter 10

'Do not go gentle into that good night. Rage, rage against the dying of the light'
Dylan Thomas

'One hour of life, crowded to the full with glorious action, and filled with noble risks, is worth whole years of those mean observances of paltry decorum' Walter Scott

IT IS 3 JANUARY 2003, the second day of the fifth Test of the Ashes series — Steve Waugh's 156th Test overall, equalling Allan Border's record for Test appearances by an Australian. It is a beautiful summer's afternoon like only Sydney makes them, with the heat of the sun slightly offset by the sea breeze, and a crystal quality to the air that can only be found in the most shining of diamond days. The SCG, that grand ol' girl that has seen the world's finest cricketers come and go over the years, is packed to the proverbials, and all are waiting for one thing. Steve Waugh, the Sydney boy, to come to the crease. At last, it happens …

At exactly 3.26 p.m., Waugh's closest friend in the team, Justin Langer, botches a hook shot and top-edges a catch down to fine-leg.

The score is now 3/56 — still over 300 shy of England's first innings total of 362 — meaning the best of all possible things. You beauty, Australia is in trouble. Just like it was in days of yore! This looks like a job for …

All eyes turn to the southern end of the green-roofed Members Stand …

There! The 40 000-strong capacity crowd sees Steve Waugh's green-helmeted head bob-bob-bobbing up and down through the heads of so many others, and a massive roar goes up, even as they leap to their feet in a spontaneous standing ovation. On he comes, down the path he has walked so many times before, out from the shadows, into the light and full view. Putting his gloves on as he walks. No smiling. He is here on business.

He barely acknowledges Langer as he passes. However close their friendship, whatever the poignancy of the moment, this is a man with a job o'work to do and he clearly has only two things on his mind. Redemption, and punishment. This day, Waugh just *looks* like a man who is going to shove it down the critics' throats one more time for the road, and England's bloody throats while he is at it — and the crowd is clearly with him every step of the way. Even the Barmy Army, the famed band of English supporters, seems to be caught up in the euphoria of the moment, as they are cheering too.

As he makes his way to the centre and the cheering continues,

'Consider the many variables Steve has to contend with every time he goes out to bat: humidity, moisture, breed of grass, length of grass, prevailing winds, cloud cover, available light, trajectory, velocity, spin, swing, bounce, age of the ball, self-expectation, human fallibility, sledging, heckling and psychological intimidation — and that's just from the non-striker's end' ANDREW DENTON LAUNCHING STEVE WAUGH'S BOOK, *NEVER SAY DIE*

Waugh barely even looks up, however much he is gratified and uplifted by it, and certainly doesn't pause to read the many banners around the ground proclaiming the people's enormous affection.

WE BELIEVE IN STEVE reads one. BEV, THANKS FOR THE TWINS, says another. In the stands, Steve's mother Bev is sitting, with tears in her eyes, with the rest of the Waugh clan including, most particularly, Steve's wife Lynette. For nigh on two decades, Lynette has been *willing* her man to do well, but never has she wanted him to crank out a good innings like she wants it now, and she has joined the ovation with all the rest, her hands clapping vigorously above her head right up until the moment her husband takes strike.

But hush ...

Waugh on strike. Andy Caddick to bowl. The *pulse* of the ground, which has been racing, now slows a little as everyone concentrates, soaking it up, wanting to savour the moment, while equally being also a little fearful that despite all their acclaim the hero of the moment might fall at their feet. Finished. Washed up.

Caddick roaring into the crease now, while up the other end all is quiet — the English long ago learnt their lesson when it came to sledging Waugh — bar the *tap-tap-tap*ping of Steve's bat on the wicket, as the ball is sent on its way.

And on its way it goes as, most particularly off the bowling of Caddick's fast-bowling partner, Steve Harmison, Waugh knocks out 9 runs before tea, including a boundary, with every scoring stroke receiving another almighty roar from the crowd.

For the previous quarter-hour, just as he has been doing nothing but focusing on the job at hand, so too has Lynette. Her eyes are intent on Steve; she is not talking to anyone around her; she *believes* he can do this.

And now, after the tea break he's back at it. Feeling good, feeling strong, taking it to them, as he clips the English attack to all parts of the ground he knows so well. Off one Andy Caddick over shortly after tea, Waugh scores 14 runs, which includes three boundaries. He is in his high 40s when drinks are called at 5 p.m.

And here is something different. For coming out on to the

ground carrying the drinks is no less than Andrew Denton, who — as the result of having bid a very high price in a charity auction — has won the right to take over the twelfth man duties. It is a difficult situation for Denton to find himself in. He's a man known for his wit and irreverence, and yet here he is right in the middle of a very serious, historic sporting moment, quite possibly the defining innings of the dominant cricketer of his generation and the most revered figure in the Australian game. How to handle it? Off the cuff.

'Don't be home before six ...' Denton says to Steve Waugh, before drifting off.


AND INDEED ...

The shadows from the Members Stand are lengthening now, reaching out towards the centre, almost as if they are wanting to claim the one who is now the sole focus of attention of the entire ground, and most of the nation. But he is not done yet.

Sweetly striking a slightly wayward half-volley from Andy Caddick, Waugh scorches an off-drive boundary to bring up his 50 and the ground explodes with acclaim, all of the crowd again on their feet. Waugh lifts his bat in token acknowledgment, but no more than that. This is not yet redemption, and nowhere *near* enough punishment for the English. Or the critics.

Now established, and seeing the ball well, with the crowd right behind him, Waugh sets about lifting the tempo further still. While still defending his wicket fiercely, he goes after the attack with gusto, and frequently sends the ball hurtling to the fence, while the Englishmen do what Australians have always loved to see them do at the SCG — *chase leather!* The spirit of Yabba, the famous barracker from the SCG Hill, who in the 1920s and '30s would yell out 'Have a go, ya mug!' to anyone dawdling at the wicket, must have been pleased.

For whatever else, Waugh really is having a go, chancing his arm, *backing himself* — to use his own mantra — to give it to the Pommies one more time. And here's another one for you, Ian Chappell, as he sends the ball roaring to the picket fence yet again!

'I don't see myself being an age. I see myself being competitive and really enjoying it. My age has got nothing to do with how I play, or my attitude. Age can be overplayed sometimes. If you still have that fire in the belly and you're good enough you can play until any time you want to' STEVE WAUGH, REPLYING TO THOSE WHO SAID HE WAS TOO OLD TO PLAY TEST CRICKET

As Waugh passes 60, the realisation grows among the crowd that they are witnessing something extraordinary, a 'Waugh Innings for the Ages', a knock that would be talked about for years to come, and *they are there* as he is doing it.

Then to the first major milestone of the afternoon ...

With a back-foot cut for a boundary, Waugh notches up his 10 000th Test cricket run, a mystical mark only reached twice before, by Allan Robert Border and the great Indian captain and batsman Sunil Gavaskar.

The crowd is on its feet once more, screaming, swaying, willing him to go on with it.

High up in the gods of the SCG Members Stand at this moment, even a visiting Englishman is clearly enjoying the whole spectacle enormously — despite the fact that his team is taking a hammering in this session — and can barely contain his excitement. So much so that when his mobile phone rings by pure happenstance, just as the crowd is finding their seats again, he answers and bursts forth with a one-sided conversation that everyone within 20 metres can hear:

'Yes, darling, it's a great day ... Steve Waugh just scored his 10 000th run!'...

'No dear, not today ...'

... 'Mmmm ... over the last week or so, I believe.'

WAUGH BATS ON. GOING even harder now, and by God he needs to. For the next question is, can he get a century before the close of play? As the shadows continue to lengthen, there is one other focal point of attention competing with Waugh now, the clock atop the Members Stand that, traditionally, the umpires follow to call the close of play.

Can he get to 100 by stumps or not? In the news room at Sydney's Channel 9 studios at this point, furious discussions are taking place. If the game goes past six o'clock, as seems likely, and Steve Waugh is within cooee of his century, can they really just leave the east coast viewers behind with regret, and say sorry, but the *six*

*o'clock* news is just that and cannot be delayed? They cannot. The decision is taken that for the bulk of Australian viewers this is the only news that counts on this day, anyway, and they will stay with Steve Waugh.

With 2 overs to go, he is on 88 runs, meaning that he has 12 balls to get 12 runs. Go for it? Or consolidate? Yabba, what do you say?

Of course, he goes for it. Flashing his bat, backing himself, scrambling through, his score races north, and finally, it has come to this ...

With three balls to go till stumps, Waugh hits a cover drive for a mighty 3 runs, to bring him up to 98, but ...

But this leaves Adam Gilchrist on strike with two balls to go. Around the ground, the chant of '*Sin-gle!*' '*Sin-gle!*' '*Sin-gle!*' goes up. The people have spoken. Their will is clear. It is up to Gilchrist to get Waugh on strike for the last ball of the day, and give him the chance to reach his century. Anything less is unthinkable, and it is simply unimaginable that after the afternoon they have all experienced, Waugh could be allowed to get to stumps without even the chance to finish the job.

The English spinner Richard Dawson dances in ...

Gilchrist — who in year nine at high school had a photo of Steve Waugh front and centre on the cover of his maths book — glides a beautifully timed nudge to mid-wicket and it is done! There may have been other occasions in the history of Test cricket when a modest single — that didn't win a match — has been cause for such a roar of appreciation, but it is unlikely. Waugh is on strike now.

The crowd continues to roar for all of the next ninety seconds as the English captain Nasser Hussain laboriously rearranges his field to maximise the pressure on Waugh and give Dawson every chance to pick up the prize wicket to beat them all.

Up in the ABC commentary box, England's Jonathan Agnew and Australia's Kerry O'Keefe are doing the honours, their words being beamed right around Australia and the United Kingdom.

Agnew: 'Well, what high drama we have here, Kerry. What will he do?'

ABOVE **Out ... finally.** Matthew Hoggard of England claims a prized scalp.

OVERLEAF, LEFT Steve leaps for joy after scoring his century, as Adam Gilchrist attempts a high-five; RIGHT Humble in triumph, Steve acknowledges the crowd's appreciation of his feat.

O'Keefe: 'He'll go for it.'

Agnew: 'But he could come back tomorrow and wait for a trundler down the leg side …'

O'Keefe: 'Stuff tomorrow, Aggers. Tomorrow is for silver medallists. We're Australians. *Poms* come back tomorrow. Australians only want the gold and we want it now ... He'll go for it.'

Two seconds later, Dawson dances in again, flights his spinning orb towards Waugh ... pitching just outside the off-stump ... while the crowd hangs in suspended animation ... as it lands and snarls up ... as Waugh moves ... on to his back foot ... and CRACKS it ... straightintothefence!

Around the SCG, and indeed around the nation, not to mention from the throats of tens of thousands of expats in the United Kingdom and around the world, there is an explosion of Australian joy in a single moment only rarely experienced — a moment right up there with Kieren Perkins's second gold-medal swim in Atlanta in 1996, the Wallabies' first World Cup victory in 1991 and the America's Cup win of 1983.

It is Steve Waugh's 29th Test century, a number that is the equal of Bradman. As the crowd continues to roar, as the umpires gather the bails for the close of the day's play, Waugh pauses for a savouring moment, waving his bat in acknowledgment of the crowd, with a special wave for Lynette as the cameras catch her covering her face with her hands as the tears of relief and joy flow.

His 102 not out at stumps has come from 130 balls and has included no fewer than 18 boundaries. From 3/56 when he arrived at the crease, he has guided Australia to a much healthier postion of 5/237, just as he has so often done in days gone by.

In the inner sanctum of the dressing room immediately afterwards, there is an extraordinary moment as Waugh sits, exhausted, head down at his locker, not saying a word, as his team-mates stand in a virtual arc of awe, themselves not speaking, just soaking it all up. Somehow, *somehow* he has done it. He fair dinkum *has* shown them all.

Soon though, as the pressure on the dressing room builds to the point where the moment must be broken, Waugh sits awash in the

'You're never sure when it will happen. It may never happen. It's something I have always striven for, to play the almost perfect innings, and today was pretty close to as good as I could play' STEVE WAUGH

congratulations of the team and officials, a few ex-players, the Prime Minister and, most importantly, Lynette and six-year-old Rosalie. Even as they talk, though, all became aware of a kind of muffled but still throbbing roar that simply never ebbs.

Steve WAUGH ... Steve WAUGH ... Steve WAUGH ... Steve WAUGH ...

It's the Australian fans, and a fair measure of the Barmy Army as well, caught up in the moment. They refuse to go home until they have seen Waugh one more time. As he has done all afternoon, Waugh obliges them. At twenty minutes to seven, Waugh emerges onto the players' balcony to wave, acknowledge their acclaim and thank them for it.

Whatever else they will say about him, no one can say that Waugh has not raged against the dying of the light.

And what can his fiercest critics do, but acknowledge the greatness of the feat?

'It typifies Waugh's career,' Ian Chappell says. 'He thrived on people saying he was not playing well or he was through, and that seems to motivate him. I think that was the best I have seen him play in 18 months.' Many others would say it was the best ever, and if not that it was certainly the innings that defined him.

# A Rock to the Very Last

# Chapter 11

'When in Rome, do as Steve Waugh...'
Stuart MacGill

'Almost, perhaps, it's my security blanket. It makes me feel proud, strong, committed and linked to a special group of people. It gives me power and the team aura'

OPPOSITE Steve Waugh shakes hands with Sachin Tendulkar after India's defeat in the third Test at the MCG, 30 December 2003.
PREVIOUS PAGES, LEFT On 2 January 2004, as Steve prepares to captain his final Test; RIGHT Howzat! Waugh claims a wicket on the third day of the fourth Ashes Test at the MCG, 28 December 2002.

IN THE AFTERMATH OF such an innings, even though England in fact went on to win the Test match, of course Waugh's position was safe. You don't drop a saint, and you certainly don't drop Steve Waugh when he is the toast of the nation and has so amply demonstrated that he can still reel off brilliant centuries.

But should he perhaps call it a day now that he's at his absolute height, now that he had *shown them all*? Would there ever come a better time?

Maybe, maybe not. But the least Waugh could say was that amidst all the hoopla, all the celebrations and back-slapping, there was no little voice inside him telling him that it was time to step down. With Lynette and Rosalie and even little Austin's blessing, he decided to push on.

So it was that he led the Australian team through the next three series victories against West Indies, Bangladesh and Zimbabwe in the full body of 2003. It was against Zimbabwe that he secured his 37th Test victory as captain, which broke the world record that had been set by the captain of the West Indies side in their own glory years, Clive Lloyd.

Lloyd had accomplished his 36 victories in 74 Tests, while Waugh did his in just 50.

Somehow though, as the summer of the 2003/04 season approached, Steve's feelings about retirement began to change.

At least one factor was the words of his seven-year-old daughter, Rosie. While the two were having breakfast at home one morning in mid-November, Rosie solemnly informed her father that she didn't want him going away any more. This was in rather strict and sobering contrast to the approach Rosie had taken just twelve months previously. Then, when the subject had come up, she had given him absolution to keep going, saying in effect that if it was in her father's heart to keep playing cricket then that was what he should do, and the family would be fine. But now she was saying, and no bones about it, enough was *enough*, Daddy.

It was a tough decision, all right. On the one hand he was still enjoying his cricket, and was still playing well enough, he thought,

to hold his place in the team. But there were no guarantees. And he had before him the example of what the selectors had done to Ian Healy a few years before. Ian Healy had infamously received a quick, brutal slaying, without even the chance to finish on his own terms or before his own crowd at the Gabba.

There could be no doubt the selectors were capable of doing exactly the same thing again — he had long before been placed on notice that he was not guaranteed of his Test spot, and would be picked on form alone — just as they had done to him before the World Cup. Still again on the *other* hand, with his 91 wickets, he was just 9 wickets shy of pulling off what one commentator had referred to as 'the unthinkable double', which was 10 000 runs and 100 wickets to his name. Only one other Australian had even had the double of 5000 runs and 50 wickets ... and that was his brother Mark, who had finished with a tally of 8029 Test runs and 59 wickets.

 On the other hand Steve still wanted to beat India in India at the end of 2004, which was effectively the last frontier. But then again he ...

This was crazy. If he was even *thinking* about retiring it was surely as good a sign as any that it was time to do precisely that and, typical of Steve Waugh, once he had decided, the rest it didn't take long.

At a packed press conference at the SCG on the afternoon of 26 November 2003, Waugh announced that, if selected, he would play his last Test at the SCG in early January against the touring Indians. It was perfect. This was where his representative career had begun, where he had some of his finest knocks, and where all the friends, family and fans who had supported him so ardently and loyally over the years could gather for the final farewell.

The reaction to Steve Waugh's retirement announcement was extraordinary to behold. While the Australian nation as a whole broke into a long burst of spontaneous applause and — led by Prime Minister John Howard — did everything but sing 'For he's a jolly good fellow', the international cricket community was equally quick

## Queen Upstaged

It was just like the old days. Two members of the rock band Queen, in Australia on a promotional tour, flew from Brisbane to Sydney on a Tuesday morning in April 2003. As they emerged from Sydney Airport, sure enough there was a whole bunch of lights, cameras and media there. Brian May and Roger Taylor were just beginning to preen when the pack started shouting questions at a bunch of blokes behind them who had also been on the flight, led by someone called Steve War who was holding some godawful ugly trophy that seemed to be called the Pure Cup or something, something they'd apparently won for the first time in years. Whatever.

TO US,
NKY WILL

FADE!!

4015

# 'It's only a game, after all. Perhaps it took me until the last innings to realise this' STEVE WAUGH

ABOVE **The captain's tools: baggy green, pads and red rag.** PREVIOUS PAGES **And now, the end is near ...**

to honour one of its greats, as luminary after luminary paid tribute to an extraordinary career. Two quotes in particular give the flavour.

'Anyone would want to play like him,' said Sachin Tendulkar. 'He was completely at a different level as far as mental toughness is concerned.'

Jonty Rhodes was also warm, and to the point, in his praise.

'He's been the hardest man in international cricket for a while,' the great South African all-rounder said. 'I can't think of anyone else in his league. He has perfected the art of gutsing things out in tight situations, for being the man for the crisis. There are some really good players around but no one who values his wicket as much as he does. He bats and bats and carries on batting and batting. Like a barnacle, he's stuck to the crease and won't move.'

Generally the mood was one of celebration for a marvellous career, well finished, though there were exceptions. At the Udayan Home for lepers, for example, many of the devastated children devoted an entire morning to writing letters to the man they called 'Steveda' — which translates to 'elder brother' — begging him to change his mind and say that he would play on, at least until such times as Australia would again be touring India, late in 2004.

At home, Steve's *real* home, the reaction was mixed. While Rosie was thrilled with the news, as was Lynette, one of the first things Steve had to do was to calm his four-year-old son Austin's fears. The little'un, having picked up that his father was to retire from international cricket, had assumed that that included playing back-yard cricket with *him* too, and had become quite upset. Once advised that his dad would now have time to play even more back-yard cricket with him though, Austin too was very pleased. As to the Waugh's third child, Lillian, who'd been born two years earlier, the best thing of all was that he would now be around for most of her early years.

So began what was effectively Steve Waugh's Farewell Tour, with Australia turning out in force to say goodbye to one of its favourite sons.

And though Waugh's own form wasn't sparking, the least the Australian captain could be assured of was that the future was in

safe and silky hands. For in December 2003, in the third Test against India at the MCG, captain-designate Ricky Ponting achieved the extraordinary feat of scoring 257 runs, not only his highest Test score, but also his *second* double century in two Tests.

Steve's own form in the series to that point had been mixed. In a mix-up with Damien Martyn in the first Test at the Gabba, Martyn — on Waugh's call — had clearly sacrificed his own wicket to be run out, prompting critics to note that of the twenty-seven times in his Test career that Steve Waugh had been involved in a run-out, on only four occasions had *he* been the one obliged to take the long walk back to the far pavilion. Against that the general celebratory mood around the nation in giving Waugh a proper farewell was so powerful, as the crowds streamed to the grounds in oft-record numbers to say goodbye, that the controversy soon passed, and after Australia's handy victory in that third Test the series was drawn at 1–1.

As that final Test for Steve Waugh approached, many cricket writers focused on trying to tabulate precisely what he had achieved, and though it wasn't easy, the stats — always beloved by the cricket world — bore testimony to the fact that Waugh's command had indeed been one out of the box. He had been in charge for a total of fifty-six Tests and his side had won no fewer than forty-one of them, giving him a win-rate of just over 70 per cent, which compared wonderfully well to Border's 34 per cent and Taylor's 52 per cent.

One writer, Steven Lynch, noted that while Waugh was 'handed a pretty useful lineup by Mark Taylor … nonetheless under Waugh the team underwent a further transformation: they lost less, drew less, won even more and scored even faster than before. That's why, although Waugh might rank behind Sachin Tendulkar and Brian Lara as batsmen pure and simple, when you add in the captaincy and character you come up with the most influential cricketer of the last decade.'

Few were arguing, and beyond simply being influential, Waugh was also revered, as was attested by the continuing calls to

'I haven't done things the same way or taken much advice from past players. Maybe that's where I went wrong. Maybe I should have spent more time at the bar with other cricketers, but I've never worried too much about that' STEVE WAUGH

talkback radio, letters to the editor and general conversation around the country.

Not that there weren't nay-sayers, with the letters pages also including a few letters from people saying that all the wins were irrelevant when the Waugh era would always be synonymous with sledging and bad behaviour by his sides, but these were mere raspberries in a general chorus of thunderous applause.

Of all the hundreds of thousands of words that were printed in Waugh valedictories though, it was Paul Keating's former speech-writer Don Watson who perhaps got closest to defining the essence of the Steve Waugh attraction.

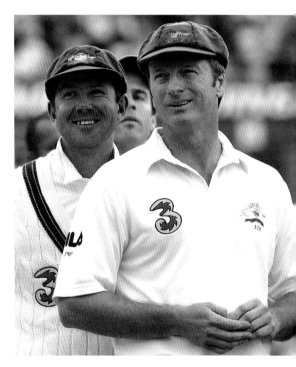

'He became immoveable and indestructible. Fearless. That was the attraction. He was Steve Waugh and you could take it or leave it. So he was the sort of man who wouldn't give you the skin from a grape: that's better than one who gives you the whole thing and thinks he's bought you with it. It's better than being a hypocrite, or a crawler, or a preacher, a pimp, a chump or a politician, etc.

'It was because he was Waugh that we forgave him things we didn't forgive in other players; we justified them, or we decided that with Waugh no justification was necessary. He claimed a catch that the cameras showed wasn't clean. He was an inveterate, unapologetic sledger. Even his most ardent fans suspected that once or twice he batted for his average.

'But he was Steve Waugh and we could take it or leave it, he didn't care. Most people took it.'

And now, the end is near, and so he faced the final curtain …

And that would be Waugh, too. On the occasion of playing his last Test — with seemingly the entire world of Australian cricket awash in heavy emotion — Waugh realised one particular thing about the extraordinary outpouring of emotion across the nation. He could use it. The team could use it. There was enough force in it that it could effectively be harnessed.

No, he didn't bang on about it at the team meeting, but he did tell them straight out.

# The Sydney Morning Herald

MONDAY, JANUARY 26, 2004

# AUSTRALIAN OF THE YEAR

# STEVE WAUGH

Photo: Mark Ray

# 'I'm a pretty emotional person. I'm basically the opposite to what I show on the cricket field' STEVE WAUGH

'The crowd will be on our side,' he said. 'Let's just use it to our advantage.'

And he certainly got that right.

For the Waugh-roar was *still* there, into the third day of that fourth Test, even though India had batted on and on since the beginning to at last declare at 7/705. Under any other circumstances it would have been clear that the very best Australia could hope for was a draw. But for Steve Waugh's last Test, who knew? If anyone could conjure a win from that position, the popular feeling went, it was him. In fact, Waugh made a handy 40 runs to help Australia to 474 runs, and by the time he revisited the crease — at 2.05 p.m. before a record fifth-day SCG crowd of 27 506 — Waugh was batting to save the match from an Indian victory. Of course — what else but? Waugh went down fighting all the way. When he was out, caught by Sachin Tendulkar on the boundary for 80 runs, just after 6 p.m., Australia had at least salvaged a draw, and the seismic acclaim of the crowd seemingly knew no limits as he made his way from the field for the last time. They cheered, they cried, they screamed, they clapped till they could clap no more. Waugh graciously acknowledged the acclaim, and walked on, jogging the last few steps into the dressing room and into the embrace of his team-mates. It was over.

Well played.

# Epilogue

'To have summer holidays, and Christmas at home, just the normal everyday things. That's what I'm looking forward to most'

Lynette Waugh

# Epilogue

## Phar Lap

Sports historian and cricket biographer Geoff Armstrong, who has worked extensively with Stephen Waugh over the years as well as having written a book about Phar Lap, makes an interesting point. Phar Lap had 51 starts for 37 wins, while Steve Waugh had 57 starts as Australian Test captain for 41 wins. Which, according to Geoff, makes him better than Phar Lap!

THERE WAS, OF COURSE, a post-script. In cricket there always is.

In a column Ian Chappell penned for *The Bulletin,* just after Steve had been announced as Australian of the Year, the influential former Australian captain charged that Steve Waugh was leaving behind a Test team that was 'sadly in disarray'.

'Australia faces some serious questions after a series in which they were outplayed by India,' Chappell wrote. 'Only two firm conclusions can be made from the drawn series and neither is particularly encouraging for the future: Australia's attack is dramatically diminished in potency without Glenn McGrath and Shane Warne, while claims of a second side capable of beating the world are clearly nothing more than jingoistic propaganda.'

As it turned out, though, the team that Waugh was leaving in such 'sad disarray' actually did very well, knocking over Sri Lanka, *in* Sri Lanka, for a 3–0 whitewash — the first time such a thing had been achieved. Not that Steve necessarily was able to see a whole lot of it, even though he tried. Problem was, each time he flicked the tele over to watch the Test, Lynette would say: 'Get that bloody cricket off!'

Which was fair enough. As Steve explained to an interviewer shortly afterwards:

'I can understand that after twenty-odd years of watching nearly every day of her life, it's probably not top of her list ...'

Though both Mark and Steve continued playing cricket for NSW, in March 2004, the two brothers played their last game for the state — a Pura Cup loss to Queensland. And when it was all over, what was the difference between the first-class averages of the slashing, dashing, flashing Mark Waugh of popular mythology and the stoic, steely stare-'em-down Steve Waugh? Mark finished with 52.04, while Steve was on 51.94.

All those years on, all those games, all those moments squinting at the bowler as he made his run-up with the backdrop of Trinidad / Manchester / Colombo / Perth / Auckland / Madras / Melbourne / Port Elizabeth right behind, and pushing two decades later, all that separated them over the 724 first-class matches and 50 907 runs was the batting average equivalent of the four minutes that had separated them at birth — 0.08.

# Timeline

## 1965

■ June 2 – Stephen Rodger Waugh is born to Beverly and Rodger Waugh in Canterbury, Sydney. Mark Edward Waugh arrives four minutes later.

## 1973

■ November – First visits the Sydney Cricket Ground to see New South Wales play South Australia.

## 1977

■ New South Wales Primary Schools team wins the national cricket carnival undefeated. Mark is captain, Steve vice, and in one innings the twins forge a 150-run partnership.

■ Both Waughs by now have represented New South Wales in cricket, soccer and tennis.

■ They win the Torch Roselands Sports Star Award after leading Panania Primary to victory in the Umbro International School soccer tournament. In the final, they beat Cardiff South, Newcastle, 3–1 (Steve scores two goals, Mark one).

## 1978–9

■ At the select Barry Richards coaching clinic, he smashes ball after ball beyond the nets, prompting a furious Richards to remove him. 'Get out of here!' says Richards. 'If you are going to bat like that, you might as well not play.'

## 1981

■ Over the 1980–81 summer, he scores more than 1500 runs, including five centuries (four unbeaten). He is overlooked for the New South Wales under-fifteens squad for scoring 'too quickly'. Mark is selected.

## 1986

■ January 9 – One-day international debut against New Zealand. Takes 1/13 and does not bat.

■ February 28 – Makes his first Test half-century in a vital stand with skipper Allan Border (140) in the second Test at Christchurch. Dismissed next day for 74, ending a 177-run partnership.

■ March 13-17 – Scores 0 and 1 as Australia loses the third Test in Auckland. It is the second series lost to New Zealand in a few months. Australian cricket reaches its nadir. An abject Border threatens to resign.

■ September 18–22 – Watches team-mate Dean Jones endure 40-degree Madras heat to score 210 in a dramatic tied Test.

## 1987

■ November 8 – Australia defeats England in the World Cup final. Waugh excels at bowling tight in the closing overs, boosting his credentials as an all-rounder.

## 1988

■ Playing for Somerset in the County Championship, he scores six centuries and tops the batting averages with 80.37.

■ November 19 – Greets Viv Richards with three bouncers in the first Test at the Gabba to air his thoughts on the West Indies' liberal use of the short-pitched ball. He draws plenty of fire when next at the crease, and scores 90.

## 1989

■ April – Named Wisden Cricketer of the Year (1988).

■ June 9–10 – Scores his maiden Test century (177no) in his 27th match, the first Test against England at Headingley.

■ June 23–24 – Scores his second Test century (152no) in the second Test at Lord's.

■ Australia regains the Ashes with a 4–0 series win. Waugh averages 126.5 for the series.

## 1990

■ December 20–23 – The Waugh twins appear in first-class match for the first time when New South Wales meet Western Australia in Perth. They post a world-record, unbroken fifth-wicket partnership of 464 (Mark 229no, Steve 216no).

## 1983

■ March 3–6 – Scores 187 in his first match at the Melbourne Cricket Ground, the third and final under-nineteens Test against Sri Lanka.

■ At his soccer club, where he and Mark play reserve grade, he is given an ultimatum: cricket or soccer. He chooses cricket.

■ Meets Lynette Dougherty, a student at the sister school to Steve's East Hills Boys Technology High School. He takes her to his formal.

## 1984

■ January – Greg Chappell, Dennis Lillee and Rod Marsh retire from Test cricket simultaneously, leaving a massive void in the Australian team.

■ Waugh attends Milperra Teachers College. Leaves after 90 minutes. In the following months he adds to his résumé the dole, indoor cricket umpiring and road maintenance for Bankstown Council.

■ December 7 – Makes his first-class debut, playing Sheffield Shield for New South Wales against Queensland at the Gabba. He bats at nine and scores 31 in a drawn match.

■ December 29 – Plays his first state limited-overs match (the McDonald's Cup), a semi-final win over Victoria. Takes 0/47 and does not bat.

## 1985

■ March 15 – Makes 71 and 21 as New South Wales beat Queensland in the Sheffield Shield final.

■ Is offered a three-year contract by Kerry Packer to prevent him joining an upcoming rebel tour of South Africa. He signs gladly. He is now a professional cricketer.

■ September–October – Tours Zimbabwe with the Young Australia team.

■ October 26 – Scores his maiden first-class century (107) against Tasmania in Hobart.

■ December 4 – With the rebel Australian XI in South Africa having depleted the senior stocks, Australia (the official team) loses a home Test series 1–2 to New Zealand.

■ December 26 – After just 11 state matches, Waugh makes his Test debut against India at the Melbourne Cricket Ground. Selected for his all-rounder potential, he is dismissed for 13 and five but takes an encouraging 2/36.

## 1991

■ January – On the eve of the fourth Ashes Test in Adelaide, Steve is dropped from the Test team. Mark takes his place.

■ January 25–26 – Mark scores a Test century (138) on debut.

■ April 5–10 – The Waugh twins play their first Test together when Steve is recalled for the third Test against the West Indies in Trindad. He makes 2 and 4no in the fourth Test and is dropped for the fifth.

■ August 16 – Marries Lynette.

## 1993

■ January 2 – Scores a vital century (100) in the third Test against the West Indies at the Sydney Cricket Ground. He had been recalled only to struggle for runs at number three in the first two Tests. This century saved his place and served as his passport to England.

■ January 23–26 – In the fourth Test in Adelaide, Australia falls two runs short of winning the match and the Frank Worrell Trophy.

■ July 22–26 – Posts a 332-run stand with Border to secure the Ashes (Border 200no, Waugh 157no) in the fourth Test at Headingley. Border's declaration at 4/653 is seen as overkill but is instructive for Waugh: the opponent is denied all hope for the match and the series.

■ Tops the Australian Ashes tour averages with 83.2 and cements his place in the team.

## 1994

■ January 28–29 – Plays a vital hand in the third Test against South Africa in Adelaide, during which Allan Border becomes the first player to amass 11 000 Test runs. Waugh compiles 164, his seventh Test century, and takes 4/26. He is named not only Man of the Match but Player of the Series, despite missing the first two Tests.

■ March 17–20 – Takes a career-best 5/28 against South Africa at Newlands, Cape Town.

■ March 29 – Having made 195 at 65.00 and taken 10 wickets at 13.00 in South Africa, Steve is again named Player of the Series.

■ Border retires and Mark Taylor becomes captain.

# Timeline

## 1995

■ Voted International Cricketer of the Year. February 28 – Shane Warne and Mark Waugh are fined by the ACB for dealing with an illegal Indian bookmaker, who paid them for supplying information. The fines are not made public.

■ April 21–22 – Steve contributes a defiant 63no to Australia's first innings total of 128 against the West Indies in the third Test in Trinidad. Exchanges words with a fired-up Curtly Ambrose, who is restrained by his skipper Richie Richardson.

■ April 30–May 1 – Scores career-high innings of 200 in the fourth Test at Sabina Park, Kingston, sharing a 231-run partnership with Mark. Australia secures its first series win (2–1) over the West Indies at home in 22 years and after a 15-year unbeaten run of 29 Test series, the Caribbean reign ends.

■ May – Moves to number one in the Coopers and Lybrand batsmen ratings.

## 1996

■ Australia loses to Sri Lanka in the World Cup final.

■ August – Daughter Rosalie is born.

■ October 10–13 – In a one-off Test against India in Delhi, Waugh produces one of his most determined, if not prettiest, innings (67no). Australia loses by seven wickets.

## 1997

■ February 28–March 4 – In the first Test against South Africa in Johannesburg, Waugh and Greg Blewett mount a 385-run partnership to set up a comprehensive win.

■ April 17 – Becomes vice-captain of the Australian Test team, replacing Ian Healy, who had been demoted for throwing his bat in South Africa.

■ July 3–7 – Playing with a broken thumb, Waugh makes 108 and 116 in the third Ashes Test at Old Trafford.

■ October – Becomes captain of the Australian one-day team as national squad is split for the first time.

■ October – After a record 30 months as the number-one batsmen in the world on the Coopers and Lybrand ratings, Waugh is dislodged by Inzamam-ul-Huq.

■ November 20 – On the first day of the second Test against New Zealand in Perth, a pay-contract dispute between the Australian Cricketers Association and the Australian Cricket Board appears to reach crisis point when Waugh (ACA secretary) and Shane Warne announce they will back the ACA's the authority to call a strike for four one-day matches. The strike is averted following intervention by Kerry Packer. (A new player agreement is not signed until September 1998.)

## 2000

■ March 1 – Australia defeats New Zealand in Napier to extend its unbeaten run to 14 wins, a new world record for one-day internationals.

■ March 31–April 4 – Victory in the second Test in Wellington gives Waugh's team nine consecutive wins, an Australian record.

■ May – The Australian cricket team is named Team of the Year at the Laureus World Sports Awards.

■ December 1–3 – Australia's win in the second Test against the West Indies at the WACA takes their consecutive run to 12, breaking the world record set by the West Indies in the 1980s. The run delivers Waugh a personal world record: 12 consecutive wins as captain.

## 2001

■ January 2–6 – Australia completes a 5–0 series win the West Indies, the first clean sweep of a five-match series in 69 years and the first time Australia has whitewashed the Windies.

■ Awarded the Allan Border medal, the honour bestowed upon Australia's most outstanding cricketer.

■ February 27–March 1 – Victory in the first Test in Mumbai extends Australia's world-record winning streak to 16 consecutive Tests. (The run is broken when India win the next Test and then the third to claim a remarkable series.)

■ In the same Test, Waugh draws criticism for not intervening when Michael Slater abuses Rahul Dravid for standing his ground in the face of Slater's unsuccessful appeal for a catch. The 'winning ugly' impression of Waugh's team firms.

■ August – On the eve of the fifth Ashes Test, Waugh drops Slater for Justin Langer, who had been dropped on the eve of the first Test.

■ September 20 – Daughter Lillian is born.

## 2002

■ February 3 – Plays his last one-day international against South Africa at the WACA. He scores 42 off 63. Australia wins but fails to make the finals.

■ October 11 – Becomes only the second player after Allan Border to appear in 150 Tests in the second Test against Pakistan in Sharjah.

■ October 19–22 – Ends a run drought (16 innings without a century) with an unbeaten 103 in the third Test.

■ The third Test is the 108th, and the last, the twins have played together, a record for any two Australia players.

■ October 28 – Mark is dropped from the Australian squad for the

## 1998

■ March 22 – Australia suffers its fourth worst Test defeat ever, losing to India in Kolkata in four days by an innings and 219 runs. With a day off, Waugh acts on a letter slipped under his hotel room door inviting him to visit Udayan, a home for children of leprosy sufferers. He becomes a committed patron of the charity.

■ October 1–5 – In the first Test against Pakistan in Rawalpindi, Waugh enters with his team on 3-28 chasing Pakistan's 269. He is dismissed for 157. Australia makes 513 and wins by an innings and 99 runs.

■ December 8 – The ACB, knowing the press are set to go to print with the story, announces it had fined Shane Warne and Mark Waugh in February 1995 for their dealings with an illegal Indian bookmaker.

## 1999

■ February 12 – Waugh becomes the fortieth captain of the Australian Test team.

■ March–April – First Test series as captain, against the West Indies, is drawn 2–2. In a courageous and tellingly impartial move, he drops an under-performing Shane Warne for the fourth Test.

■ June 13 – Scores 120no against South Africa in a do-or-die Super Six match to keep Australia's hopes of winning the World Cup alive. It is only his second one-day century in 266 matches and stands as his highest one-day innings. Herschelle Gibbs, after dropping Waugh on 56, hears this from the batsman: 'I hope you realise you've just lost the game for your team.'

■ June 20 – Australia wins the World Cup, defeating Pakistan in the final.

■ September 10 – In the first Test against Sri Lanka in Kandy, Waugh collides with Jason Gillespie in the outfield and breaks his nose.

■ October 27 – Named Wisden Australia Cricketer of the Year 2000–01.

■ November 11 – Son Austin is born.

■ November 18–22 – At 5/126 chasing 369 for victory in the second Test against Pakistan at Hobart, Adam Gilchrist and Justin Langer blaze a 238-run partnership to secure the third-highest fourth innings run chase in history.

## 2003

first Test against England. He then retires from international cricket. Selectors make it known that Steve has their backing only for the Ashes series.

■ December 26–30 – Fourth Test victory is Waugh's 33rd as captain, overtaking Border's Australian record.

■ January 3 – Scores his 29th century (102no) in the fifth Test before a sell-out crowd at the SCG with a boundary off the last delivery of the day. Becomes the third batsman to score 10 000 Test runs, after Sunil Gavaskar (India, 10 122) and Allan Border (11 174).

■ April 10 – The first Test against the West Indies in Guyana is Waugh's 157th. He thus overtakes Allan Border as the most capped player in Test cricket history.

■ May 1–5 – Posts his 30th century (115) in the third Test in Barbados, breaking Bradman's Australian record of 29.

■ May 9–13 – In the heated fourth Test, the West Indies face the prospect of an unprecedented whitewash series defeat at home. They score a record 418 runs in the final innings to win. Glenn McGrath's verbal abuse of Ramnaresh Sarwan (105) highlights the ill-spirited behaviour of Waugh's Australians, and his disinclination to douse tempers when required.

■ June 9 – Honoured with the Order of Australia.

■ July 20 – His 37th win as captain comes at the expense of Bangladesh in the first Test in Darwin and makes him the most successful captain in Test cricket history, passing Clive Lloyd.

■ In the same Test, he becomes the second batsman (after South Africa's Gary Kirsten) to score a century against every Test-playing nation.

■ July 25–28 – In the second Test, he scores 156no, his 32nd and final Test century.

■ November 26 – Announces his retirement from international cricket at a press conference held at the SCG.

■ December 26–30 – Australia's victory over India in the third Test at the MCG is Waugh's last win as captain. He is the most successful captain ever, with 41 wins from 57 matches for an unprecedented success rate of 72 per cent.

## 2004

■ January 2 - Plays his final, 168th Test against India at the SCG. Scores 40 in first innings and then 80 in the second to ensure a drawn match and series.

■ Named Australian of the Year.

# Statistics

'It doesn't matter how pretty you look, it's how many runs you get'
Steve Waugh

# STEPHEN RODGER WAUGH

(Born 2 June, 1965 at 8:14pm Canterbury Hospital, Canterbury, NSW)

| | M | Runs | H.S | 100 | Avrge | Ct | Wkt | Avrge | Best |
|---|---|---|---|---|---|---|---|---|---|
| Sheffield Shield-Pura Cup | 85 | 6609 | 216* | 22 | 49.69 | 83 | 85 | 30.79 | 6/51 |
| Test Cricket | 168 | 10927 | 200 | 32 | 51.06 | 112 | 92 | 37.45 | 5/28 |
| Other First-Class | 103 | 6515 | 161 | 25 | 56.16 | 78 | 72 | 29.07 | 4/71 |
| First-Class | 356 | 24051 | 216* | 79 | 51.95 | 273 | 249 | 32.75 | 6/51 |
| International Limited-Overs | 325 | 7569 | 120* | 3 | 32.19 | 111 | 195 | 34.69 | 4/33 |
| Domestic Limited-Overs | 55 | 2269 | 131 | 5 | 51.57 | 19 | 34 | 25.09 | 4/32 |

## Abbreviations

| | | | |
|---|---|---|---|
| 0s = 0 | Bwd = Bowled | HW = Hit Wicket | R = Runs |
| 5 = 5 Wickets/Innings | C&B = Caught & Bowled | Inn = Innings | RO = Run out |
| 10 = 10 Wickets/Match | Cfd = Caught Fielder | LBW = Leg Before Wicket | RPO = Runs/Overs |
| 50 = 50 | Ct = Catches | M = Matches | Stk/Rt = Strike Rate |
| 100 = 100 | Cwk = Caught Wicket-Keeper | Mdns = Maidens | Stp = Stumped |
| Avrge = Average | H.S = Highest Score | NO or * = Not Out | Wks or W = Wickets |
| Best = Best Bowling Figures | HB = Handled Ball | O = Overs | |

# BATTING AND FIELDING

(Right hand batsman, right arm medium bowler)

## First-Class Career

Debut: 1984-85 New South Wales v. Queensland, Brisbane

| Season | Country | M | Inn | NO | Runs | H.S | 0s | 50 | 100 | Avrge | Ct |
|---|---|---|---|---|---|---|---|---|---|---|---|
| 1984-85 | Australia | 5 | 7 | - | 223 | 94 | 1 | 2 | - | 31.86 | 8 |
| 1985-86 | Zimbabwe | 1 | 1 | - | 30 | 30 | - | - | - | 30.00 | - |
| 1985-86 | Australia | 7 | 12 | 2 | 378 | 119* | 1 | - | 2 | 37.80 | 4 |
| 1985-86 | New Zealand | 5 | 8 | - | 124 | 74 | 2 | 1 | - | 15.50 | 4 |
| 1986-87 | India | 6 | 7 | 3 | 227 | 82 | - | 2 | - | 56.75 | 4 |
| 1986-87 | Australia | 13 | 21 | 2 | 741 | 89 | 3 | 6 | - | 39.00 | 24 |
| 1987 | England | 4 | 6 | 3 | 340 | 137* | - | 1 | 2 | 113.33 | 4 |
| 1987-88 | Australia | 10 | 15 | 1 | 517 | 170 | - | 3 | 1 | 36.93 | 12 |
| 1988 | England | 15 | 24 | 6 | 1314 | 161 | 1 | 4 | 6 | 73.00 | 20 |
| 1988-89 | Pakistan | 6 | 9 | - | 160 | 59 | 1 | 1 | - | 17.78 | 4 |
| 1988-89 | Australia | 14 | 24 | 1 | 711 | 118 | 1 | 3 | 1 | 30.91 | 12 |
| 1989 | England | 16 | 24 | 8 | 1030 | 177* | 2 | 3 | 4 | 64.38 | 6 |
| 1989-90 | Australia | 12 | 19 | 3 | 704 | 196 | - | 3 | 2 | 44.00 | 5 |
| 1989-90 | New Zealand | 1 | 2 | - | 50 | 25 | - | - | - | 25.00 | - |
| 1990-91 | Australia | 8 | 11 | 1 | 598 | 216* | - | 4 | 1 | 59.80 | 3 |
| 1990-91 | West Indies | 6 | 7 | 2 | 229 | 96* | - | 2 | - | 45.80 | 1 |
| 1991-92 | Zimbabwe | 2 | 2 | - | 130 | 119 | - | - | 1 | 65.00 | 3 |
| 1991-92 | Australia | 8 | 11 | - | 472 | 115 | - | 2 | 2 | 42.91 | 9 |
| 1992-93 | Australia | 9 | 16 | 1 | 523 | 100* | 2 | 1 | 2 | 34.87 | 11 |
| 1992-93 | New Zealand | 4 | 6 | 1 | 250 | 75 | 1 | 2 | - | 50.00 | 2 |
| 1993 | England | 16 | 21 | 8 | 875 | 157* | 1 | 2 | 3 | 67.31 | 7 |
| 1993-94 | Australia | 9 | 15 | 4 | 976 | 190* | - | 2 | 4 | 88.73 | 5 |
| 1993-94 | South Africa | 5 | 7 | 1 | 400 | 102 | 1 | 3 | 1 | 66.67 | 7 |
| 1994-95 | Pakistan | 3 | 4 | 1 | 224 | 98 | 1 | 3 | - | 74.67 | 4 |
| 1994-95 | Australia | 9 | 17 | 4 | 849 | 206 | 2 | 6 | 1 | 65.31 | 9 |
| 1994-95 | West Indies | 6 | 8 | 3 | 510 | 200 | - | 4 | 1 | 102.00 | 7 |
| 1995-96 | Australia | 10 | 18 | 3 | 952 | 170 | 2 | 3 | 4 | 63.47 | 5 |
| 1996-97 | India | 2 | 3 | 1 | 94 | 67* | 1 | 1 | - | 47.00 | - |
| 1996-97 | Australia | 7 | 12 | 1 | 609 | 186* | 1 | 3 | 2 | 55.36 | 8 |

| Season | Country | M | Inn | NO | Runs | H.S | 0s | 50 | 100 | Avrge | Ct |
|---|---|---|---|---|---|---|---|---|---|---|---|
| 1996-97 | South Africa | 5 | 7 | 1 | 404 | 160 | - | 3 | 1 | 67.33 | 5 |
| 1997 | England | 13 | 17 | - | 924 | 154 | 1 | 4 | 4 | 54.35 | 9 |
| 1997-98 | Australia | 10 | 17 | 4 | 720 | 202* | - | 5 | 1 | 55.38 | 9 |
| 1997-98 | India | 4 | 5 | - | 259 | 107 | - | 1 | 1 | 51.80 | 2 |
| 1997-98 | Ireland | 1 | 2 | - | 76 | 45 | - | - | - | 38.00 | - |
| 1998-99 | Pakistan | 4 | 6 | 1 | 327 | 157 | 1 | 1 | 1 | 65.40 | 1 |
| 1998-99 | Australia | 6 | 12 | 4 | 619 | 122* | - | 2 | 3 | 77.38 | - |
| 1998-99 | West Indies | 6 | 11 | 1 | 483 | 199 | 1 | 2 | 2 | 48.30 | 3 |
| 1999-00 | Sri Lanka | 4 | 5 | - | 115 | 42 | - | - | - | 23.00 | 1 |
| 1999-00 | Zimbabwe | 2 | 3 | 1 | 339 | 161 | - | - | 2 | 169.50 | 1 |
| 1999-00 | Australia | 7 | 11 | - | 471 | 150 | - | 1 | 2 | 42.82 | 7 |
| 1999-00 | New Zealand | 4 | 8 | 2 | 243 | 151* | - | - | 1 | 40.50 | 5 |
| 2000-01 | Australia | 6 | 9 | 1 | 394 | 121* | - | - | 2 | 49.25 | 1 |
| 2000-01 | India | 6 | 10 | 2 | 509 | 110 | 1 | - | 3 | 63.63 | 6 |
| 2001 | England | 7 | 11 | 2 | 583 | 157* | - | - | 3 | 64.78 | 5 |
| 2001-02 | Australia | 6 | 8 | - | 219 | 90 | 1 | 2 | - | 27.38 | 3 |
| 2001-02 | South Africa | 5 | 7 | 1 | 201 | 102* | 1 | - | 1 | 33.50 | 2 |
| 2002 | England | 4 | 6 | 1 | 224 | 146 | 1 | - | 1 | 44.80 | 3 |
| 2002-03 | Sri Lanka | 1 | 2 | - | 31 | 31 | 1 | - | - | 15.50 | 2 |
| 2002-03 | United Arab Emirates | 2 | 2 | 1 | 103 | 103* | 1 | - | 1 | 103.00 | 2 |
| 2002-03 | Australia | 12 | 21 | - | 964 | 211 | 2 | 3 | 4 | 45.90 | 10 |
| 2002-03 | West Indies | 6 | 8 | 2 | 381 | 115 | - | - | 2 | 63.50 | 2 |
| 2003-04 | Australia | 16 | 24 | 4 | 1222 | 157 | 4 | 6 | 4 | 55.55 | 6 |
| **Total** | | **356** | **551** | **88** | **24051** | **216*** | **39** | **97** | **79** | **51.95** | **273** |

| | Country | M | Inn | NO | Runs | H.S | 0s | 50 | 100 | Avrge | Ct |
|---|---|---|---|---|---|---|---|---|---|---|---|
| | Australia | 184 | 302 | 36 | 12862 | 216* | 20 | 57 | 38 | 48.35 | 151 |
| | England | 75 | 109 | 28 | 5290 | 177* | 6 | 14 | 23 | 65.31 | 54 |
| | India | 18 | 25 | 6 | 1089 | 110 | 2 | 4 | 4 | 57.32 | 12 |
| | Ireland | 1 | 2 | - | 76 | 45 | - | - | - | 38.00 | - |
| | New Zealand | 14 | 24 | 3 | 667 | 151* | 3 | 3 | 1 | 31.76 | 11 |
| | Pakistan | 13 | 19 | 2 | 711 | 157 | 3 | 5 | 1 | 41.82 | 9 |
| | South Africa | 15 | 21 | 3 | 1005 | 160 | 2 | 6 | 3 | 55.83 | 14 |
| | Sri Lanka | 5 | 7 | - | 146 | 42 | 1 | - | - | 20.86 | 3 |
| | United Arab Emirates | 2 | 2 | 1 | 103 | 103* | 1 | - | 1 | 103.00 | 2 |
| | West Indies | 24 | 34 | 8 | 1603 | 200 | 1 | 8 | 5 | 61.65 | 13 |
| | Zimbabwe | 5 | 6 | 1 | 499 | 161 | - | - | 3 | 99.80 | 4 |

| Batting Position | | Inn | NO | Runs | H.S | 0s | 50 | 100 | Avrge |
|---|---|---|---|---|---|---|---|---|---|
| 1/2 | | 2 | - | 16 | 15 | - | - | - | 8.00 |
| 3 | | 81 | 8 | 3957 | 206 | 4 | 13 | 15 | 54.21 |
| 4 | | 114 | 15 | 5080 | 211 | 10 | 15 | 20 | 51.31 |
| 5 | | 205 | 34 | 9842 | 200 | 11 | 46 | 34 | 57.56 |
| 6 | | 115 | 25 | 4302 | 216* | 11 | 19 | 8 | 47.80 |
| 7 | | 24 | 4 | 708 | 134* | 1 | 3 | 2 | 35.40 |
| 8 | | 9 | 2 | 115 | 71 | 2 | 1 | - | 16.43 |
| 9 | | 1 | - | 31 | 31 | - | - | - | 31.00 |

| Team | M | Inn | NO | Runs | H.S | 0s | 50 | 100 | Avrge | Ct |
|---|---|---|---|---|---|---|---|---|---|---|
| AUSTRALIA | 168 | 260 | 46 | 10927 | 200 | 22 | 50 | 32 | 51.06 | 112 |
| Australian XI | 70 | 93 | 17 | 4194 | 161 | 4 | 16 | 16 | 55.18 | 41 |
| Ireland | 1 | 2 | - | 76 | 45 | - | - | - | 38.00 | - |
| Kent | 4 | 6 | 1 | 224 | 146 | 1 | - | 1 | 44.80 | 3 |
| New South Wales | 93 | 159 | 15 | 6946 | 216* | 11 | 26 | 22 | 48.24 | 93 |
| Somerset | 19 | 30 | 9 | 1654 | 161 | 1 | 5 | 8 | 78.76 | 24 |
| Young Australians | 1 | 1 | - | 30 | 30 | - | - | - | 30.00 | - |

| How Dismissed | Inns | NO | Bwd | Cfd | Cwk | LBW | Stp | RO | HB | HW |
|---|---|---|---|---|---|---|---|---|---|---|
| | 551 | 88 | 85 | 185 | 113 | 60 | 5 | 13 | 1 | 1 |

## Centuries

Highest Score: 216* New South Wales v. Western Australia, Perth, 1990-91

| 100s | Team | Opponent | Venue | Season |
|---|---|---|---|---|
| 107* | New South Wales | Tasmania | Hobart | 1985-86 |
| 119* | New South Wales | South Australia | Sydney | 1985-86 |
| 111* | Somerset | Surrey | The Oval | 1987 |
| 137* | Somerset | Gloucestershire | Bristol | 1987 |
| 170 | New South Wales | Victoria | Sydney | 1987-88 |
| 115* | Somerset | Hampshire | Southampton | 1988 |
| 103* | Somerset | Warwickshire | Bath | 1988 |
| 137 | Somerset | Sussex | Bath | 1988 |
| 101* | Somerset | Glamorgan | Taunton | 1988 |
| 161 | Somerset | Kent | Canterbury | 1988 |
| 112* | Somerset | Middlesex | Uxbridge | 1988 |
| 118 | New South Wales | Queensland | Brisbane | 1988-89 |
| 177* | AUSTRALIA | ENGLAND | Leeds | 1989 |
| 152* | AUSTRALIA | ENGLAND | Lord's | 1989 |
| 112 | Australian XI | Hampshire | Southampton | 1989 |
| 100* | Australian XI | Essex | Chelmsford | 1989 |
| 134* | AUSTRALIA | SRI LANKA | Hobart | 1989-90 |
| 196 | New South Wales | Tasmania | Hobart | 1989-90 |
| 216* | New South Wales | Western Australia | Perth | 1990-91 |
| 119 | Australian XI | Zimbabweans | Bulawayo | 1991-92 |
| 115 | New South Wales | Western Australia | Perth | 1991-92 |
| 113 | New South Wales | Western Australia | Perth | 1991-92 |
| 100* | Australian XI | West Indians | Hobart | 1992-93 |
| 100 | AUSTRALIA | WEST INDIES | Sydney | 1992-93 |
| 124 | Australian XI | Sussex | Hove | 1993 |
| 157* | AUSTRALIA | ENGLAND | Leeds | 1993 |
| 123 | Australian XI | Kent | Canterbury | 1993 |
| 122 | New South Wales | Victoria | Melbourne | 1993-94 |
| 147* | AUSTRALIA | NEW ZEALAND | Brisbane | 1993-94 |
| 190* | New South Wales | Tasmania | Hobart | 1993-94 |
| 164 | AUSTRALIA | SOUTH AFRICA | Adelaide | 1993-94 |
| 102 | Australian XI | Orange Free State | Bloemfontein | 1993-94 |
| 206 | New South Wales | Tasmania | Hobart | 1994-95 |
| 200 | AUSTRALIA | WEST INDIES | Kingston | 1994-95 |
| 107 | New South Wales | Tasmania | Sydney | 1995-96 |
| 112* | AUSTRALIA | PAKISTAN | Brisbane | 1995-96 |
| 131* | AUSTRALIA | SRI LANKA | Melbourne | 1995-96 |
| 170 | AUSTRALIA | SRI LANKA | Adelaide | 1995-96 |
| 106 | New South Wales | Queensland | Bankstown | 1996-97 |
| 186* | New South Wales | Queensland | Brisbane | 1996-97 |
| 160 | AUSTRALIA | SOUTH AFRICA | Johannesburg | 1996-97 |
| 115 | Australian XI | Nottinghamshire | Nottingham | 1997 |
| 108 | AUSTRALIA | ENGLAND | Manchester | 1997 |
| 116 | AUSTRALIA | ENGLAND | Manchester | 1997 |
| 154 | Australian XI | Kent | Canterbury | 1997 |
| 202* | New South Wales | Victoria | Sydney | 1997-98 |
| 107 | Australian XI | India 'A' | Jamshedpur | 1997-98 |
| 157 | AUSTRALIA | PAKISTAN | Rawalpindi | 1998-99 |
| 112 | AUSTRALIA | ENGLAND | Brisbane | 1998-99 |
| 116 | New South Wales | Victoria | Sydney | 1998-99 |
| 122* | AUSTRALIA | ENGLAND | Melbourne | 1998-99 |
| 100 | AUSTRALIA | WEST INDIES | Kingston | 1998-99 |
| 199 | AUSTRALIA | WEST INDIES | Bridgetown | 1998-99 |
| 161 | Australian XI | Zimbabwe President's XI | Bulawayo | 1999-00 |
| 151* | AUSTRALIA | ZIMBABWE | Harare | 1999-00 |
| 150 | AUSTRALIA | INDIA | Adelaide | 1999-00 |
| 128 | New South Wales | Western Australia | Perth | 1999-00 |
| 151* | AUSTRALIA | NEW ZEALAND | Wellington | 1999-00 |
| 121* | AUSTRALIA | WEST INDIES | Melbourne | 2000-01 |
| 103 | AUSTRALIA | WEST INDIES | Sydney | 2000-01 |
| 106* | Australian XI | Mumbai | Mumbai | 2000-01 |
| 109 | Australian XI | Indian Board President's XI | Delhi | 2000-01 |
| 110 | AUSTRALIA | INDIA | Kolkata | 2000-01 |
| 105 | Australian XI | MCC | Arundel | 2001 |
| 105 | AUSTRALIA | ENGLAND | Birmingham | 2001 |
| 157* | AUSTRALIA | ENGLAND | The Oval | 2001 |
| 102* | Australian XI | South Africa A | Potchefstroom | 2001-02 |
| 146 | Kent | Yorkshire | Leeds | 2002 |
| 103* | AUSTRALIA | PAKISTAN | Sharjah | 2002-03 |
| 135 | New South Wales | South Australia | Sydney | 2002-03 |
| 102 | AUSTRALIA | ENGLAND | Sydney | 2002-03 |
| 211 | New South Wales | Victoria | Melbourne | 2002-03 |
| 138 | New South Wales | Queensland | Sydney | 2002-03 |
| 106* | Australian XI | Carib Beer XI | Georgetown | 2002-03 |
| 115 | AUSTRALIA | WEST INDIES | Bridgetown | 2002-03 |
| 100* | AUSTRALIA | BANGLADESH | Darwin | 2003-04 |
| 156* | AUSTRALIA | BANGLADESH | Cairns | 2003-04 |
| 117* | New South Wales | Western Australia | Sydney | 2003-04 |
| 157 | New South Wales | Tasmania | Hobart | 2003-04 |

## Test Career

Debut: 1985-86 Australia v. India, Melbourne

| Season | Opponent | Venue | M | Inn | NO | Runs | H.S | 0s | 50 | 100 | Avrge | Ct |
|---|---|---|---|---|---|---|---|---|---|---|---|---|
| 1985-86 | India | Australia | 2 | 4 | - | 26 | 13 | 1 | - | - | 6.50 | - |
| 1985-86 | New Zealand | New Zealand | 3 | 5 | - | 87 | 74 | 1 | 1 | - | 17.40 | 2 |
| 1986-87 | India | India | 3 | 4 | 3 | 59 | 39* | - | - | - | 59.00 | 2 |
| 1986-87 | England | Australia | 5 | 8 | 1 | 310 | 79* | 2 | 3 | - | 44.29 | 8 |
| 1987-88 | New Zealand | Australia | 3 | 4 | - | 147 | 61 | - | 2 | - | 36.75 | 3 |
| 1987-88 | England | Australia | 1 | 1 | - | 27 | 27 | - | - | - | 27.00 | - |
| 1987-88 | Sri Lanka | Australia | 1 | 1 | - | 20 | 20 | - | - | - | 20.00 | 3 |
| 1988-89 | Pakistan | Pakistan | 3 | 5 | - | 92 | 59 | 1 | 1 | - | 18.40 | 2 |

| Season | Opponent | Venue | M | Inn | NO | Runs | H.S | Os | 50 | 100 | Avrge | Ct |
|--------|----------|-------|---|-----|----|------|-----|----|----|-----|-------|----|
| 1988-89 | West Indies | Australia | 5 | 9 | 1 | 331 | 91 | - | 3 | - | 41.38 | 3 |
| 1989 | England | England | 6 | 8 | 4 | 506 | 177* | 1 | 1 | 2 | 126.50 | 4 |
| 1989-90 | New Zealand | Australia | 1 | 1 | - | 17 | 17 | - | - | - | 17.00 | - |
| 1989-90 | Sri Lanka | Australia | 2 | 4 | 1 | 267 | 134* | - | 2 | 1 | 89.00 | 2 |
| 1989-90 | Pakistan | Australia | 3 | 4 | - | 44 | 20 | - | - | - | 11.00 | 1 |
| 1989-90 | New Zealand | New Zealand | 1 | 2 | - | 50 | 25 | - | - | - | 25.00 | - |
| 1990-91 | England | Australia | 3 | 4 | - | 82 | 48 | - | - | - | 20.50 | 1 |
| 1990-91 | West Indies | West Indies | 2 | 3 | 1 | 32 | 26 | - | - | - | 16.00 | 1 |
| 1992-93 | West Indies | Australia | 5 | 9 | - | 228 | 100 | 1 | - | 1 | 25.33 | 5 |
| 1992-93 | New Zealand | New Zealand | 3 | 4 | - | 178 | 75 | 1 | 2 | - | 44.50 | 1 |
| 1993 | England | England | 6 | 9 | 4 | 416 | 157* | - | 2 | 1 | 83.20 | 5 |
| 1993-94 | New Zealand | Australia | 3 | 3 | 2 | 216 | 147* | - | - | 1 | 216.00 | 1 |
| 1993-94 | South Africa | Australia | 1 | 2 | - | 165 | 164 | - | - | 1 | 82.50 | 1 |
| 1993-94 | South Africa | South Africa | 3 | 4 | 1 | 195 | 86 | 1 | 2 | - | 65.00 | 3 |
| 1994-95 | Pakistan | Pakistan | 2 | 3 | - | 171 | 98 | 1 | 2 | - | 57.00 | 2 |
| 1994-95 | England | Australia | 5 | 10 | 3 | 345 | 99* | 2 | 3 | - | 49.29 | 3 |
| 1994-95 | West Indies | West Indies | 4 | 6 | 2 | 429 | 200 | - | 3 | 1 | 107.25 | 6 |
| 1995-96 | Pakistan | Australia | 3 | 5 | 1 | 200 | 112* | - | - | 1 | 50.00 | 1 |
| 1995-96 | Sri Lanka | Australia | 2 | 3 | 2 | 362 | 170 | - | 1 | 2 | 362.00 | 1 |
| 1996-97 | India | India | 1 | 2 | 1 | 67 | 67* | 1 | 1 | - | 67.00 | - |
| 1996-97 | West Indies | Australia | 4 | 6 | - | 188 | 66 | 1 | 2 | - | 31.33 | 2 |
| 1996-97 | South Africa | South Africa | 3 | 5 | 1 | 313 | 160 | - | 2 | 1 | 78.25 | 3 |
| 1997 | England | England | 6 | 10 | - | 390 | 116 | 1 | 1 | 2 | 39.00 | 4 |
| 1997-98 | New Zealand | Australia | 3 | 5 | 1 | 130 | 96 | - | 1 | - | 32.50 | 4 |
| 1997-98 | South Africa | Australia | 3 | 5 | - | 238 | 96 | - | 2 | - | 47.60 | 1 |
| 1997-98 | India | India | 2 | 4 | - | 152 | 80 | - | 1 | - | 38.00 | 2 |
| 1998-99 | Pakistan | Pakistan | 3 | 5 | 1 | 235 | 157 | 1 | - | 1 | 58.75 | 1 |
| 1998-99 | England | Australia | 5 | 10 | 4 | 498 | 122* | - | 2 | 2 | 83.00 | - |
| 1998-99 | West Indies | West Indies | 4 | 8 | 1 | 409 | 199 | 1 | 1 | 2 | 58.43 | 1 |
| 1999-00 | Sri Lanka | Sri Lanka | 3 | 3 | - | 52 | 19 | - | - | - | 17.33 | 1 |
| 1999-00 | Zimbabwe | Zimbabwe | 1 | 1 | 1 | 151 | 151* | - | - | 1 | - | 1 |
| 1999-00 | Pakistan | Australia | 3 | 4 | - | 58 | 28 | - | - | - | 14.50 | 3 |
| 1999-00 | India | Australia | 3 | 5 | - | 276 | 150 | - | 1 | 1 | 55.20 | 4 |
| 1999-00 | New Zealand | New Zealand | 3 | 6 | 2 | 214 | 151* | - | - | 1 | 53.50 | 4 |
| 2000-01 | West Indies | Australia | 4 | 6 | 1 | 349 | 121* | - | - | 2 | 69.80 | - |
| 2000-01 | India | India | 3 | 5 | - | 243 | 110 | - | - | 1 | 48.60 | 4 |
| 2001 | England | England | 4 | 5 | 2 | 321 | 157* | - | - | 2 | 107.00 | 2 |
| 2001-02 | New Zealand | Australia | 3 | 4 | - | 78 | 67 | 1 | 1 | - | 19.50 | 3 |
| 2001-02 | South Africa | Australia | 3 | 4 | - | 141 | 90 | - | 1 | - | 35.25 | - |
| 2001-02 | South Africa | South Africa | 3 | 5 | - | 95 | 42 | 1 | - | - | 19.00 | 1 |
| 2002-03 | Pakistan | SRL/U.A.E. | 3 | 4 | 1 | 134 | 103* | 2 | - | 1 | 44.67 | 4 |
| 2002-03 | England | Australia | 5 | 8 | - | 305 | 102 | - | 2 | 1 | 38.13 | 2 |
| 2002-03 | West Indies | West Indies | 4 | 4 | 1 | 226 | 115 | - | - | 1 | 75.33 | 1 |
| 2003-04 | Bangladesh | Australia | 2 | 2 | 2 | 256 | 156* | - | - | 2 | - | - |
| 2003-04 | Zimbabwe | Australia | 2 | 2 | - | 139 | 78 | - | 2 | - | 69.50 | 3 |
| 2003-04 | India | Australia | 4 | 7 | 1 | 267 | 80 | 1 | 2 | - | 44.50 | - |
| **Total** | | | **168** | **260** | **46** | **10927** | **200** | **22** | **50** | **32** | **51.06** | **112** |

| | Opponents | | M | Inn | NO | Runs | H.S | Os | 50 | 100 | Avrge | Ct |
|--|-----------|--|---|-----|----|------|-----|----|----|-----|-------|----|
| | Bangladesh | | 2 | 2 | 2 | 256 | 156* | - | - | 2 | - | - |
| | England | | 46 | 73 | 18 | 3200 | 177* | 6 | 14 | 10 | 58.18 | 29 |
| | India | | 18 | 31 | 5 | 1090 | 150 | 3 | 5 | 2 | 41.92 | 12 |
| | New Zealand | | 23 | 34 | 5 | 1117 | 151* | 3 | 7 | 2 | 38.52 | 18 |
| | Pakistan | | 20 | 30 | 3 | 934 | 157 | 5 | 3 | 3 | 34.59 | 14 |
| | South Africa | | 16 | 25 | 2 | 1147 | 164 | 2 | 7 | 2 | 49.87 | 9 |
| | Sri Lanka | | 8 | 11 | 3 | 701 | 170 | - | 3 | 3 | 87.63 | 7 |
| | West Indies | | 32 | 51 | 7 | 2192 | 200 | 3 | 9 | 7 | 49.82 | 19 |
| | Zimbabwe | | 3 | 3 | 1 | 290 | 151* | - | 2 | 1 | 145.00 | 4 |

| Innings | Inn | NO | Runs | H.S | 0s | 50 | 100 | Avrge | Ct |
|---------|-----|-----|------|------|-----|-----|------|-------|-----|
| First | 94 | 16 | 4855 | 199 | 6 | 22 | 17 | 62.24 | 33 |
| Second | 72 | 9 | 3703 | 200 | 5 | 16 | 13 | 58.78 | 28 |
| Third | 63 | 14 | 1756 | 134* | 8 | 10 | 2 | 35.84 | 17 |
| Fourth | 31 | 7 | 613 | 80 | 3 | 2 | - | 25.54 | 34 |

## Batting at Each Venue

| Venue | M | Inn | NO | Runs | H.S | 0s | 50 | 100 | Avrge | Ct |
|-------|-----|-----|-----|------|------|-----|-----|------|-------|-----|
| **in Australia** | | | | | | | | | | |
| Adelaide | 15 | 26 | 2 | 1056 | 170 | 1 | 4 | 3 | 44.00 | 13 |
| Brisbane | 17 | 26 | 4 | 915 | 147* | 2 | 5 | 3 | 41.59 | 10 |
| Cairns | 1 | 1 | 1 | 156 | 156* | - | - | 1 | - | - |
| Darwin | 1 | 1 | 1 | 100 | 100* | - | - | 1 | - | - |
| Hobart | 6 | 10 | 3 | 272 | 134* | 1 | - | 1 | 38.86 | 2 |
| Melbourne | 17 | 30 | 6 | 1284 | 131* | - | 6 | 3 | 53.50 | 4 |
| Perth | 15 | 21 | 2 | 843 | 99* | 2 | 8 | - | 44.37 | 20 |
| Sydney | 17 | 25 | 1 | 1084 | 103 | 3 | 7 | 3 | 45.17 | 6 |
| **in England** | | | | | | | | | | |
| Birmingham | 4 | 5 | - | 252 | 105 | - | 1 | 1 | 50.40 | 3 |
| Leeds | 3 | 3 | 2 | 338 | 177* | - | - | 2 | 338.00 | 1 |
| Lord's | 4 | 5 | 3 | 231 | 152* | 1 | - | 1 | 115.50 | - |
| Manchester | 3 | 5 | 1 | 397 | 116 | - | 2 | 2 | 99.25 | 1 |
| Nottingham | 4 | 7 | 2 | 163 | 75 | 1 | 1 | - | 32.60 | 5 |
| The Oval | 4 | 7 | 2 | 252 | 157* | - | - | 1 | 50.40 | 5 |
| **in India** | | | | | | | | | | |
| Chennai | 3 | 6 | 2 | 147 | 47 | - | - | - | 36.75 | 5 |
| Delhi | 2 | 3 | 2 | 106 | 67* | 1 | 1 | - | 106.00 | - |
| Kolkata | 2 | 4 | - | 247 | 110 | - | 1 | 1 | 61.75 | 1 |
| Mumbai | 2 | 2 | - | 21 | 15 | - | - | - | 10.50 | 2 |
| **in New Zealand** | | | | | | | | | | |
| Auckland | 3 | 6 | - | 69 | 41 | 2 | - | - | 11.50 | 3 |
| Christchurch | 2 | 3 | - | 137 | 74 | - | 2 | - | 45.67 | 1 |
| Hamilton | 1 | 2 | 1 | 21 | 18+ | - | - | - | 21.00 | - |
| Wellington | 4 | 6 | 1 | 302 | 151* | - | 1 | 1 | 60.40 | 3 |
| **in Pakistan** | | | | | | | | | | |
| Faisalabad | 1 | 2 | - | 20 | 19 | - | - | - | 10.00 | 1 |
| Karachi | 3 | 6 | - | 114 | 73 | 3 | 1 | - | 19.00 | - |
| Lahore | 1 | 1 | - | 59 | 59 | - | 1 | - | 59.00 | 1 |
| Peshawar | 1 | 2 | 1 | 50 | 49* | - | - | - | 50.00 | 1 |
| Rawalpindi | 2 | 2 | - | 255 | 157 | - | 1 | 1 | 127.50 | 2 |
| **in South Africa** | | | | | | | | | | |
| Cape Town | 2 | 3 | - | 100 | 86 | 1 | 1 | - | 33.33 | 1 |
| Centurion | 1 | 2 | 1 | 127 | 67 | - | 2 | - | 127.00 | 1 |
| Durban | 2 | 3 | - | 113 | 64 | - | 1 | - | 37.67 | 1 |
| Johannesburg | 3 | 4 | 1 | 237 | 160 | 1 | - | 1 | 79.00 | 3 |
| Port Elizabeth | 1 | 2 | - | 26 | 18 | - | - | - | 13.00 | 1 |
| **in Sri Lanka** | | | | | | | | | | |
| Colombo (PSS) | 1 | 2 | - | 31 | 31 | 1 | - | - | 15.50 | 2 |
| Colombo (SSC) | 1 | 1 | - | 14 | 14 | - | - | - | 14.00 | - |
| Galle | 1 | 1 | - | 19 | 19 | - | - | - | 19.00 | 1 |
| Kandy | 1 | 1 | - | 19 | 19 | - | - | - | 19.00 | - |

| Venue | M | Inn | NO | Runs | H.S | Os | 50 | 100 | Avrge | Ct |
|---|---|---|---|---|---|---|---|---|---|---|
| **in West Indies** | | | | | | | | | | |
| Bridgetown | 4 | 6 | 1 | 396 | 199 | - | 1 | 2 | 79.20 | 5 |
| Georgetown | 1 | 1 | - | 25 | 25 | - | - | - | 25.00 | - |
| Kingston | 2 | 3 | - | 309 | 200 | - | - | 2 | 103.00 | 1 |
| Port-of-Spain | 4 | 5 | 1 | 124 | 63* | 1 | 1 | - | 31.00 | 1 |
| St John's | 3 | 6 | 3 | 242 | 72* | - | 2 | - | 80.67 | 2 |
| **in United Arab Emirates** | | | | | | | | | | |
| Sharjah | 2 | 2 | 1 | 103 | 103* | 1 | - | 1 | 103.00 | 2 |
| **in Zimbabwe** | | | | | | | | | | |
| Harare | 1 | 1 | 1 | 151 | 151* | - | - | 1 | - | 1 |

| Country | M | Inn | NO | Runs | H.S | Os | 50 | 100 | Avrge | Ct |
|---|---|---|---|---|---|---|---|---|---|---|
| Australia | 89 | 140 | 20 | 5710 | 170 | 9 | 30 | 15 | 47.58 | 55 |
| England | 22 | 32 | 10 | 1633 | 177* | 2 | 4 | 7 | 74.23 | 15 |
| India | 9 | 15 | 4 | 521 | 110 | 1 | 2 | 1 | 47.36 | 8 |
| New Zealand | 10 | 17 | 2 | 529 | 151* | 2 | 3 | 1 | 35.27 | 7 |
| Pakistan | 8 | 13 | 1 | 498 | 157 | 3 | 3 | 1 | 41.50 | 5 |
| South Africa | 9 | 14 | 2 | 603 | 160 | 2 | 4 | 1 | 50.25 | 7 |
| Sri Lanka | 4 | 5 | - | 83 | 31 | 1 | - | - | 16.60 | 3 |
| United Arab Emirates | 2 | 2 | 1 | 103 | 103* | 1 | - | 1 | 103.00 | 2 |
| West Indies | 14 | 21 | 5 | 1096 | 200 | 1 | 4 | 4 | 68.50 | 9 |
| Zimbabwe | 1 | 1 | 1 | 151 | 151* | - | - | 1 | - | 1 |

| Batting Position | | Inn | NO | Runs | H.S | Os | 50 | 100 | Avrge | |
|---|---|---|---|---|---|---|---|---|---|---|
| 3 | | 7 | - | 252 | 100 | 1 | 1 | 1 | 36.00 | |
| 4 | | 8 | 2 | 196 | 90 | 1 | 1 | - | 32.67 | |
| 5 | | 143 | 23 | 6821 | 200 | 11 | 30 | 24 | 56.84 | |
| 6 | | 78 | 16 | 3098 | 177* | 7 | 15 | 6 | 49.97 | |
| 7 | | 19 | 3 | 543 | 134* | - | 3 | 1 | 33.94 | |
| 8 | | 5 | 2 | 17 | 12* | 2 | - | - | 5.67 | |

| How Dismissed | Inns | NO | Bwd | Cfd | Cwk | LBW | Stp | RO | HB | HW |
|---|---|---|---|---|---|---|---|---|---|---|
| | 260 | 46 | 39 | 80 | 60 | 26 | 3 | 4 | 1 | 1 |

## Centuries

Highest Score: 200 Australia v. West Indies, Kingston, 1994-95

| 100s | Opponent | Venue | Season |
|---|---|---|---|
| 177* | England | Leeds | 1989 |
| 152* | England | Lord's | 1989 |
| 134* | Sri Lanka | Hobart | 1989-90 |
| 100 | West Indies | Sydney | 1992-93 |
| 157* | England | Leeds | 1993 |
| 147* | New Zealand | Brisbane | 1993-94 |
| 164 | South Africa | Adelaide | 1993-94 |
| 200 | West Indies | Kingston | 1994-95 |
| 112* | Pakistan | Brisbane | 1995-96 |
| 131* | Sri Lanka | Melbourne | 1995-96 |
| 170 | Sri Lanka | Adelaide | 1995-96 |
| 160 | South Africa | Johannesburg | 1996-97 |
| 108 | England | Manchester | 1997 |
| 116 | England | Manchester | 1997 |
| 157 | Pakistan | Rawalpindi | 1998-99 |
| 112 | England | Brisbane | 1998-99 |

| 100s | Opponent | Venue | Season |
|---|---|---|---|
| 122* | England | Melbourne | 1998-99 |
| 100 | West Indies | Kingston | 1998-99 |
| 199 | West Indies | Bridgetown | 1998-99 |
| 151* | Zimbabwe | Harare | 1999-00 |
| 150 | India | Adelaide | 1999-00 |
| 151* | New Zealand | Wellington | 1999-00 |
| 121* | West Indies | Melbourne | 2000-01 |
| 103 | West Indies | Sydney | 2000-01 |
| 110 | India | Kolkata | 2000-01 |
| 105 | England | Birmingham | 2001 |
| 157* | England | The Oval | 2001 |
| 103* | Pakistan | Sharjah | 2002-03 |
| 102 | England | Sydney | 2002-03 |
| 115 | West Indies | Bridgetown | 2002-03 |
| 100* | Bangladesh | Darwin | 2003-04 |
| 156* | Bangladesh | Cairns | 2003-04 |

## Nineties

| 90s | Opponent | Venue | Season |
|---|---|---|---|
| 90 | West Indies | Brisbane | 1988-89 |
| 91 | West Indies | Perth | 1988-89 |
| 92 | England | Manchester | 1989 |
| 98 | Pakistan | Rawalpindi | 1994-95 |
| 94* | England | Melbourne | 1994-95 |
| 99* | England | Perth | 1994-95 |
| 96 | New Zealand | Perth | 1997-98 |
| 96 | South Africa | Melbourne | 1997-98 |
| 96 | England | Sydney | 1998-99 |
| 90 | South Africa | Melbourne | 2001-02 |

## Sheffield Shield-Pura Cup Career

Debut: 1984-85 New South Wales v. Queensland, Brisbane

| Season | M | Inn | NO | Runs | H.S | 0s | 50 | 100 | Avrge | Ct |
|---|---|---|---|---|---|---|---|---|---|---|
| 1984-85 | 5 | 7 | - | 223 | 94 | 1 | 2 | - | 31.86 | 8 |
| 1985-86 | 4 | 6 | 2 | 325 | 119* | - | - | 2 | 81.25 | 3 |
| 1986-87 | 7 | 12 | 1 | 384 | 89 | 1 | 3 | - | 34.91 | 14 |
| 1987-88 | 5 | 9 | 1 | 323 | 170 | - | 1 | 1 | 40.38 | 6 |
| 1988-89 | 8 | 14 | - | 359 | 118 | 1 | - | 1 | 25.64 | 7 |
| 1989-90 | 5 | 8 | 1 | 308 | 196 | - | - | 1 | 44.00 | 1 |
| 1990-91 | 5 | 7 | 1 | 516 | 216* | - | 4 | 1 | 86.00 | 2 |
| 1991-92 | 6 | 9 | - | 448 | 115 | - | 2 | 2 | 49.78 | 7 |
| 1992-93 | 2 | 4 | - | 78 | 38 | 1 | - | - | 19.50 | 2 |
| 1993-94 | 4 | 8 | 2 | 503 | 190* | - | 1 | 2 | 83.83 | 3 |
| 1994-95 | 4 | 7 | 1 | 504 | 206 | - | 3 | 1 | 84.00 | 6 |
| 1995-96 | 4 | 8 | - | 343 | 107 | 1 | 2 | 1 | 42.88 | 2 |
| 1996-97 | 3 | 6 | 1 | 421 | 186* | - | 1 | 2 | 84.20 | 6 |
| 1997-98 | 4 | 7 | 3 | 352 | 202* | - | 2 | 1 | 88.00 | 4 |
| 1998-99 | 1 | 2 | - | 121 | 116 | - | - | 1 | 60.50 | - |
| 1999-00 | 1 | 2 | - | 137 | 128 | - | - | 1 | 68.50 | - |
| 2000-01 | 2 | 3 | - | 45 | 25 | - | - | - | 15.00 | 1 |
| 2001-02 | - | - | - | - | - | - | - | - | - | - |
| 2002-03 | 7 | 13 | - | 659 | 211 | 2 | 1 | 3 | 50.69 | 8 |
| 2003-04 | 8 | 15 | 1 | 560 | 157 | 3 | 2 | 2 | 40.00 | 3 |
| **Total** | **85** | **147** | **14** | **6609** | **216*** | **10** | **24** | **22** | **49.69** | **83** |

| Opponents | M | Inn | NO | Runs | H.S | 0s | 50 | 100 | Avrge | Ct |
|---|---|---|---|---|---|---|---|---|---|---|
| Queensland | 21 | 38 | 4 | 1348 | 186* | 2 | 6 | 4 | 39.65 | 18 |
| South Australia | 15 | 24 | 1 | 847 | 135 | 1 | 2 | 2 | 36.83 | 17 |
| Tasmania | 14 | 23 | 4 | 1508 | 206 | 1 | 6 | 6 | 79.37 | 11 |
| Victoria | 21 | 38 | 3 | 1788 | 211 | 2 | 7 | 5 | 51.09 | 26 |
| Western Australia | 14 | 24 | 2 | 1118 | 216* | 4 | 3 | 5 | 50.82 | 11 |

| Innings | Inn | NO | Runs | H.S | 0s | 50 | 100 | Avrge | Ct |
|---|---|---|---|---|---|---|---|---|---|
| First | 48 | 2 | 2806 | 216* | 3 | 5 | 12 | 61.00 | 25 |
| Second | 37 | 2 | 1682 | 202* | 4 | 10 | 5 | 48.06 | 22 |
| Third | 38 | 5 | 1414 | 186* | 3 | 5 | 4 | 42.85 | 16 |
| Fourth | 24 | 5 | 707 | 117* | - | 4 | 1 | 37.21 | 20 |

## Batting at Each Venue

| Venue | M | Inn | NO | Runs | H.S | 0s | 50 | 100 | Avrge | Ct |
|---|---|---|---|---|---|---|---|---|---|---|
| Adelaide | 6 | 10 | - | 301 | 73 | 1 | 1 | - | 30.10 | 5 |
| Bankstown | 1 | 2 | - | 141 | 106 | - | - | 1 | 70.50 | - |
| Brisbane | 9 | 17 | 3 | 633 | 186* | - | 2 | 2 | 45.21 | 8 |
| Devonport | 1 | 1 | - | 39 | 39 | - | - | - | 39.00 | 1 |
| Hobart (Bellerive) | 5 | 9 | 3 | 867 | 206 | 1 | 1 | 4 | 144.50 | 2 |
| Hobart (TCA) | 2 | 2 | - | 172 | 107 | - | 1 | 1 | 86.00 | 4 |
| Melbourne | 6 | 11 | 1 | 528 | 211 | - | 1 | 2 | 52.80 | 5 |
| Newcastle | 7 | 14 | 1 | 188 | 53 | 1 | 1 | - | 14.46 | 3 |
| North Sydney | 1 | 2 | 2 | 262 | 202* | - | 1 | 1 | - | 2 |
| Perth | 9 | 16 | 1 | 864 | 216* | 2 | 2 | 4 | 57.60 | 9 |
| Richmond | 1 | 2 | - | 38 | 25 | - | - | - | 19.00 | 1 |
| St Kilda | 2 | 4 | - | 160 | 59 | - | 2 | - | 40.00 | 2 |
| Sydney | 35 | 57 | 3 | 2416 | 170 | 5 | 12 | 7 | 44.74 | 41 |

| Batting Position | Inn | NO | Runs | H.S | 0s | 50 | 100 | Avrge |
|---|---|---|---|---|---|---|---|---|
| 3 | 57 | 6 | 3060 | 206 | 1 | 10 | 12 | 60.00 |
| 4 | 49 | 4 | 2045 | 211 | 6 | 6 | 7 | 45.44 |
| 5 | 20 | 2 | 729 | 119* | - | 5 | 1 | 40.50 |
| 6 | 15 | 2 | 647 | 216* | 2 | 2 | 2 | 49.77 |
| 7 | 2 | - | 1 | 1 | 1 | - | - | 0.50 |
| 8 | 3 | - | 96 | 71 | - | 1 | - | 32.00 |
| 9 | 1 | - | 3 | 31 | - | - | - | 31.00 |

| How Dismissed | Inns | NO | Bwd | Cfd | Cwk | LBW | Stp | RO |
|---|---|---|---|---|---|---|---|---|
| | 147 | 14 | 25 | 51 | 31 | 17 | 1 | 8 |

## Centuries

**Highest Score: 216* New South Wales v. Western Australia, Perth, 1990-91**

| 100s | Team | Opponent | Venue | Season |
|---|---|---|---|---|
| 107* | New South Wales | Tasmania | Hobart | 1985-86 |
| 119* | New South Wales | South Australia | Sydney | 1985-86 |
| 170 | New South Wales | Victoria | Sydney | 1987-88 |
| 118 | New South Wales | Queensland | Brisbane | 1988-89 |
| 196 | New South Wales | Tasmania | Hobart | 1989-90 |
| 216* | New South Wales | Western Australia | Perth | 1990-91 |
| 115 | New South Wales | Western Australia | Perth | 1991-92 |
| 113 | New South Wales | Western Australia | Perth | 1991-92 |
| 122 | New South Wales | Victoria | Melbourne | 1993-94 |
| 190* | New South Wales | Tasmania | Hobart | 1993-94 |
| 206 | New South Wales | Tasmania | Hobart | 1994-95 |
| 107 | New South Wales | Tasmania | Sydney | 1995-96 |
| 106 | New South Wales | Queensland | Bankstown | 1996-97 |
| 186* | New South Wales | Queensland | Brisbane | 1996-97 |
| 202* | New South Wales | Victoria | Sydney | 1997-98 |
| 116 | New South Wales | Victoria | Sydney | 1998-99 |
| 128 | New South Wales | Western Australia | Perth | 1999-00 |
| 135 | New South Wales | South Australia | Sydney | 2002-03 |
| 211 | New South Wales | Victoria | Melbourne | 2002-03 |
| 138 | New South Wales | Queensland | Sydney | 2002-03 |
| 117* | New South Wales | Western Australia | Sydney | 2003-04 |
| 157 | New South Wales | Tasmania | Hobart | 2003-04 |

# International Limited-Overs Career

Debut: 1985-86 Australia v. New Zealand, Melbourne

| Season | Tournament | Venue | M | Inn | NO | Runs | H.S | 0s | 50 | 100 | Avrge | Stk/Rt | Ct |
|--------|-----------|-------|---|-----|-----|------|-----|-----|----|-----|-------|--------|-----|
| 1985-86 | World Series Cup | AUS | 12 | 10 | 3 | 266 | 81 | - | 2 | - | 38.00 | 65.04 | 2 |
| 1985-86 | Rothman's Cup | N.Z | 4 | 4 | - | 111 | 71 | - | 1 | - | 27.75 | 78.17 | 2 |
| 1985-86 | Austral-Asia Cup | UAE | 1 | 1 | - | 26 | 26 | - | - | - | 26.00 | 70.27 | - |
| 1986-87 | India v. Australia | IND | 6 | 4 | 2 | 111 | 57* | - | 1 | - | 55.50 | 86.05 | - |
| 1986-87 | Challenge Cup | AUS | 3 | 3 | - | 127 | 82 | - | 1 | - | 42.33 | 73.41 | - |
| 1986-87 | World Series Cup | AUS | 10 | 10 | 3 | 245 | 83* | - | 1 | - | 35.00 | 65.68 | 3 |
| 1986-87 | Sharjah Cup | UAE | 3 | 3 | - | 42 | 20 | - | - | - | 14.00 | 47.19 | 1 |
| 1987-88 | World Cup | IND/PAK | 8 | 8 | 5 | 167 | 45 | - | - | - | 55.67 | 97.66 | 3 |
| 1987-88 | World Series Cup | AUS | 10 | 8 | 2 | 199 | 68 | 2 | 1 | - | 33.17 | 83.26 | 3 |
| 1987-88 | Australia v. England | AUS | 1 | 1 | - | 27 | 27 | - | - | - | 27.00 | 108.00 | - |
| 1988-89 | Pakistan v. Australia | PAK | 1 | 1 | - | 7 | 7 | - | - | - | 7.00 | 77.78 | - |
| 1988-89 | World Series Cup | AUS | 11 | 10 | 3 | 270 | 54 | 1 | 1 | - | 38.57 | 86.54 | 4 |
| 1989 | England v. Australia | ENG | 3 | 3 | - | 113 | 43 | - | - | - | 37.67 | 67.26 | - |
| 1989-90 | Nehru Cup | IND | 5 | 4 | 1 | 83 | 53* | 1 | 1 | - | 27.67 | 112.16 | 3 |
| 1989-90 | World Series | AUS | 9 | 8 | 2 | 104 | 31* | 1 | - | - | 17.33 | 50.98 | 4 |
| 1989-90 | Rothman's Series | N.Z | 5 | 4 | - | 72 | 36 | - | - | - | 18.00 | 53.73 | 3 |
| 1989-90 | Austral-Asia Cup | UAE | 4 | 2 | - | 98 | 64 | - | 1 | - | 49.00 | 74.81 | 1 |
| 1990-91 | World Series | AUS | 10 | 9 | 5 | 141 | 65* | - | 1 | - | 35.25 | 68.45 | 4 |
| 1990-91 | West Indies v. Australia | W.I | 5 | 5 | 2 | 86 | 26* | - | - | - | 28.67 | 84.31 | 3 |
| 1991-92 | World Series | AUS | 10 | 7 | 2 | 60 | 34 | - | - | - | 12.00 | 57.69 | 9 |
| 1991-92 | World Cup | ANZ | 8 | 7 | - | 187 | 55 | - | 1 | - | 26.71 | 78.24 | 2 |
| 1992-93 | World Series | AUS | 10 | 10 | 1 | 213 | 64 | - | 1 | - | 23.67 | 59.66 | 4 |
| 1992-93 | New Zealand v. Australia | N.Z | 5 | 5 | 1 | 120 | 39 | - | - | - | 30.00 | 68.97 | 3 |
| 1993 | England v. Australia | ENG | 3 | 3 | 1 | 41 | 27 | - | - | - | 20.50 | 97.62 | - |
| 1993-94 | World Series | AUS | 9 | 8 | 2 | 141 | 33 | - | - | - | 23.50 | 66.20 | 2 |
| 1993-94 | South Africa v. Australia | SAF | 8 | 8 | 2 | 291 | 86 | - | 2 | - | 48.50 | 90.37 | 2 |
| 1993-94 | Austral-Asia Cup | UAE | 3 | 1 | - | 53 | 53 | - | 1 | - | 53.00 | 73.61 | - |
| 1994-95 | Singer World Series | S.L | 3 | 3 | - | 53 | 30 | - | - | - | 17.67 | 63.10 | - |
| 1994-95 | Wills Triangular Series | PAK | 5 | 5 | 1 | 153 | 59* | - | 2 | - | 38.25 | 75.37 | 2 |
| 1994-95 | World Series | AUS | 1 | 1 | - | 0 | 0 | 1 | - | - | 0.00 | 0.00 | 1 |
| 1994-95 | New Zealand Centenary | N.Z | 4 | 4 | 1 | 81 | 44* | - | - | - | 27.00 | 52.94 | 1 |
| 1994-95 | West Indies v. Australia | W.I | 5 | 5 | - | 164 | 58 | - | 1 | - | 32.80 | 90.61 | - |
| 1995-96 | World Series | AUS | 4 | 4 | 1 | 128 | 102* | - | - | 1 | 42.67 | 73.99 | 2 |
| 1995-96 | World Cup | ASIA | 7 | 7 | 2 | 226 | 82 | - | 3 | - | 45.20 | 76.87 | 3 |
| 1996-97 | Singer World Series | S.L | 4 | 4 | - | 214 | 82 | - | 3 | - | 53.50 | 89.17 | 3 |
| 1996-97 | Titan Cup | IND | 5 | 5 | - | 152 | 41 | - | - | - | 30.40 | 64.14 | 1 |
| 1996-97 | CUB Series | AUS | 6 | 6 | - | 159 | 57 | - | 1 | - | 26.50 | 67.37 | 3 |
| 1996-97 | South Africa v. Australia | SAF | 7 | 7 | 1 | 301 | 91 | 1 | 4 | - | 50.17 | 88.27 | 3 |
| 1997 | England v. Australia | ENG | 3 | 3 | - | 60 | 24 | - | - | - | 20.00 | 62.50 | 2 |
| 1997-98 | CUB Series | AUS | 10 | 9 | 1 | 181 | 71 | 3 | 2 | - | 22.63 | 73.88 | 2 |
| 1997-98 | New Zealand v. Australia | N.Z | 4 | 3 | - | 112 | 47 | - | - | - | 37.33 | 81.16 | 1 |
| 1997-98 | Triangular Cup | IND | 5 | 4 | - | 131 | 57 | 1 | 1 | - | 32.75 | 98.50 | 2 |
| 1997-98 | Coca-Cola Cup | UAE | 5 | 5 | - | 123 | 70 | - | 1 | - | 24.60 | 82.55 | - |
| 1998-99 | Wills International | BAN | 1 | 1 | - | 7 | 7 | - | - | - | 7.00 | 53.85 | - |
| 1998-99 | Pakistan v. Australia | PAK | 3 | 3 | - | 40 | 30 | 1 | - | - | 13.33 | 76.92 | 1 |
| 1998-99 | CUB Series | AUS | 2 | 2 | - | 20 | 20 | 1 | - | - | 10.00 | 86.96 | - |
| 1998-99 | West Indies v. Australia | W.I | 7 | 7 | 1 | 135 | 72* | 1 | 1 | - | 22.50 | 76.27 | 2 |
| 1999 | World Cup | ENG | 10 | 8 | 3 | 398 | 120* | - | 2 | 1 | 79.60 | 77.58 | 6 |
| 1999-00 | Aiwa Cup | S.L | 5 | 4 | - | 67 | 43 | - | - | - | 16.75 | 63.21 | 1 |
| 1999-00 | Zimbabwe v. Australia | ZIM | 3 | 1 | - | 14 | 14 | - | - | - | 14.00 | 82.35 | - |
| 1999-00 | CUB Series | AUS | 10 | 9 | 2 | 195 | 81* | 1 | 1 | - | 27.86 | 73.86 | 5 |
| 1999-00 | New Zealand v. Australia | N.Z | 6 | 5 | 3 | 145 | 54 | - | 1 | - | 72.50 | 108.21 | 2 |
| 1999-00 | South Africa v. Australia | SAF | 3 | 2 | - | 53 | 51 | - | 1 | - | 26.50 | 54.64 | 1 |

| Season | Tournament | Venue | M | Inn | NO | Runs | H.S | Os | 50 | 100 | Avrge | Stk/Rt | Ct |
|---|---|---|---|---|---|---|---|---|---|---|---|---|---|
| 2000-01 | Australia v. South Africa | AUS | 3 | 3 | 1 | 161 | 114* | - | - | 1 | 80.50 | 99.38 | - |
| 2000-01 | ICC Trophy | KYA | 1 | 1 | - | 23 | 23 | - | - | - | 23.00 | 67.65 | - |
| 2000-01 | Carlton Series | AUS | 7 | 5 | 1 | 192 | 79 | - | 1 | - | 48.00 | 95.05 | 3 |
| 2000-01 | India v. Australia | IND | 5 | 4 | - | 93 | 35 | - | - | - | 23.25 | 84.55 | 3 |
| 2001 | NatWest Series | ENG | 6 | 4 | 2 | 200 | 64 | - | 3 | - | 100.00 | 77.52 | - |
| 2001-02 | VB Series | AUS | 8 | 7 | 1 | 187 | 62 | - | 1 | - | 31.17 | 69.00 | 3 |
| **Total** | | | **325** | **288** | **58** | **7569** | **120*** | **15** | **45** | **3** | **32.91** | **75.81** | **111** |

| Opponents | M | Inn | NO | Runs | H.S | Os | 50 | 100 | Avrge | Stk/Rt | Ct |
|---|---|---|---|---|---|---|---|---|---|---|---|
| Bangladesh | 2 | - | - | - | - | - | - | - | - | - | - |
| England | 30 | 28 | 9 | 666 | 83* | 2 | 3 | - | 35.05 | 74.50 | 7 |
| India | 53 | 45 | 7 | 1117 | 81 | 1 | 7 | - | 29.39 | 72.58 | 16 |
| Kenya | 1 | 1 | - | 82 | 82 | - | 1 | - | 82.00 | 89.13 | - |
| New Zealand | 60 | 51 | 12 | 1088 | 71 | 3 | 4 | - | 27.90 | 73.61 | 20 |
| Pakistan | 43 | 40 | 8 | 1003 | 82 | 4 | 8 | - | 31.34 | 72.89 | 19 |
| Sri Lanka | 24 | 20 | 4 | 433 | 102* | 1 | 1 | 1 | 27.06 | 76.50 | 6 |
| South Africa | 47 | 44 | 7 | 1581 | 120* | 3 | 12 | 2 | 42.73 | 78.42 | 14 |
| Scotland | 1 | 1 | 1 | 49 | 49* | - | - | - | - | 70.00 | 1 |
| West Indies | 50 | 48 | 8 | 1114 | 72* | 1 | 5 | - | 27.85 | 72.10 | 23 |
| Zimbabwe | 14 | 10 | 2 | 436 | 82 | - | 4 | - | 54.50 | 106.86 | 5 |

| Innings | Inn | NO | Runs | H.S | Os | 50 | 100 | Avrge | Stk/Rt | Ct |
|---|---|---|---|---|---|---|---|---|---|---|
| First | 171 | 30 | 4398 | 114* | 6 | 25 | 2 | 31.19 | 78.83 | 61 |
| Second | 117 | 28 | 3171 | 120* | 9 | 20 | 1 | 35.63 | 71.99 | 50 |

| Country | M | Inn | NO | Runs | H.S | Os | 50 | 100 | Avrge | Stk/Rt | Ct |
|---|---|---|---|---|---|---|---|---|---|---|---|
| Australia | 123 | 110 | 25 | 2410 | 102* | 8 | 12 | 1 | 28.35 | 69.31 | 45 |
| England | 9 | 9 | 1 | 214 | 43 | - | - | - | 26.75 | 69.93 | 2 |
| India | 34 | 30 | 9 | 825 | 82 | 2 | 6 | - | 39.29 | 83.76 | 12 |
| New Zealand | 23 | 21 | 2 | 534 | 71 | - | 1 | - | 28.11 | 68.90 | 10 |
| Pakistan | 8 | 8 | 2 | 205 | 59* | - | 2 | - | 34.17 | 77.36 | 2 |
| Sri Lanka | 7 | 7 | - | 267 | 82 | - | 3 | - | 38.14 | 82.41 | 3 |
| South Africa | 15 | 15 | 3 | 592 | 91 | 1 | 6 | - | 49.33 | 89.29 | 5 |
| Sharjah | 16 | 12 | - | 342 | 70 | - | 3 | - | 28.50 | 71.55 | 2 |
| West Indies | 10 | 10 | 2 | 250 | 58 | - | 1 | - | 31.25 | 88.34 | 3 |

| Batting Position | Inn | NO | Runs | H.S | Os | 50 | 100 | Avrge | Stk/Rt |
|---|---|---|---|---|---|---|---|---|---|
| 3 | 10 | - | 191 | 37 | 1 | - | - | 19.10 | 59.13 |
| 4 | 51 | 5 | 1411 | 102* | 3 | 11 | 1 | 30.67 | 70.59 |
| 5 | 89 | 16 | 2604 | 91 | 5 | 16 | - | 35.67 | 76.41 |
| 6 | 57 | 17 | 1186 | 73* | 2 | 6 | - | 29.65 | 77.31 |
| 7 | 15 | 6 | 247 | 57* | - | 1 | - | 27.44 | 84.59 |

| How Dismissed | Inns | NO | Bwd | Cfd | Cwk | LBW | Stp | RO | HW |
|---|---|---|---|---|---|---|---|---|---|
| | 288 | 58 | 63 | 80 | 33 | 18 | 8 | 27 | 1 |

# Centuries

Highest Score: 120* Australia v. South Africa, Leeds, 1999

| 100s | Team | Opponent | Venue | Season |
|---|---|---|---|---|
| 102* | Australia | Sri Lanka | Melbourne | 1995-96 |
| 120* | Australia | South Africa | Leeds | 1999 |
| 104* | Australia | South Africa | Melbourne | 2000-01 |

# Domestic Limited-Overs Career

Debut: 1984-85 New South Wales v. Victoria, Melbourne

| Season | M | Inn | NO | Runs | H.S | Os | 50 | 100 | Avrge | Stk/Rt | Ct |
|--------|---|-----|-----|------|-----|-----|-----|-----|-------|--------|-----|
| 1984-85 | 1 | - | - | - | - | - | - | - | - | - | 1 |
| 1985-86 | 1 | 1 | - | 47 | 47 | - | - | - | 47.00 | 66.20 | - |
| 1986-87 | 2 | 2 | - | 2 | 2 | 1 | - | - | 1.00 | 33.33 | 1 |
| 1987-88 | 4 | 4 | - | 101 | 56 | - | 1 | - | 25.25 | 78.91 | - |
| 1988-89 | 3 | 3 | 1 | 82 | 81* | 1 | 1 | - | 41.00 | 109.33 | 1 |
| 1989-90 | - | - | - | - | - | - | - | - | - | - | - |
| 1990-91 | 4 | 4 | 2 | 88 | 66* | - | 1 | - | 44.00 | 60.69 | 1 |
| 1991-92 | 4 | 4 | - | 239 | 126 | - | 1 | 1 | 59.75 | 86.28 | - |
| 1992-93 | 4 | 4 | 1 | 269 | 131 | - | 1 | 1 | 89.67 | 85.13 | 1 |
| 1993-94 | 2 | 2 | - | 94 | 59 | - | 1 | - | 47.00 | 97.92 | 2 |
| 1994-95 | - | - | - | - | - | - | - | - | - | - | - |
| 1995-96 | 3 | 3 | - | 140 | 90 | - | 1 | - | 46.67 | 73.68 | 2 |
| 1996-97 | - | - | - | - | - | - | - | - | - | - | - |
| 1997-98 | 3 | 3 | - | 96 | 72 | - | 1 | - | 32.00 | 90.57 | 4 |
| 1998-99 | 1 | 1 | - | 29 | 29 | - | - | - | 29.00 | 85.29 | - |
| 1999-00 | - | - | - | - | - | - | - | - | - | - | - |
| 2000-01 | 5 | 5 | 2 | 228 | 75* | - | 1 | - | 76.00 | 78.08 | 1 |
| 2001-02 | 2 | 2 | 2 | 133 | 101* | - | - | 1 | - | 90.48 | - |
| 2002-03 | 7 | 7 | - | 343 | 104 | - | 2 | 1 | 49.00 | 104.89 | 3 |
| 2003-04 | 9 | 9 | 2 | 378 | 101* | - | 2 | 1 | 54.00 | 78.26 | 2 |
| **Total** | **55** | **54** | **10** | **2269** | **131** | **2** | **13** | **5** | **51.57** | **84.26** | **19** |

| Opponents | M | Inn | NO | Runs | H.S | Os | 50 | 100 | Avrge | Stk/Rt | Ct |
|-----------|---|-----|-----|------|-----|-----|-----|-----|-------|--------|-----|
| Queensland | 11 | 11 | 1 | 604 | 131 | - | 3 | 2 | 60.40 | 85.80 | 2 |
| South Australia | 9 | 9 | 1 | 455 | 85* | - | 4 | - | 56.88 | 80.39 | 5 |
| Tasmania | 11 | 11 | 5 | 511 | 104 | - | 4 | 1 | 85.17 | 94.45 | 3 |
| Victoria | 13 | 12 | 2 | 313 | 126 | 2 | - | 1 | 31.30 | 66.31 | 4 |
| Western Australia | 11 | 11 | 1 | 386 | 101* | - | 2 | 1 | 38.60 | 94.15 | 5 |

| Innings | | Inn | NO | Runs | H.S | Os | 50 | 100 | Avrge | Stk/Rt | Ct |
|---------|--|-----|-----|------|-----|-----|-----|-----|-------|--------|-----|
| First | | 26 | 2 | 1131 | 131 | - | 6 | 3 | 47.13 | 86.47 | 10 |
| Second | | 28 | 8 | 1138 | 101* | 2 | 7 | 2 | 56.90 | 82.17 | 9 |

## Batting at Each Venue

| Venue | M | Inn | NO | Runs | H.S | Os | 50 | 100 | Avrge | Stk/Rt | Ct |
|-------|---|-----|-----|------|-----|-----|-----|-----|-------|--------|-----|
| Adelaide | 3 | 3 | 1 | 187 | 85* | - | 2 | - | 93.50 | 76.02 | 2 |
| Bankstown | 1 | 1 | - | 49 | 49 | - | - | - | 49.00 | 100.00 | 1 |
| Bowral | 1 | 1 | - | 38 | 38 | - | - | - | 38.00 | 65.52 | - |
| Brisbane | 7 | 7 | - | 357 | 131 | - | 3 | 1 | 51.00 | 87.71 | 1 |
| Coffs Harbour | 1 | 1 | - | 12 | 12 | - | - | - | 12.00 | 133.33 | - |
| Devonport | 1 | 1 | 1 | 32 | 32* | - | - | - | - | 118.52 | - |
| Drummoyne | 2 | 2 | - | 118 | 104 | - | - | 1 | 59.00 | 82.52 | 1 |
| Hobart | 3 | 3 | 1 | 118 | 75* | - | 1 | - | 59.00 | 96.72 | - |
| Homebush | 2 | 2 | - | 119 | 71 | - | 1 | - | 59.50 | 91.54 | - |
| Melbourne | 4 | 3 | - | 5 | 4 | 1 | - | - | 1.67 | 25.00 | 3 |
| North Sydney | 9 | 9 | 2 | 478 | 126 | - | 1 | 2 | 68.29 | 87.55 | 5 |
| Perth | 9 | 9 | - | 273 | 90 | - | 2 | - | 30.33 | 88.93 | 5 |
| Sydney | 11 | 11 | 5 | 447 | 101* | 1 | 3 | 1 | 74.50 | 79.40 | 1 |

| Batting Position | | Inn | NO | Runs | H.S | Os | 50 | 100 | Avrge | Stk/Rt | |
|------------------|--|-----|-----|------|-----|-----|-----|-----|-------|--------|--|
| 3 | | 30 | 4 | 1392 | 131 | 1 | 7 | 4 | 53.54 | 85.35 | |
| 4 | | 15 | 3 | 697 | 101* | - | 5 | 1 | 58.08 | 87.67 | |
| 5 | | 9 | 3 | 180 | 66* | 1 | 1 | - | 30.00 | 67.42 | |

| How Dismissed | | Inns | NO | Bwd | Cfd | Cwk | LBW | Stp | RO | HW | |
|---------------|--|------|-----|-----|-----|-----|-----|-----|-----|-----|--|
| | | 54 | 10 | 3 | 21 | 14 | 2 | - | 4 | - | |

## Centuries

Highest Score: 131 New South Wales v. Queensland, Brisbane, 1992-93

| 100s | Team | Opponent | Venue | Season |
|------|------|----------|-------|--------|
| 126 | New South Wales | Victoria | North Sydney | 1991-92 |
| 131 | New South Wales | Queensland | Brisbane | 1992-93 |
| 101* | New South Wales | Queensland | Sydney | 2001-02 |
| 104 | New South Wales | Tasmania | Drummoyne | 2002-03 |
| 101* | New South Wales | Western Australia | North Sydney | 2003-04 |

# BOWLING

## First-Class Career

Debut: 1984-85 New South Wales v. Queensland, Brisbane

| Season | Country | M | Overs | Mdns | Runs | Wkts | Avrge | 5 | 10 | Best |
|--------|---------|---|-------|------|------|------|-------|---|----|----|
| 1984-85 | Australia | 5 | 72.0 | 25 | 156 | 3 | 52.00 | - | - | 1/15 |
| 1985-86 | Zimbabwe | 1 | 20.5 | 2 | 85 | 2 | 42.50 | - | - | 2/57 |
| 1985-86 | Australia | 7 | 68.0 | 18 | 190 | 4 | 47.50 | - | - | 2/36 |
| 1985-86 | New Zealand | 5 | 53.0 | 12 | 151 | 7 | 21.57 | - | - | 4/56 |
| 1986-87 | India | 6 | 97.0 | 15 | 367 | 10 | 36.70 | - | - | 4/71 |
| 1986-87 | Australia | 13 | 258.3 | 49 | 772 | 25 | 30.88 | 1 | - | 5/69 |
| 1987 | England | 4 | 112.0 | 22 | 348 | 11 | 31.64 | - | - | 3/48 |
| 1987-88 | Australia | 10 | 218.3 | 59 | 499 | 23 | 21.70 | 1 | - | 5/50 |
| 1988 | England | 15 | 23.0 | 5 | 60 | 3 | 20.00 | - | - | 2/33 |
| 1988-89 | Pakistan | 6 | 126.0 | 33 | 362 | 4 | 90.50 | - | - | 1/15 |
| 1988-89 | Australia | 14 | 365.0 | 68 | 1114 | 36 | 30.94 | 2 | - | 6/51 |
| 1989 | England | 16 | 176.1 | 39 | 571 | 23 | 24.83 | - | - | 3/10 |
| 1989-90 | Australia | 12 | 9.0 | 3 | 19 | 1 | 19.00 | - | - | 1/13 |
| 1989-90 | New Zealand | 1 | - | - | - | - | - | - | - | - |
| 1990-91 | Australia | 8 | 107.0 | 26 | 319 | 4 | 79.75 | - | - | 1/7 |
| 1990-91 | West Indies | 6 | 78.0 | 16 | 234 | 3 | 78.00 | - | - | 3/76 |
| 1991-92 | Zimbabwe | 2 | 27.0 | 14 | 21 | 2 | 10.50 | - | - | 2/2 |
| 1991-92 | Australia | 8 | 125.0 | 35 | 342 | 12 | 28.50 | - | - | 3/23 |
| 1992-93 | Australia | 9 | 130.0 | 34 | 389 | 7 | 55.57 | - | - | 3/90 |
| 1992-93 | New Zealand | 4 | 55.0 | 21 | 108 | 5 | 21.60 | - | - | 2/21 |
| 1993 | England | 16 | 73.1 | 19 | 229 | 7 | 32.71 | - | - | 2/9 |
| 1993-94 | Australia | 9 | 80.0 | 22 | 190 | 7 | 27.14 | - | - | 4/26 |
| 1993-94 | South Africa | 5 | 89.5 | 31 | 157 | 11 | 14.27 | 1 | - | 5/28 |
| 1994-95 | Pakistan | 3 | 38.0 | 8 | 90 | 1 | 90.00 | - | - | 1/28 |
| 1994-95 | Australia | 9 | - | - | - | - | - | - | - | - |
| 1994-95 | West Indies | 6 | 37.0 | 8 | 100 | 8 | 12.50 | - | - | 2/14 |
| 1995-96 | Australia | 10 | 81.0 | 21 | 200 | 10 | 20.00 | - | - | 4/34 |
| 1996-97 | India | 2 | 13.0 | 5 | 25 | 1 | 25.00 | - | - | 1/25 |
| 1996-97 | Australia | 7 | 47.1 | 15 | 116 | 1 | 116.00 | - | - | 1/15 |
| 1996-97 | South Africa | 5 | 27.3 | 3 | 94 | 2 | 47.00 | - | - | 1/4 |
| 1997 | England | 13 | 26.0 | 5 | 97 | 1 | 97.00 | - | - | 1/13 |
| 1997-98 | Australia | 10 | 55.0 | 17 | 151 | 6 | 25.17 | - | - | 3/20 |
| 1997-98 | India | 4 | 17.0 | 2 | 44 | - | - | - | - | - |
| 1998-99 | Ireland | 1 | 6.0 | 1 | 27 | - | - | - | - | - |
| 1998-99 | Pakistan | 4 | 20.0 | 6 | 41 | 1 | 41.00 | - | - | 1/19 |
| 1998-99 | Australia | 6 | 11.0 | 3 | 28 | 2 | 14.00 | - | - | 2/8 |
| 1998-99 | West Indies | 6 | 5.0 | - | 19 | - | - | - | - | - |
| 1999-00 | Sri Lanka | 4 | - | - | - | - | - | - | - | - |
| 1999-00 | Zimbabwe | 2 | 4.0 | 1 | 17 | - | - | - | - | - |
| 1999-00 | Australia | 7 | 5.0 | 1 | 20 | - | - | - | - | - |
| 1999-00 | New Zealand | 4 | 7.0 | - | 20 | - | - | - | - | - |

| Season | Country | M | Overs | Mdns | Runs | Wkts | Avrge | 5 | 10 | Best |
|---|---|---|---|---|---|---|---|---|---|---|
| 2000-01 | Australia | 6 | 6.0 | 3 | 11 | - | - | - | - | - |
| 2000-01 | India | 6 | - | - | - | - | - | - | - | - |
| 2001 | England | 7 | - | - | - | - | - | - | - | - |
| 2001-02 | Australia | 6 | - | - | - | - | - | - | - | - |
| 2001-02 | South Africa | 5 | 3.0 | - | 16 | - | - | - | - | - |
| 2002 | England | 4 | 3.0 | - | 15 | - | - | - | - | - |
| 2002-03 | Sri Lanka | 1 | - | - | - | - | - | - | - | - |
| 2002-03 | United Arab Emirates | 2 | - | - | - | - | - | - | - | - |
| 2002-03 | Australia | 12 | 36.0 | 10 | 71 | 4 | 17.75 | - | - | 2/15 |
| 2002-03 | West Indies | 6 | 24.0 | 4 | 76 | - | - | - | - | - |
| 2003-04 | Australia | 16 | 69.0 | 11 | 194 | 2 | 97.00 | - | - | 1/23 |
| **Total** | | **356** | **2904.4** | **692** | **8155** | **249** | **32.75** | **5** | **-** | **6/51** |

| Team | M | Overs | Mdns | Runs | Wkts | Avrge | 5 | 10 | Best |
|---|---|---|---|---|---|---|---|---|---|
| AUSTRALIA | 168 | 1300.5 | 332 | 3445 | 92 | 37.45 | 3 | - | 5/28 |
| Australian XI | 70 | 461.2 | 109 | 1431 | 54 | 26.50 | - | - | 4/71 |
| Ireland | 1 | 6.0 | 1 | 27 | - | - | - | - | - |
| Kent | 4 | 3.0 | - | 15 | - | - | - | - | - |
| New South Wales | 93 | 977.4 | 221 | 2744 | 87 | 31.54 | 2 | - | 6/51 |
| Somerset | 19 | 135.0 | 27 | 408 | 14 | 29.14 | - | - | 3/48 |
| Young Australians | 1 | 20.5 | 2 | 85 | 2 | 42.50 | - | - | 2/57 |

| Wickets Taken | Wkts | Bwd | Cfd | Cwk | LBW | Stp | HW | | | |
|---|---|---|---|---|---|---|---|---|---|---|
| | 249 | 44 | 111 | 49 | 43 | 2 | - | | | |

| Batsmen Dismissed | Wkts | 1/2 | 3 | 4 | 5 | 6 | 7 | 8 | 9 | 10 | 11 |
|---|---|---|---|---|---|---|---|---|---|---|---|
| | 249 | 48 | 30 | 31 | 39 | 32 | 17 | 18 | 17 | 10 | 7 |

## Five Wickets in an Innings

**Best Bowling: 6/51 New South Wales v. Queensland, Sydney, 1988-89**

| Wkts | Team | Opponent | Venue | Season |
|---|---|---|---|---|
| 5/69 | Australia | England | Perth | 1986-87 |
| 5/50 | New South Wales | Tasmania | Sydney | 1987-88 |
| 5/92 | Australia | West Indies | Melbourne | 1988-89 |
| 6/51 | New South Wales | Queensland | Sydney | 1988-89 |
| 5/28 | Australia | South Africa | Cape Town | 1993-94 |

## Test Career

**Debut: 1985-86 Australia v. India, Melbourne**

| Season | Opponent | Venue | M | Overs | Mdns | Runs | Wkts | Avrge | 5 | 10 | Best |
|---|---|---|---|---|---|---|---|---|---|---|---|
| 1985-86 | India | Australia | 2 | 18.0 | 5 | 69 | 2 | 34.50 | - | - | 2/36 |
| 1985-86 | New Zealand | New Zealand | 3 | 36.0 | 9 | 83 | 5 | 16.60 | - | - | 4/56 |
| 1986-87 | India | India | 3 | 35.0 | 5 | 130 | 2 | 65.00 | - | - | 1/29 |
| 1986-87 | England | Australia | 5 | 108.3 | 26 | 336 | 10 | 33.60 | 1 | - | 5/69 |
| 1987-88 | New Zealand | Australia | 3 | 75.0 | 26 | 169 | 2 | 84.50 | - | - | 1/2 |
| 1987-88 | England | Australia | 1 | 22.5 | 5 | 51 | 3 | 17.00 | - | - | 3/51 |
| 1987-88 | Sri Lanka | Australia | 1 | 28.0 | 11 | 47 | 4 | 11.75 | - | - | 4/33 |
| 1988-89 | Pakistan | Pakistan | 3 | 78.0 | 17 | 216 | 2 | 108.00 | - | - | 1/44 |
| 1988-89 | West Indies | Australia | 5 | 139.0 | 17 | 472 | 10 | 47.20 | 1 | - | 5/92 |
| 1989 | England | England | 6 | 57.0 | 15 | 208 | 2 | 104.00 | - | - | 1/38 |
| 1989-90 | New Zealand | Australia | 1 | - | - | - | - | - | - | - | - |
| 1989-90 | Sri Lanka | Australia | 2 | 6.0 | 3 | 6 | - | - | - | - | - |
| 1989-90 | Pakistan | Australia | 3 | 3.0 | - | 13 | 1 | 13.00 | - | - | 1/13 |
| 1989-90 | New Zealand | New Zealand | 1 | - | - | - | - | - | - | - | - |
| 1990-91 | England | Australia | 3 | 38.0 | 15 | 90 | 1 | 90.00 | - | - | 1/7 |
| 1990-91 | West Indies | West Indies | 2 | 35.0 | 6 | 90 | - | - | - | - | - |
| 1992-93 | West Indies | Australia | 5 | 58.0 | 14 | 162 | 3 | 54.00 | - | - | 1/14 |
| 1992-93 | New Zealand | New Zealand | 3 | 41.0 | 18 | 71 | 2 | 35.50 | - | - | 1/15 |

| Season | Opponent | Venue | M | Overs | Mdns | Runs | Wkts | Avrge | 5 | 10 | Best |
|---|---|---|---|---|---|---|---|---|---|---|---|
| 1993 | England | England | 6 | 32.0 | 9 | 82 | 2 | 41.00 | - | - | 2/45 |
| 1993-94 | New Zealand | Australia | 3 | 18.0 | 3 | 41 | 1 | 41.00 | - | - | 1/10 |
| 1993-94 | South Africa | Australia | 1 | 24.0 | 10 | 30 | 4 | 7.50 | - | - | 4/26 |
| 1993-94 | South Africa | South Africa | 3 | 77.5 | 29 | 130 | 10 | 13.00 | 1 | - | 5/28 |
| 1994-95 | Pakistan | Pakistan | 2 | 30.0 | 5 | 78 | 1 | 78.00 | - | - | 1/28 |
| 1994-95 | England | Australia | 5 | - | - | - | - | - | - | - | - |
| 1994-95 | West Indies | West Indies | 4 | 24.0 | 7 | 62 | 5 | 12.40 | - | - | 2/14 |
| 1995-96 | Pakistan | Australia | 3 | 16.0 | 2 | 40 | 1 | 40.00 | - | - | 1/18 |
| 1995-96 | Sri Lanka | Australia | 2 | 19.0 | 8 | 34 | 4 | 8.50 | - | - | 4/34 |
| 1996-97 | India | India | 1 | 13.0 | 5 | 25 | 1 | 25.00 | - | - | 1/25 |
| 1996-97 | West Indies | Australia | 4 | 25.1 | 7 | 63 | 1 | 63.00 | - | - | 1/15 |
| 1996-97 | South Africa | South Africa | 3 | 8.3 | 1 | 20 | 1 | 20.00 | - | - | 1/4 |
| 1997 | England | England | 6 | 20.0 | 3 | 76 | - | - | - | - | - |
| 1997-98 | New Zealand | Australia | 3 | 15.0 | 6 | 30 | 4 | 7.50 | - | - | 3/20 |
| 1997-98 | South Africa | Australia | 3 | 31.0 | 10 | 74 | 2 | 37.00 | - | - | 1/12 |
| 1997-98 | India | India | 2 | 12.0 | 1 | 38 | - | - | - | - | - |
| 1998-99 | Pakistan | Pakistan | 3 | 20.0 | 6 | 41 | 1 | 41.00 | - | - | 1/19 |
| 1998-99 | England | Australia | 5 | 11.0 | 3 | 28 | 2 | 14.00 | - | - | 2/8 |
| 1998-99 | West Indies | West Indies | 4 | 5.0 | - | 19 | - | - | - | - | - |
| 1999-00 | Sri Lanka | Sri Lanka | 3 | - | - | - | - | - | - | - | - |
| 1999-00 | Zimbabwe | Zimbabwe | 1 | 4.0 | 1 | 17 | - | - | - | - | - |
| 1999-00 | Pakistan | Australia | 3 | 5.0 | 1 | 20 | - | - | - | - | - |
| 1999-00 | India | Australia | 3 | - | - | - | - | - | - | - | - |
| 1999-00 | New Zealand | New Zealand | 3 | 7.0 | - | 20 | - | - | - | - | - |
| 2000-01 | West Indies | Australia | 4 | - | - | - | - | - | - | - | - |
| 2000-01 | India | India | 3 | - | - | - | - | - | - | - | - |
| 2001 | England | England | 4 | - | - | - | - | - | - | - | - |
| 2001-02 | New Zealand | Australia | 3 | - | - | - | - | - | - | - | - |
| 2001-02 | South Africa | Australia | 3 | - | - | - | - | - | - | - | - |
| 2001-02 | South Africa | South Africa | 3 | 3.0 | - | 16 | - | - | - | - | - |
| 2002-03 | Pakistan | SRL/U.A.E. | 3 | - | - | - | - | - | - | - | - |
| 2002-03 | England | Australia | 5 | 25.0 | 8 | 43 | 2 | 21.50 | - | - | 1/2 |
| 2002-03 | West Indies | West Indies | 4 | 24.0 | 4 | 76 | - | - | - | - | - |
| 2002-03 | Bangladesh | Australia | 2 | 5.0 | 3 | 4 | - | - | - | - | - |
| 2003-04 | Zimbabwe | Australia | 2 | 17.0 | 3 | 43 | - | - | - | - | - |
| 2003-04 | India | Australia | 4 | 31.0 | 5 | 82 | 1 | 82.00 | - | - | 1/35 |
| **Total** | | | **168** | **1300.5** | **332** | **3445** | **92** | **37.45** | **3** | **-** | **5/28** |

| | Opponents | | M | Overs | Mdns | Runs | Wkts | Avrge | 5 | 10 | Best |
|---|---|---|---|---|---|---|---|---|---|---|---|
| | Bangladesh | | 2 | 5.0 | 3 | 4 | - | - | - | - | - |
| | England | | 46 | 314.2 | 84 | 914 | 22 | 41.55 | 1 | - | 5/69 |
| | India | | 18 | 109.0 | 21 | 344 | 6 | 57.33 | - | - | 2/36 |
| | New Zealand | | 23 | 192.0 | 62 | 414 | 14 | 29.57 | - | - | 4/56 |
| | Pakistan | | 20 | 152.0 | 31 | 408 | 6 | 68.00 | - | - | 1/13 |
| | South Africa | | 16 | 144.2 | 50 | 270 | 17 | 15.88 | 1 | - | 5/28 |
| | Sri Lanka | | 8 | 53.0 | 22 | 87 | 8 | 10.88 | - | - | 4/33 |
| | West Indies | | 32 | 310.1 | 55 | 944 | 19 | 49.68 | 1 | - | 5/92 |
| | Zimbabwe | | 3 | 21.0 | 4 | 60 | - | - | - | - | - |

| | Innings | | | Overs | Mdns | Runs | Wkts | Avrge | 5 | 10 | Best |
|---|---|---|---|---|---|---|---|---|---|---|---|
| | First Innings | | | 410.5 | 100 | 1169 | 23 | 50.83 | - | - | 3/51 |
| | Second Innings | | | 459.3 | 122 | 1183 | 38 | 31.13 | - | - | 4/26 |
| | Third Innings | | | 287.3 | 69 | 787 | 20 | 39.35 | 3 | - | 5/28 |
| | Fourth Innings | | | 143.0 | 41 | 306 | 11 | 27.82 | - | - | 4/34 |

# Bowling at Each Venue

| Venue | M | Overs | Mdns | Runs | Wkts | Avrge | 5 | 10 | Best |
|---|---|---|---|---|---|---|---|---|---|
| **in Australia** | | | | | | | | | |
| Adelaide | 15 | 170.0 | 54 | 380 | 11 | 34.55 | - | - | 4/26 |
| Brisbane | 17 | 127.1 | 30 | 337 | 10 | 33.70 | - | - | 3/76 |
| Cairns | 1 | 5.0 | 3 | 4 | - | - | - | - | - |
| Darwin | 1 | - | - | - | - | - | - | - | - |
| Hobart | 6 | 43.0 | 12 | 100 | 5 | 20.00 | - | - | 3/20 |
| Melbourne | 17 | 134.0 | 36 | 426 | 17 | 25.06 | 1 | - | 5/92 |
| Perth | 15 | 161.3 | 32 | 456 | 10 | 45.60 | 1 | - | 5/69 |
| Sydney | 17 | 97.5 | 24 | 244 | 5 | 48.80 | - | - | 3/51 |
| **in England** | | | | | | | | | |
| Birmingham | 4 | 28.0 | 7 | 87 | 1 | 87.00 | - | - | 1/38 |
| Leeds | 3 | 10.0 | 3 | 38 | - | - | - | - | - |
| Lord's | 4 | 26.0 | 6 | 107 | 1 | 107.00 | - | - | 1/49 |
| Manchester | 3 | 10.0 | 1 | 40 | - | - | - | - | - |
| Nottingham | 4 | 20.0 | 8 | 38 | - | - | - | - | - |
| The Oval | 4 | 15.0 | 2 | 56 | 2 | 28.00 | - | - | 2/45 |
| **in India** | | | | | | | | | |
| Chennai | 3 | 27.0 | 4 | 98 | 1 | 98.00 | - | - | 1/44 |
| Delhi | 2 | 19.0 | 5 | 54 | 2 | 27.00 | - | - | 1/25 |
| Kolkata | 2 | - | - | - | - | - | - | - | - |
| Mumbai | 2 | 14.0 | 2 | 41 | - | - | - | - | - |
| **in New Zealand** | | | | | | | | | |
| Auckland | 3 | 29.0 | 9 | 52 | 3 | 17.33 | - | - | 1/14 |
| Christchurch | 2 | 29.0 | 10 | 65 | 4 | 16.25 | - | - | 4/56 |
| Hamilton | 1 | 3.0 | - | 10 | - | - | - | - | - |
| Wellington | 4 | 23.0 | 8 | 47 | - | - | - | - | - |
| **in Pakistan** | | | | | | | | | |
| Faisalabad | 1 | 29.0 | 9 | 80 | 1 | 80.00 | - | - | 1/44 |
| Karachi | 3 | 53.0 | 11 | 147 | 2 | 73.50 | - | - | 1/28 |
| Lahore | 1 | 23.0 | 5 | 42 | - | - | - | - | - |
| Peshawar | 1 | 8.0 | 1 | 19 | 1 | 19.00 | - | - | 1/19 |
| Rawalpindi | 2 | 15.0 | 2 | 47 | - | - | - | - | - |
| **in South Africa** | | | | | | | | | |
| Cape Town | 2 | 34.3 | 12 | 64 | 5 | 12.80 | 1 | - | 5/28 |
| Centurion | 1 | - | - | - | - | - | - | - | - |
| Durban | 2 | 27.2 | 12 | 40 | 3 | 13.33 | - | - | 3/40 |
| Johannesburg | 3 | 23.0 | 6 | 46 | 3 | 15.33 | - | - | 1/4 |
| Port Elizabeth | 1 | 4.3 | - | 16 | - | - | - | - | - |
| **in Sri Lanka** | | | | | | | | | |
| Colombo (PSS) | 1 | - | - | - | - | - | - | - | - |
| Colombo (SSC) | 1 | - | - | - | - | - | - | - | - |
| Galle | 1 | - | - | - | - | - | - | - | - |
| Kandy | 1 | - | - | - | - | - | - | - | - |
| **in United Arab Emirates** | | | | | | | | | |
| Sharjah | 2 | - | - | - | - | - | - | - | - |
| **in West Indies** | | | | | | | | | |
| Bridgetown | 4 | 39.0 | 7 | 105 | - | - | - | - | - |
| Georgetown | 1 | 8.0 | 1 | 29 | - | - | - | - | - |
| Kingston | 2 | 15.0 | 5 | 23 | 2 | 11.50 | - | - | 2/14 |
| Port-of-Spain | 4 | 15.0 | 3 | 45 | 1 | 45.00 | - | - | 1/19 |
| St John's | 3 | 11.0 | 1 | 45 | 2 | 22.50 | - | - | 2/20 |

| Venue | | | M | Overs | Mdns | Runs | Wkts | Avrge | 5 | 10 | Best |
|---|---|---|---|---|---|---|---|---|---|---|---|
| in Zimbabwe | | | | | | | | | | | |
| Harare | | | 1 | 4.0 | 1 | 17 | - | - | - | - | - |

| Country | | | M | Overs | Mdns | Runs | Wkts | Avrge | 5 | 10 | Best |
|---|---|---|---|---|---|---|---|---|---|---|---|
| Australia | | | 89 | 738.3 | 191 | 1947 | 58 | 33.57 | 2 | - | 5/69 |
| England | | | 22 | 109.0 | 27 | 366 | 4 | 91.50 | - | - | 2/45 |
| India | | | 9 | 60.0 | 11 | 193 | 3 | 64.33 | - | - | 1/25 |
| New Zealand | | | 10 | 84.0 | 27 | 174 | 7 | 24.86 | - | - | 4/56 |
| Pakistan | | | 8 | 128.0 | 28 | 335 | 4 | 83.75 | - | - | 1/19 |
| South Africa | | | 9 | 89.2 | 30 | 166 | 11 | 15.09 | 1 | - | 5/28 |
| Sri Lanka | | | 4 | - | - | - | - | - | - | - | - |
| United Arab Emirates | | | 2 | - | - | - | - | - | - | - | - |
| West Indies | | | 14 | 88.0 | 17 | 247 | 5 | 49.40 | - | - | 2/14 |
| Zimbabwe | | | 1 | 4.0 | 1 | 17 | - | - | - | - | - |

| Wickets Taken | Wkts | Bwd | Cfd | Cwk | LBW | Stp | HW | | | | |
|---|---|---|---|---|---|---|---|---|---|---|---|
| | 92 | 12 | 33 | 24 | 23 | - | - | | | | |

| Batsmen Dismissed | Wkts | 1/2 | 3 | 4 | 5 | 6 | 7 | 8 | 9 | 10 | 11 |
|---|---|---|---|---|---|---|---|---|---|---|---|
| | 92 | 12 | 10 | 9 | 18 | 12 | 6 | 9 | 7 | 5 | 4 |

## Five Wickets in an Innings

Best Bowling: 5/28 Australia v. South Africa, Cape Town, 1993-94

| Wkts | Team | Opponent | Venue | Season |
|---|---|---|---|---|
| 5/69 | Australia | England | Perth | 1986-87 |
| 5/92 | Australia | West Indies | Melbourne | 1988-89 |
| 5/28 | Australia | South Africa | Cape Town | 1993-94 |

## Sheffield Shield Career

Debut: 1984-85 New South Wales v. Queensland, Brisbane

| Season | M | Overs | Mdns | Runs | Wkts | Avrge | 5 | 10 | Best |
|---|---|---|---|---|---|---|---|---|---|
| 1984-85 | 5 | 72.0 | 25 | 156 | 3 | 52.00 | - | - | 1/15 |
| 1985-86 | 4 | 50.0 | 13 | 121 | 2 | 60.50 | - | - | 1/15 |
| 1986-87 | 7 | 145.0 | 23 | 424 | 15 | 28.27 | - | - | 3/33 |
| 1987-88 | 5 | 92.4 | 17 | 232 | 14 | 16.57 | 1 | - | 5/50 |
| 1988-89 | 8 | 216.0 | 49 | 620 | 26 | 23.85 | 1 | - | 6/51 |
| 1989-90 | 5 | - | - | - | - | - | - | - | - |
| 1990-91 | 5 | 69.0 | 11 | 229 | 3 | 76.33 | - | - | 1/33 |
| 1991-92 | 6 | 94.0 | 25 | 261 | 9 | 29.00 | - | - | 3/23 |
| 1992-93 | 2 | 41.0 | 12 | 131 | 3 | 43.67 | - | - | 3/90 |
| 1993-94 | 4 | 33.0 | 8 | 113 | 2 | 56.50 | - | - | 1/15 |
| 1994-95 | 4 | - | - | - | - | - | - | - | - |
| 1995-96 | 4 | 46.0 | 11 | 126 | 5 | 25.20 | - | - | 2/25 |
| 1996-97 | 3 | 22.0 | 8 | 53 | - | - | - | - | - |
| 1997-98 | 4 | 9.0 | 1 | 47 | - | - | - | - | - |
| 1998-99 | 1 | - | - | - | - | - | - | - | - |
| 1999-00 | 1 | - | - | - | - | - | - | - | - |
| 2000-01 | 2 | 6.0 | 3 | 11 | - | - | - | - | - |
| 2001-02 | - | - | - | - | - | - | - | - | - |
| 2002-03 | 7 | 11.0 | 2 | 28 | 2 | 14.00 | - | - | 2/15 |
| 2003-04 | 8 | 16.0 | - | 65 | 1 | 65.00 | - | - | 1/23 |
| **Total** | **85** | **922.4** | **208** | **2617** | **85** | **30.79** | **2** | **-** | **6/51** |

| Opponents | M | Overs | Mdns | Runs | Wkts | Avrge | 5 | 10 | Best |
|---|---|---|---|---|---|---|---|---|---|
| Queensland | 21 | 238.3 | 60 | 693 | 26 | 26.65 | 1 | - | 6/51 |
| South Australia | 15 | 126.0 | 32 | 341 | 7 | 48.71 | - | - | 1/15 |
| Tasmania | 14 | 154.4 | 28 | 433 | 16 | 27.06 | 1 | - | 5/50 |
| Victoria | 21 | 240.3 | 58 | 627 | 17 | 36.88 | - | - | 3/23 |
| Western Australia | 14 | 163.0 | 30 | 523 | 19 | 27.53 | - | - | 4/30 |

| Innings | Overs | Mdns | Runs | Wkts | Avrge | 5 | 10 | Best |
|---|---|---|---|---|---|---|---|---|
| First | 324.0 | 77 | 876 | 25 | 35.04 | - | - | 3/23 |
| Second | 293.1 | 74 | 731 | 25 | 29.24 | 1 | - | 5/50 |
| Third | 134.3 | 26 | 448 | 22 | 20.36 | 1 | - | 6/51 |
| Fourth | 171.0 | 31 | 562 | 13 | 43.23 | - | - | 2/25 |

## Bowling at Each Venue

| Venue | M | Overs | Mdns | Runs | Wkts | Avrge | 5 | 10 | Best |
|---|---|---|---|---|---|---|---|---|---|
| Adelaide | 6 | 20.0 | 6 | 67 | - | - | - | - | - |
| Bankstown | 1 | 10.0 | 5 | 16 | - | - | - | - | - |
| Brisbane | 9 | 148.3 | 39 | 416 | 13 | 32.00 | - | - | 3/33 |
| Devonport | 1 | 29.0 | 7 | 68 | 2 | 34.00 | - | - | 2/68 |
| Hobart (Bellerive) | 5 | 16.0 | 3 | 56 | - | - | - | - | - |
| Hobart (TCA) | 2 | 34.0 | 4 | 106 | 4 | 26.50 | - | - | 2/36 |
| Melbourne | 6 | 59.0 | 16 | 124 | 4 | 31.00 | - | - | 3/23 |
| Newcastle | 7 | 66.0 | 12 | 196 | 5 | 39.20 | - | - | 3/38 |
| North Sydney | 1 | - | - | - | - | - | - | - | - |
| Perth | 9 | 125.0 | 23 | 416 | 13 | 32.00 | - | - | 3/49 |
| Richmond | 1 | - | - | - | - | - | - | - | - |
| St Kilda | 2 | 50.3 | 9 | 151 | 3 | 50.33 | - | - | 2/39 |
| Sydney | 35 | 364.4 | 84 | 1001 | 41 | 24.41 | 2 | - | 6/51 |

| Wickets Taken | Wkts | Bwd | Cfd | Cwk | LBW | Stp | HW |
|---|---|---|---|---|---|---|---|
| | 85 | 15 | 41 | 18 | 9 | - | - |

| Batsmen Dismissed | Wkts | 1/2 | 3 | 4 | 5 | 6 | 7 | 8 | 9 | 10 | 11 |
|---|---|---|---|---|---|---|---|---|---|---|---|
| | 85 | 20 | 10 | 10 | 11 | 12 | 4 | 4 | 9 | 3 | 2 |

## Five Wickets in an Innings

Best Bowling: 6/51 New South Wales v. Queensland, Sydney, 1988-89

| Wkts | Team | Opponent | Venue | Season |
|---|---|---|---|---|
| 5/50 | New South Wales | Tasmania | Sydney | 1987-88 |
| 6/51 | New South Wales | Queensland | Sydney | 1988-89 |

## International Limited-Overs Career

Debut: 1985-86 Australia v. New Zealand, Melbourne

| Season | Tournament | Venue | M | Overs | Mdns | Runs | Wkts | Avrge | 5 | Best | Stk/Rt | RPO |
|---|---|---|---|---|---|---|---|---|---|---|---|---|
| 1985-86 | World Series Cup | AUS | 12 | 53.0 | 4 | 231 | 7 | 33.00 | - | 2/28 | 45.43 | 4.36 |
| 1985-86 | Rothman's Cup | NZ | 4 | 35.0 | 1 | 159 | 4 | 39.75 | - | 1/31 | 52.50 | 4.54 |
| 1985-86 | Austral-Asia Cup | UAE | 1 | 6.0 | 1 | 25 | - | - | - | - | - | 4.17 |
| 1986-87 | India v. Australia | IND | 6 | 46.0 | 1 | 229 | 7 | 32.71 | - | 2/44 | 39.43 | 4.98 |
| 1986-87 | Challenge Cup | AUS | 3 | 24.5 | - | 113 | 6 | 18.83 | - | 4/48 | 24.83 | 4.55 |
| 1986-87 | World Series Cup | AUS | 10 | 85.0 | 4 | 345 | 15 | 23.00 | - | 3/26 | 34.00 | 4.06 |
| 1986-87 | Sharjah Cup | UAE | 3 | 24.0 | 1 | 116 | 2 | 58.00 | - | 1/33 | 72.00 | 4.83 |
| 1987-88 | World Cup | IND/PAK | 8 | 63.3 | 4 | 288 | 11 | 26.18 | - | 2/36 | 34.64 | 4.54 |
| 1987-88 | World Series Cup | AUS | 10 | 89.5 | 3 | 381 | 17 | 22.41 | - | 4/33 | 31.71 | 4.24 |
| 1987-88 | Australia v. England | AUS | 1 | 10.0 | - | 42 | 1 | 42.00 | - | 1/42 | 60.00 | 4.20 |
| 1988-89 | Pakistan v. Australia | PAK | 1 | 8.0 | - | 42 | 1 | 42.00 | - | 1/42 | 48.00 | 5.25 |
| 1988-89 | World Series Cup | AUS | 11 | 78.0 | - | 373 | 8 | 46.63 | - | 3/57 | 58.50 | 4.78 |
| 1989 | England v. Australia | ENG | 3 | 33.0 | 2 | 162 | 3 | 54.00 | - | 2/45 | 66.00 | 4.91 |
| 1989-90 | Nehru Cup | IND | 5 | - | - | - | - | - | - | - | - | - |
| 1989-90 | World Series | AUS | 9 | 16.0 | - | 77 | 2 | 38.50 | - | 1/26 | 48.00 | 4.81 |
| 1989-90 | Rothman's Series | NZ | 5 | - | - | - | - | - | - | - | - | - |

| Season | Tournament | Venue | M | Overs | Mdns | Runs | Wkts | Avrge | 5 | Best | Stk/Rt | RPO |
|--------|-----------|-------|---|-------|------|------|------|-------|---|------|--------|-----|
| 1989-90 | Austral-Asia Cup | UAE | 4 | 29.0 | 2 | 112 | 4 | 28.00 | - | 2/22 | 43.50 | 3.86 |
| 1990-91 | World Series | AUS | 10 | 76.0 | 5 | 346 | 7 | 49.43 | - | 2/39 | 65.14 | 4.55 |
| 1990-91 | West Indies v. Australia | WI | 5 | 32.0 | 1 | 153 | 5 | 30.60 | - | 2/25 | 38.40 | 4.78 |
| 1991-92 | World Series | AUS | 10 | 80.3 | 5 | 304 | 16 | 19.00 | - | 3/31 | 30.19 | 3.78 |
| 1991-92 | World Cup | ANZ | 8 | 60.4 | 1 | 277 | 8 | 34.63 | - | 3/36 | 45.50 | 4.57 |
| 1992-93 | World Series | AUS | 10 | 82.3 | 4 | 353 | 9 | 39.22 | - | 2/25 | 55.00 | 4.28 |
| 1992-93 | New Zealand v. Australia | NZ | 5 | 35.4 | - | 173 | 3 | 57.67 | - | 2/27 | 71.33 | 4.85 |
| 1993 | England v. Australia | ENG | 3 | 29.0 | - | 151 | 5 | 30.20 | - | 3/53 | 34.80 | 5.21 |
| 1993-94 | World Series | AUS | 9 | 61.0 | 2 | 218 | 4 | 54.50 | - | 2/20 | 91.50 | 3.57 |
| 1993-94 | South Africa v. Australia | SAF | 8 | 56.0 | 2 | 282 | 5 | 56.40 | - | 2/48 | 67.20 | 5.04 |
| 1993-94 | Austral-Asia Cup | UAE | 3 | 24.0 | 1 | 117 | 2 | 58.50 | - | 2/17 | 72.00 | 4.88 |
| 1994-95 | Singer World Series | SL | 3 | 24.0 | 1 | 81 | 5 | 16.20 | - | 3/16 | 28.80 | 3.38 |
| 1994-95 | Wills Triangular Series | PAK | 5 | 37.0 | 2 | 144 | 2 | 72.00 | - | 2/35 | 111.00 | 3.89 |
| 1994-95 | World Series | AUS | 1 | - | - | - | - | - | - | - | - | - |
| 1994-95 | New Zealand Centenary | NZ | 4 | - | - | - | - | - | - | - | - | - |
| 1994-95 | West Indies v. Australia | WI | 5 | 22.3 | 1 | 123 | 3 | 41.00 | - | 2/61 | 45.00 | 5.47 |
| 1995-96 | World Series | AUS | 4 | 4.0 | - | 28 | - | - | - | - | - | 7.00 |
| 1995-96 | World Cup | ASIA | 7 | 31.0 | 2 | 157 | 5 | 31.40 | - | 2/22 | 37.20 | 5.06 |
| 1996-97 | Singer World Series | SL | 4 | 25.0 | 3 | 111 | 3 | 37.00 | - | 1/20 | 50.00 | 4.44 |
| 1996-97 | Titan Cup | IND | 5 | 13.0 | - | 76 | 2 | 38.00 | - | 2/52 | 39.00 | 5.85 |
| 1996-97 | CUB Series | AUS | 6 | 3.0 | - | 24 | - | - | - | - | - | 8.00 |
| 1996-97 | South Africa v. Australia | SAF | 7 | 5.0 | - | 25 | - | - | - | - | - | 5.00 |
| 1997 | England v. Australia | ENG | 3 | 7.0 | - | 42 | - | - | - | - | - | 6.00 |
| 1997-98 | CUB Series | AUS | 10 | 4.0 | - | 14 | 1 | 14.00 | - | 1/14 | 24.00 | 3.50 |
| 1997-98 | New Zealand v. Australia | NZ | 4 | 29.3 | 1 | 126 | 3 | 42.00 | - | 2/46 | 59.00 | 4.27 |
| 1997-98 | Triangular Cup | IND | 5 | 17.0 | - | 97 | 3 | 32.33 | - | 2/42 | 34.00 | 5.71 |
| 1997-98 | Coca Cola Cup | UAE | 5 | 28.0 | - | 171 | 5 | 34.20 | - | 4/40 | 33.60 | 6.11 |
| 1998-99 | Wills International Cup | BAN | 1 | 3.0 | - | 23 | - | - | - | - | - | 7.67 |
| 1998-99 | Pakistan v. Australia | PAK | 3 | 19.2 | - | 97 | 1 | 97.00 | - | 1/22 | 116.00 | 5.02 |
| 1998-99 | CUB Series | AUS | 2 | - | - | - | - | - | - | - | - | - |
| 1998-99 | W.Indies v. Australia | WI | 7 | 16.3 | - | 66 | 2 | 33.00 | - | 1/13 | 49.50 | 4.00 |
| 1999 | World Cup | ENG | 10 | 18.0 | - | 92 | 3 | 30.67 | - | 2/8 | 36.00 | 5.11 |
| 1999-00 | Aiwa Cup | SL | 5 | 6.1 | - | 42 | 1 | 42.00 | - | 1/26 | 37.00 | 6.81 |
| 1999-00 | Zimbabwe v. Australia | ZIM | 3 | - | - | - | - | - | - | - | - | - |
| 1999-00 | CUB Series | AUS | 10 | 6.0 | - | 22 | - | - | - | - | - | 3.67 |
| 1999-00 | New Zealand v. Australia | NZ | 6 | - | - | - | - | - | - | - | - | - |
| 1999-00 | South Africa v. Australia | SAF | 3 | 3.0 | - | 18 | - | - | - | - | - | 6.00 |
| 2000-01 | Australia v. South Africa | AUS | 3 | - | - | - | - | - | - | - | - | - |
| 2000-01 | ICC Trophy | KYA | 1 | 4.0 | - | 28 | 1 | 28.00 | - | 1/28 | 24.00 | 7.00 |
| 2000-01 | Carlton Series | AUS | 7 | - | - | - | - | - | - | - | - | - |
| 2000-01 | India v. Australia | IND | 5 | 6.0 | - | 29 | 3 | 9.67 | - | 3/29 | 12.00 | 4.83 |
| 2001 | NatWest Series | ENG | 6 | - | - | - | - | - | - | - | - | - |
| 2001-02 | VB Series | AUS | 8 | 10.0 | - | 59 | - | - | - | - | - | 5.90 |
| **Total** | | | 325 | 1480.3 | 54 | 6764 | 195 | 34.69 | - | 4/33 | 45.55 | 4.57 |

| | Opponents | | M | Overs | Mdns | Runs | Wkts | Avrge | 5 | Best | Stk/Rt | R/O |
|---|-----------|---|---|-------|------|------|------|-------|---|------|--------|-----|
| | Bangladesh | | 2 | 10.0 | 2 | 22 | 2 | 11.00 | - | 2/22 | 30.00 | 2.20 |
| | England | | 30 | 188.0 | 7 | 870 | 26 | 33.46 | - | 3/26 | 43.38 | 4.63 |
| | India | | 53 | 257.3 | 5 | 1270 | 43 | 29.53 | - | 4/40 | 35.93 | 4.93 |
| | Kenya | | 1 | 7.0 | - | 43 | - | - | - | - | - | 6.14 |
| | New Zealand | | 60 | 294.4 | 10 | 1365 | 31 | 44.03 | - | 2/23 | 57.03 | 4.63 |
| | Pakistan | | 43 | 168.5 | 4 | 774 | 20 | 38.70 | - | 4/48 | 50.65 | 4.58 |
| | Scotland | | 1 | 6.0 | - | 22 | 1 | 22.00 | - | 1/22 | 36.00 | 3.67 |
| | South Africa | | 47 | 144.0 | 6 | 646 | 12 | 53.83 | - | 2/20 | 72.00 | 4.49 |
| | Sri Lanka | | 24 | 103.1 | 3 | 479 | 16 | 29.94 | - | 4/33 | 38.69 | 4.64 |
| | West Indies | | 50 | 260.2 | 10 | 1128 | 37 | 30.49 | - | 3/31 | 42.22 | 4.33 |
| | Zimbabwe | | 14 | 41.0 | 7 | 145 | 7 | 20.71 | - | 2/22 | 35.14 | 3.54 |

| Innings | | Overs | Mdns | Runs | Wkts | Avrge | 5 | Best | Stk/Rt | R/O |
|---|---|---|---|---|---|---|---|---|---|---|
| First | | 824.4 | 27 | 3741 | 112 | 33.40 | - | 4/40 | 44.18 | 4.54 |
| Second | | 655.5 | 27 | 3023 | 83 | 36.42 | - | 4/33 | 47.41 | 4.61 |

| Country | M | Overs | Mdns | Runs | Wkts | Avrge | 5 | Best | Stk/Rt | R/O |
|---|---|---|---|---|---|---|---|---|---|---|
| Australia | 153 | 734.2 | 28 | 3147 | 101 | 31.16 | - | 4/33 | 43.62 | 4.29 |
| Bangladesh | 1 | 3.0 | - | 23 | - | - | - | - | - | 7.67 |
| England | 25 | 87.0 | 2 | 447 | 11 | 40.64 | - | 3/53 | 47.45 | 5.14 |
| India | 39 | 164.3 | 6 | 810 | 30 | 27.00 | - | 3/29 | 32.90 | 4.92 |
| Kenya | 1 | 4.0 | - | 28 | 1 | 28.00 | - | 1/28 | 24.00 | 7.00 |
| New Zealand | 29 | 110.1 | 2 | 518 | 10 | 51.80 | - | 2/27 | 66.10 | 4.70 |
| Pakistan | 11 | 76.2 | 3 | 349 | 5 | 69.80 | - | 2/35 | 91.60 | 4.57 |
| Sri Lanka | 12 | 55.1 | 4 | 234 | 9 | 26.00 | - | 3/16 | 36.78 | 4.24 |
| South Africa | 18 | 64.0 | 2 | 325 | 5 | 65.00 | - | 2/48 | 76.80 | 5.08 |
| United Arab Emirates | 16 | 111.0 | 5 | 541 | 13 | 41.62 | - | 4/40 | 51.23 | 4.87 |
| West Indies | 17 | 71.0 | 2 | 342 | 10 | 34.20 | - | 2/25 | 42.60 | 4.82 |
| Zimbabwe | 3 | - | - | - | - | - | - | - | - | - |

| Wickets Taken | Wkts | Bwd | Cfd | Cwk | LBW | Stp | HW | | | |
|---|---|---|---|---|---|---|---|---|---|---|
| | 195 | 44 | 99 | 30 | 22 | - | - | | | |

| Batsmen Dismissed | Wkts | 1/2 | 3 | 4 | 5 | 6 | 7 | 8 | 9 | 10 | 11 |
|---|---|---|---|---|---|---|---|---|---|---|---|
| | 195 | 37 | 23 | 22 | 37 | 16 | 12 | 19 | 13 | 10 | 6 |

Best Bowling: 4/33 Australia v. Sri Lanka, Sydney, 1987-88

# Domestic Limited-Overs Career

Debut: 1984-85 New South Wales v. Victoria, Melbourne

| Season | M | Overs | Mdns | Runs | Wkts | Avrge | 5 | Best | Stk/Rt | RPO |
|---|---|---|---|---|---|---|---|---|---|---|
| 1984-85 | 1 | 10.0 | 4 | 47 | - | - | - | - | - | 4.70 |
| 1985-86 | 1 | 10.0 | 2 | 37 | 3 | 12.33 | - | 3/37 | 20.00 | 3.70 |
| 1986-87 | 2 | 17.0 | 2 | 102 | 2 | 51.00 | - | 1/50 | 51.00 | 6.00 |
| 1987-88 | 4 | 33.4 | 3 | 132 | 5 | 26.40 | - | 2/21 | 40.40 | 3.92 |
| 1988-89 | 3 | 20.0 | 2 | 97 | 5 | 19.40 | - | 3/29 | 24.00 | 4.85 |
| 1989-90 | - | - | - | - | - | - | - | - | - | - |
| 1990-91 | 4 | 28.2 | 2 | 116 | 5 | 23.20 | - | 4/32 | 34.00 | 4.09 |
| 1991-92 | 4 | 29.0 | 3 | 127 | 7 | 18.14 | - | 3/25 | 24.86 | 4.38 |
| 1992-93 | 4 | 23.0 | - | 122 | 5 | 24.40 | - | 3/50 | 27.60 | 5.30 |
| 1993-94 | 2 | 5.0 | - | 34 | 1 | 34.00 | - | 1/34 | 30.00 | 6.80 |
| 1994-95 | - | - | - | - | - | - | - | - | - | - |
| 1995-96 | 3 | 4.0 | - | 19 | - | - | - | - | - | 4.75 |
| 1996-97 | - | - | - | - | - | - | - | - | - | - |
| 1997-98 | 3 | 2.0 | - | 12 | 1 | 12.00 | - | 1/12 | 12.00 | 6.00 |
| 1998-99 | 1 | - | - | - | - | - | - | - | - | - |
| 1999-00 | - | - | - | - | - | - | - | - | - | - |
| 2000-01 | 5 | - | - | - | - | - | - | - | - | - |
| 2001-02 | 2 | - | - | - | - | - | - | - | - | - |
| 2002-03 | 7 | - | - | - | - | - | - | - | - | - |
| 2003-04 | 9 | 2.0 | - | 8 | - | - | - | - | - | - |
| **Total** | **55** | **184.0** | **18** | **853** | **34** | **25.09** | **-** | **4/32** | **32.47** | **4.64** |

| Opponents | M | Overs | Mdns | Runs | Wkts | Avrge | 5 | Best | Stk/Rt | R/O |
|---|---|---|---|---|---|---|---|---|---|---|
| Queensland | 11 | 31.0 | 4 | 145 | 8 | 18.13 | - | 3/25 | 23.25 | 4.68 |
| South Australia | 9 | 30.0 | 4 | 112 | 8 | 14.00 | - | 3/37 | 22.50 | 3.73 |
| Tasmania | 11 | 35.4 | - | 163 | 7 | 23.29 | - | 2/21 | 30.57 | 4.57 |
| Victoria | 13 | 46.2 | 8 | 230 | 7 | 32.86 | - | 4/32 | 39.71 | 4.96 |
| Western Australia | 11 | 41.0 | 2 | 203 | 4 | 50.75 | - | 3/29 | 61.50 | 4.95 |

| Innings | | Overs | Mdns | Runs | Wkts | Avrge | 5 | Best | Stk/Rt | R/O |
|---|---|---|---|---|---|---|---|---|---|---|
| First | | 102.0 | 6 | 496 | 18 | 27.56 | - | 3/29 | 34.00 | 4.86 |
| Second | | 82.0 | 12 | 357 | 16 | 22.31 | - | 4/32 | 30.75 | 4.35 |

## Bowling at Each Venue

| Venue | M | Overs | Mdns | Runs | Wkts | Avrge | 5 | Best | Stk/Rt | R/O |
|---|---|---|---|---|---|---|---|---|---|---|
| Adelaide | 3 | 8.0 | - | 26 | 2 | 13.00 | - | 2/18 | 24.00 | 3.25 |
| Bankstown | 1 | - | - | - | - | - | - | - | - | - |
| Bowral | 1 | - | - | - | - | - | - | - | - | - |
| Brisbane | 7 | 31.0 | 4 | 145 | 8 | 18.13 | - | 3/25 | 23.25 | 4.68 |
| Coffs Harbour | 1 | - | - | - | - | - | - | - | - | - |
| Devonport | 1 | - | - | - | - | - | - | - | - | - |
| Drummoyne | 2 | - | - | - | - | - | - | - | - | - |
| Hobart | 3 | - | - | - | - | - | - | - | - | - |
| Homebush | 2 | - | - | - | - | - | - | - | - | - |
| Melbourne | 4 | 15.0 | 4 | 78 | - | - | - | - | - | 5.20 |
| North Sydney | 9 | 23.0 | 1 | 123 | 6 | 20.50 | - | 2/30 | 23.00 | 5.35 |
| Perth | 9 | 47.0 | 2 | 203 | 4 | 50.75 | - | 3/29 | 61.50 | 4.95 |
| Richmond | 1 | - | - | - | - | - | - | - | - | - |
| Sydney | 11 | 66.0 | 7 | 278 | 14 | 19.86 | - | 4/32 | 28.29 | 4.21 |

| Wickets Taken | Wkts | Bwd | Cfd | Cwk | LBW | Stp | HW | | | |
|---|---|---|---|---|---|---|---|---|---|---|
| | 34 | 9 | 19 | 5 | 1 | - | - | | | |

| Batsmen Dismissed | Wkts | 1/2 | 3 | 4 | 5 | 6 | 7 | 8 | 9 | 10 | 11 |
|---|---|---|---|---|---|---|---|---|---|---|---|
| | 34 | 6 | 5 | 4 | 3 | 4 | 4 | 3 | 3 | 2 | - |

Best Bowling: 4/32 New South Wales v. Victoria, Sydney, 1990-91

# MAJOR CRICKET MATCHES

| Start Date | Grade | Team | Opponent | Venue | How Out | Runs | O | M | R | W | Ct |
|---|---|---|---|---|---|---|---|---|---|---|---|
| 07/12/1984 | Pura | New South Wales | Queensland | Brisbane | c BA Courtice b JR Thomson | 31 | 23.0 | 12 | 34 | - | - |
| | | | | | | - | | | | | - |
| 29/12/1984 | ING | New South Wales | Victoria | Melbourne | | - | 10.0 | 4 | 47 | - | 1 |
| 17/01/1985 | Pura | New South Wales | Tasmania | Newcastle | b MP Tame | 4 | 6.0 | 2 | 11 | - | 1 |
| | | | | | cwk RD Woolley b RL Brown | 2 | 11.0 | 1 | 47 | 1 | - |
| 25/01/1985 | Pura | New South Wales | Victoria | Melbourne | | - | | | | | - |
| 16/02/1985 | ING | New South Wales | South Australia | Sydney | | - | | | | | - |
| 22/02/1985 | Pura | New South Wales | Queensland | Sydney | cwk RB Phillips b JN Maguire | 0 | | | | | 1 |
| | | | | | | - | | | | | 1 |
| 01/03/1985 | Pura | New South Wales | Victoria | Sydney | c DF Whatmore b RCAM McCarthy | 94 | 9.0 | 2 | 15 | 1 | 1 |
| | | | | | | - | 5.0 | 1 | 13 | - | 3 |
| 15/03/1985 | Pura | New South Wales | Queensland | Sydney | c JN Maguire b JR Thomson | 71 | 12.0 | 6 | 15 | 1 | 1 |
| | | | | | c RB Phillips b CG Rackemann | 21 | 6.0 | 1 | 21 | - | 1 |
| 01/10/1985 | Tour | Young Australians | Zimbabweans | Harare | c DL Houghton b KM Curran | 30 | 6.5 | - | 28 | - | - |
| | | | | | | - | 14.0 | 2 | 57 | 2 | - |
| 25/10/1985 | Pura | New South Wales | Tasmania | Hobart | b WW Davis | 107 | 5.0 | - | 22 | - | 1 |
| 01/11/1985 | Pura | New South Wales | Victoria | Newcastle | lbw b SP O'Donnell | 15 | 14.0 | 5 | 25 | 1 | - |
| | | | | | c DF Whatmore b AIC Dodemaide | 11 | 5.0 | - | 17 | - | - |
| 15/11/1985 | Tour | New South Wales | New Zealanders | Sydney | c JJ Crowe b VR Brown | 21 | | | | | - |
| | | | | | c JG Wright b SL Boock | 6 | | | | | 1 |
| 13/12/1985 | Pura | New South Wales | South Australia | Sydney | not out | 119* | 5.0 | 1 | 12 | - | 1 |
| | | | | | | - | 5.0 | 2 | 15 | 1 | 1 |
| 18/12/1985 | ING | New South Wales | South Australia | Sydney | lbw b PR Sleep | 47 | 10.0 | 2 | 37 | 3 | - |
| 20/12/1985 | Pura | New South Wales | Victoria | Melbourne | c JD Siddons b RJ Bright | 32 | 16.0 | 5 | 30 | - | - |
| | | | | | not out | 41* | | | | | - |
| 26/12/1985 | Test | Australia | India | Melbourne | c Kapil Dev b L Sivaramakrishnan | 13 | 11.0 | 5 | 36 | 2 | - |
| | | | | | b RJ Shastri | 5 | | | | | - |
| 02/01/1986 | Test | Australia | India | Sydney | c L Sivaramakrishnan b NS Yadav | 8 | 7.0 | - | 33 | - | - |
| | | | | | lbw b RJ Shastri | 0 | | | | | |

| Start Date | Grade | Team | Opponent | Venue | How Out | Runs | O | M | R | W | Ct |
|---|---|---|---|---|---|---|---|---|---|---|---|
| 09/01/1986 | ODI | Australia | New Zealand | Melbourne | | - | 2.0 | - | 13 | 1 | 1 |
| 12/01/1986 | ODI | Australia | India | Brisbane | b NS Yadav | 40 | 10.0 | - | 46 | 2 | - |
| 14/01/1986 | ODI | Australia | New Zealand | Sydney | not out | 19* | 3.0 | - | 12 | 1 | - |
| 16/01/1986 | ODI | Australia | India | Melbourne | not out | 73* | 3.0 | - | 16 | - | - |
| 19/01/1986 | ODI | Australia | New Zealand | Perth | c JJ Crowe b EJ Chatfield | 23 | 10.0 | 3 | 28 | 2 | - |
| 21/01/1986 | ODI | Australia | India | Sydney | not out | 6* | 3.0 | - | 10 | - | - |
| 26/01/1986 | ODI | Australia | India | Adelaide | c Kapil Dev b C Sharma | 81 | 5.0 | - | 26 | - | - |
| 27/01/1986 | ODI | Australia | New Zealand | Adelaide | c JV Coney b EJ Chatfield | 3 | | | | | - |
| 29/01/1986 | ODI | Australia | New Zealand | Sydney | run out | 17 | | | | | 1 |
| 31/01/1986 | ODI | Australia | India | Melbourne | b Kapil Dev | 3 | 6.0 | - | 34 | - | - |
| 05/02/1986 | ODI | Australia | India | Sydney | b M Azharuddin | 1 | 8.0 | 1 | 31 | 1 | - |
| 09/02/1986 | ODI | Australia | India | Melbourne | | - | 3.0 | - | 15 | - | - |
| 16/02/1986 | Tour | Australian XI | Northern Districts | Hamilton | | - | | | | | - |
| | | | | | cwk BA Young b K Treiber | 3 | 4.0 | 2 | 11 | - | 2 |
| 21/02/1986 | Test | Australia | New Zealand | Wellington | cwk IDS Smith b JV Coney | 11 | 4.0 | 1 | 9 | - | 1 |
| 28/02/1986 | Test | Australia | New Zealand | Christchurch | lbw b RJ Hadlee | 74 | 23.0 | 6 | 56 | 4 | 1 |
| | | | | | cwk IDS Smith b JG Bracewell | 1 | | | | | - |
| 08/03/1986 | Tour | Australian XI | Central Districts | New Plymouth | cwk TE Blain b GK Robertson | 34 | 13.0 | 1 | 57 | 2 | - |
| | | | | | c (sub)KW Martin b DA Stirling | 0 | | | | | - |
| 13/03/1986 | Test | Australia | New Zealand | Auckland | c JF Reid b JG Bracewell | 1 | 5.0 | 1 | 14 | 1 | - |
| | | | | | b JG Bracewell | 0 | 4.0 | 1 | 4 | - | - |
| 19/03/1986 | ODI | Australia | New Zealand | Dunedin | c MD Crowe b RJ Hadlee | 29 | 10.0 | - | 36 | 1 | 1 |
| 22/03/1986 | ODI | Australia | New Zealand | Christchurch | b RJ Hadlee | 10 | 9.0 | - | 47 | 1 | 1 |
| 26/03/1986 | ODI | Australia | New Zealand | Wellington | run out | 71 | 7.0 | - | 31 | 1 | - |
| 29/03/1986 | ODI | Australia | New Zealand | Auckland | run out | 1 | 9.0 | 1 | 45 | 1 | - |
| 11/04/1986 | ODI | Australia | Pakistan | Sharjah | cwk Zulqarnain b Wasim Akram | 26 | 6.0 | 1 | 25 | - | - |
| 04/09/1986 | Tour | Australian XI | Mumbai | Gwalior | c SM Patil b P Kasliwal | 82 | 10.0 | - | 70 | 1 | 1 |
| | | | | | | - | | | | | - |
| 07/09/1986 | ODI | Australia | India | Jaipur | | - | 7.0 | - | 42 | - | - |
| 09/09/1986 | ODI | Australia | India | Srinagar | st CS Pandit b RJ Shastri | 20 | 9.0 | - | 44 | 2 | - |
| 12/09/1986 | Tour | Australian XI | Indian Under-25's | Chandigarh | b B Arun | 4 | 19.0 | 5 | 46 | 3 | - |
| | | | | | | - | 21.0 | 5 | 71 | 4 | - |
| 18/09/1986 | Test | Australia | India | Chennai | not out | 12* | 11.0 | 2 | 44 | 1 | 1 |
| | | | | | not out | 2* | 4.0 | 1 | 16 | - | 1 |
| 24/09/1986 | ODI | Australia | India | Hyderabad | not out | 25* | | | | | - |
| 26/09/1986 | Test | Australia | India | Delhi | not out | 39* | 6.0 | - | 29 | 1 | - |
| 02/10/1986 | ODI | Australia | India | Delhi | not out | 57* | 10.0 | - | 48 | 2 | - |
| 05/10/1986 | ODI | Australia | India | Ahmedabad | cwk CS Pandit b RJ Shastri | 9 | 10.0 | - | 46 | 1 | - |
| 07/10/1986 | ODI | Australia | India | Rajkot | | - | 10.0 | 1 | 49 | 2 | - |
| 10/10/1986 | Tour | Australian XI | Delhi | Vadodara | c M Nayar b K Azad | 82 | 12.0 | - | 50 | - | 1 |
| 15/10/1986 | Test | Australia | India | Mumbai | b NS Yadav | 6 | 14.0 | 2 | 41 | - | - |
| | | | | | | - | | | | | - |
| 29/10/1986 | Pura | New South Wales | Western Australia | Perth | cwk TJ Zoehrer b CD Matthews | 37 | 18.0 | 3 | 51 | - | 2 |
| | | | | | c (sub)B Butler b TM Moody | 0 | | | | | - |
| 02/11/1986 | ING | New South Wales | Western Australia | Perth | run out | 2 | 8.0 | - | 50 | 1 | 1 |
| 05/11/1986 | Pura | New South Wales | Victoria | St Kilda | b MG Hughes | 6 | 19.0 | 5 | 42 | 1 | - |
| | | | | | b SP Davis | 59 | 8.3 | - | 39 | 2 | 1 |
| 09/11/1986 | ING | New South Wales | Victoria | Sydney | run out | 0 | 9.0 | 2 | 52 | 1 | - |
| 14/11/1986 | Test | Australia | England | Brisbane | cwk CJ. Richards b GR Dilley | 0 | 21.0 | 3 | 76 | 3 | 1 |
| | | | | | b JE Emburey | 28 | | | | | 1 |
| 21/11/1986 | Tour | New South Wales | England XI | Newcastle | c BN French b GC Small | 47 | 5.0 | - | 12 | - | 1 |
| 28/11/1986 | Test | Australia | England | Perth | c IT Botham b JE Emburey | 71 | 24.0 | 4 | 90 | - | 3 |
| | | | | | | - | 21.3 | 4 | 69 | 5 | - |
| 05/12/1986 | Pura | New South Wales | Queensland | Brisbane | cwk PW Anderson b CJ McDermott | 1 | 20.3 | 7 | 33 | 3 | - |
| | | | | | not out | 41* | 13.0 | - | 60 | 2 | 1 |
| 12/12/1986 | Test | Australia | England | Adelaide | not out | 79* | 19.0 | 4 | 56 | 1 | 1 |
| | | | | | | - | 3.0 | 1 | 10 | - | - |

| Start Date | Grade | Team | Opponent | Venue | How Out | Runs | O | M | R | W | Ct |
|---|---|---|---|---|---|---|---|---|---|---|---|
| 18/12/1986 | Pura | New South Wales | South Australia | Sydney | b AK Zesers | 14 | 9.0 | 1 | 28 | - | - |
| | | | | | cwk JTW Birchall b PR Sleep | 10 | | | | | - |
| 26/12/1986 | Test | Australia | England | Melbourne | c IT Botham b GC Small | 10 | 8.0 | 4 | 16 | - | - |
| | | | | | b PH Edmonds | 49 | | | | | - |
| 01/01/1987 | ODI | Australia | England | Perth | cwk CJ. Richards b GC Small | 16 | 5.0 | - | 24 | 1 | |
| 02/01/1987 | ODI | Australia | Pakistan | Perth | b Imran Khan | 82 | 9.5 | - | 48 | 4 | |
| 04/01/1987 | ODI | Australia | West Indies | Perth | b RA Harper | 29 | 10.0 | - | 41 | 1 | - |
| 10/01/1987 | Test | Australia | England | Sydney | cwk CJ. Richards b GC Small | 0 | 6.0 | 4 | 6 | - | - |
| | | | | | c CWJ Athey b JE Emburey | 73 | 6.0 | 2 | 13 | 1 | 2 |
| 18/01/1987 | ODI | Australia | England | Brisbane | not out | 14* | 9.0 | - | 56 | 2 | - |
| 20/01/1987 | ODI | Australia | West Indies | Melbourne | hit wicket b MA Holding | 15 | 7.0 | - | 30 | 1 | - |
| 22/01/1987 | ODI | Australia | England | Sydney | c CWJ Athey b GR Dilley | 10 | 5.0 | - | 22 | 1 | 1 |
| 25/01/1987 | ODI | Australia | West Indies | Adelaide | c IVA Richards b RA Harper | 24 | 7.0 | - | 41 | 2 | - |
| 26/01/1987 | ODI | Australia | England | Adelaide | not out | 83* | 10.0 | 1 | 30 | 2 | 1 |
| 28/01/1987 | ODI | Australia | West Indies | Sydney | run out | 16 | 10.0 | 1 | 21 | 2 | 1 |
| 01/02/1987 | ODI | Australia | England | Melbourne | not out | 49* | 10.0 | - | 26 | 3 | - |
| 06/02/1987 | ODI | Australia | West Indies | Sydney | st PJL Dujon b IVA Richards | 11 | 9.0 | 1 | 41 | 1 | - |
| 08/02/1987 | ODI | Australia | England | Melbourne | c PAJ DeFreitas b JE Emburey | 1 | 8.0 | 1 | 36 | - | - |
| 11/02/1987 | ODI | Australia | England | Sydney | run out | 22 | 10.0 | - | 42 | 1 | - |
| 20/02/1987 | Pura | New South Wales | Tasmania | Hobart | b GD Campbell | 65 | 12.0 | 1 | 48 | 2 | 1 |
| | | | | | | - | 17.0 | 3 | 36 | 2 | 2 |
| 27/02/1987 | Pura | New South Wales | Queensland | Sydney | c AR Border b JG Hill | 44 | 12.0 | 1 | 49 | 3 | 2 |
| | | | | | | - | | | | | |
| 06/03/1987 | Pura | New South Wales | Victoria | Sydney | c JD Siddons b AIC Dodemaide | 18 | 16.0 | 2 | 38 | - | 4 |
| | | | | | c MG Hughes b PW Jackson | 89 | | | | | 1 |
| 03/04/1987 | ODI | Australia | Pakistan | Sharjah | c Manzoor Elahi b Mudassar Nazar | 8 | 6.0 | - | 34 | - | 1 |
| 05/04/1987 | ODI | Australia | India | Sharjah | c G Sharma b Maninder Singh | 20 | 8.0 | - | 33 | 1 | - |
| 09/04/1987 | ODI | Australia | England | Sharjah | b NA Foster | 14 | 10.0 | 1 | 49 | 1 | - |
| 05/08/1987 | County | Somerset | Hampshire | Weston-super-Mare | lbw b RJ Maru | 1 | 20.0 | 3 | 63 | 3 | 1 |
| | | | | | not out | 71* | 14.0 | 3 | 33 | 1 | - |
| 19/08/1987 | County | Somerset | Surrey | The Oval | b MP Bicknell | 8 | 18.0 | 5 | 63 | 1 | 1 |
| | | | | | not out | 111* | 11.0 | - | 48 | 3 | - |
| 26/08/1987 | County | Somerset | Sussex | Hove | | - | | | | | 1 |
| | | | | | | - | 9.0 | 3 | 22 | 2 | - |
| 02/09/1987 | County | Somerset | Gloucestershire | Bristol | not out | 137* | 26.0 | 7 | 72 | 1 | 1 |
| | | | | | lbw b P Bainbridge | 12 | 14.0 | 1 | 47 | - | - |
| 09/10/1987 | ODI | Australia | India | Chennai | not out | 19* | 9.5 | - | 52 | 2 | - |
| 13/10/1987 | ODI | Australia | Zimbabwe | Chennai | run out | 45 | 6.0 | 3 | 7 | - | - |
| 19/10/1987 | ODI | Australia | New Zealand | Indore | not out | 13* | 6.0 | - | 36 | 2 | - |
| 22/10/1987 | ODI | Australia | India | Delhi | c NS Sidhu b Kapil Dev | 42 | 10.0 | - | 59 | 1 | 1 |
| 27/10/1987 | ODI | Australia | New Zealand | Chandigarh | b W Watson | 1 | 9.4 | - | 37 | 2 | - |
| 30/10/1987 | ODI | Australia | Zimbabwe | Cuttack | not out | 10* | 4.0 | - | 9 | 1 | 2 |
| 04/11/1987 | ODI | Australia | Pakistan | Lahore | not out | 32* | 9.0 | 1 | 51 | 1 | - |
| 08/11/1987 | ODI | Australia | England | Kolkata | not out | 5* | 9.0 | - | 37 | 2 | - |
| 14/11/1987 | Pura | New South Wales | South Australia | Sydney | c WB Phillips b PR Sleep | 6 | 12.0 | 5 | 16 | 1 | - |
| | | | | | c AMJ Hilditch b AK Zesers | 36 | 5.0 | - | 14 | - | 2 |
| 27/11/1987 | Pura | New South Wales | Queensland | Newcastle | c RB Kerr b CJ McDermott | 9 | 14.0 | 4 | 38 | 3 | 1 |
| | | | | | b CJ McDermott | 15 | 12.0 | - | 45 | - | - |
| 04/12/1987 | Test | Australia | New Zealand | Brisbane | c AH Jones b DK Morrison | 21 | 22.0 | 9 | 35 | 1 | 2 |
| | | | | | | - | 2.0 | 1 | 2 | 1 | - |
| 11/12/1987 | Test | Australia | New Zealand | Adelaide | lbw b MC Snedden | 61 | 31.0 | 11 | 71 | - | 1 |
| | | | | | | - | 10.0 | 4 | 17 | - | - |
| 18/12/1987 | Pura | New South Wales | Victoria | Sydney | cwk M Dimattina b A Dodemaide | 170 | | | | | 1 |
| 26/12/1987 | Test | Australia | New Zealand | Melbourne | c AH Jones b JG Bracewell | 55 | 10.0 | 1 | 44 | - | - |
| | | | | | c DN Patel b EJ Chatfield | 10 | | | | | - |
| 02/01/1988 | ODI | Australia | Sri Lanka | Perth | not out | 35* | 10.0 | 2 | 34 | 3 | - |
| 03/01/1988 | ODI | Australia | New Zealand | Perth | cwk TE Blain b RJ Hadlee | 0 | 10.0 | - | 49 | 1 | - |

| Start Date | Grade | Team | Opponent | Venue | How Out | Runs | O | M | R | W | Ct |
|---|---|---|---|---|---|---|---|---|---|---|---|
| 07/01/1988 | ODI | Australia | New Zealand | Melbourne | b MC Snedden | 68 | 10.0 | - | 41 | 1 | 1 |
| 10/01/1988 | ODI | Australia | Sri Lanka | Adelaide | not out | 8* | 10.0 | - | 37 | - | - |
| 14/01/1988 | ODI | Australia | Sri Lanka | Melbourne | cwk RG De Alwis b GF Labrooy | 27 | 7.0 | - | 33 | 1 | - |
| 17/01/1988 | ODI | Australia | New Zealand | Brisbane | cwk TE Blain b MC Snedden | 45 | 8.0 | 1 | 23 | 2 | - |
| 19/01/1988 | ODI | Australia | Sri Lanka | Sydney | c RS Mahanama b CPH Ramanayake | 16 | 10.0 | - | 33 | 4 | - |
| 20/01/1988 | ODI | Australia | New Zealand | Sydney | c JJ Crowe b W Watson | 0 | 7.5 | - | 33 | 2 | - |
| 22/01/1988 | ODI | Australia | New Zealand | Melbourne | | - | 10.0 | - | 47 | 2 | 1 |
| 24/01/1988 | ODI | Australia | New Zealand | Sydney | | - | 7.0 | - | 51 | 1 | 1 |
| 29/01/1988 | Test | Australia | England | Sydney | cwk BN French b GR Dilley | 27 | 22.5 | 5 | 51 | 3 | - |
| | | | | | | | | | | | - |
| 04/02/1988 | ODI | Australia | England | Melbourne | run out | 27 | 10.0 | - | 42 | 1 | - |
| 12/02/1988 | Test | Australia | Sri Lanka | Perth | c GF Labrooy b KN Amalean | 20 | 20.0 | 7 | 33 | 4 | 1 |
| | | | | | | | 8.0 | 4 | 14 | - | 2 |
| 21/02/1988 | ING | New South Wales | Queensland | Brisbane | c TJ Barsby b D Tazelaar | 56 | 10.0 | 1 | 48 | 1 | - |
| 24/02/1988 | Pura | New South Wales | Western Australia | Sydney | b TM Alderman | 9 | 8.0 | 1 | 19 | 1 | 1 |
| | | | | | cwk TJ Zoehrer b CD Matthews | 14 | 13.0 | 5 | 30 | 4 | 1 |
| 02/03/1988 | Pura | New South Wales | Tasmania | Sydney | st RE Soule b CL Broadby | 55 | 23.4 | 2 | 50 | 5 | - |
| | | | | | not out | 9* | 5.0 | - | 20 | - | - |
| 06/03/1988 | ING | New South Wales | Tasmania | Sydney | cwk RE Soule b AJ De Winter | 3 | 7.4 | - | 21 | 2 | - |
| 13/03/1988 | ING | New South Wales | Victoria | Sydney | cwk MGD Dimattina b SP Davis | 19 | 6.0 | - | 26 | - | - |
| 27/03/1988 | ING | New South Wales | South Australia | Sydney | c DW Hookes b DB Scott | 23 | 10.0 | 2 | 37 | 2 | - |
| 28/04/1988 | County | Somerset | Glamorgan | Cardiff | c CP Metson b RC Ontong | 53 | 11.0 | 1 | 33 | 2 | - |
| | | | | | | | | | | | - |
| 14/05/1988 | County | Somerset | West Indians | Taunton | lbw b WKM Benjamin | 1 | | | | | 1 |
| | | | | | c KLT Arthurton b WKM Benjamin | 27 | | | | | - |
| 01/06/1988 | County | Somerset | Hampshire | Southampton | not out | 115* | | | | | 3 |
| | | | | | | | | | | | - |
| 04/06/1988 | County | Somerset | Northamptonshire | Taunton | c W Larkins b WW Davis | 37 | 9.0 | 3 | 17 | 1 | 1 |
| | | | | | c D Ripley b WW Davis | 40 | | | | | - |
| 11/06/1988 | County | Somerset | Warwickshire | Bath | not out | 103* | | | | | - |
| | | | | | b N Gifford | 79 | | | | | 2 |
| 15/06/1988 | County | Somerset | Sussex | Bath | b AR Clarke | 137 | 3.0 | 1 | 10 | - | - |
| | | | | | c SJS Kimber b CM Wells | 85 | | | | | - |
| 29/06/1988 | County | Somerset | Glamorgan | Taunton | not out | 101* | | | | | - |
| | | | | | | | | | | | 1 |
| 02/07/1988 | County | Somerset | Essex | Taunton | | - | | | | | - |
| | | | | | not out | 33* | | | | | - |
| 16/07/1988 | County | Somerset | Gloucestershire | Bristol | cwk RC Russell b TM Alderman | 33 | | | | | 1 |
| | | | | | not out | 1* | | | | | - |
| 23/07/1988 | County | Somerset | Nottinghamshire | Taunton | lbw b FD Stephenson | 0 | | | | | 2 |
| | | | | | | - | | | | | 1 |
| 30/07/1988 | County | Somerset | Kent | Canterbury | b RF Pienaar | 161 | | | | | 2 |
| | | | | | | - | | | | | - |
| 03/08/1988 | County | Somerset | Surrey | Weston-super-Mare | b MA Feltham | 31 | | | | | - |
| | | | | | cwk AJ Stewart b KT Medlycott | 4 | | | | | 2 |
| 06/08/1988 | County | Somerset | Derbyshire | Weston-super-Mare | c BJM Maher b AE Warner | 44 | | | | | 3 |
| | | | | | lbw b AE Warner | 1 | | | | | - |
| 13/08/1988 | County | Somerset | Yorkshire | Scarborough | lbw b A Sidebottom | 2 | | | | | - |
| | | | | | b SD Fletcher | 31 | | | | | - |
| 17/08/1988 | County | Somerset | Middlesex | Uxbridge | b PCR Tufnell | 83 | | | | | 1 |
| | | | | | not out | 112* | | | | | - |
| 05/09/1988 | Tour | Australian XI | BCCP Patron's XI | Lahore | | - | 12.0 | 5 | 41 | - | 1 |
| | | | | | lbw b Mohsin Kamal | 15 | 5.0 | 4 | 1 | - | - |
| 09/09/1988 | Tour | Australian XI | Governor of Baluchistan's XI | Quetta | lbw b Iqbal Qasim | 22 | 9.0 | - | 38 | - | - |
| | | | | | c Anwar Shahid b Iqbal Qasim | 29 | 7.0 | 3 | 15 | 1 | 1 |
| 15/09/1988 | Test | Australia | Pakistan | Karachi | lbw b Iqbal Qasim | 0 | 26.0 | 3 | 94 | 1 | - |
| | | | | | st Salim Yousuf b Iqbal Qasim | 13 | | | | | - |

| Start Date | Grade | Team | Opponent | Venue | How Out | Runs | O | M | R | W | Ct |
|---|---|---|---|---|---|---|---|---|---|---|---|
| 23/09/1988 | Test | Australia | Pakistan | Faisalabad | st Salim Yousuf b Tauseef Ahmed | 1 | 11.0 | 3 | 36 | - | - |
| | | | | | c and b Shoaib Mohammad | 19 | 18.0 | 6 | 44 | 1 | 1 |
| 02/10/1988 | Tour | Australian XI | NW Frontier Province Governor's XI | Peshawar | c (sub)Shahid Hussain b Masood Anwar | 2 | 15.0 | 4 | 51 | 1 | - |
| 07/10/1988 | Test | Australia | Pakistan | Lahore | c Ijaz Ahmed b Iqbal Qasim | 59 | 18.0 | 4 | 34 | - | - |
| | | | | | | - | 5.0 | 1 | 8 | - | 1 |
| 14/10/1988 | ODI | Australia | Pakistan | Lahore | run out | 7 | 8.0 | - | 42 | 1 | - |
| 28/10/1988 | Pura | New South Wales | Queensland | Brisbane | cwk IA Healy b D Tazelaar | 118 | 22.0 | 7 | 48 | 3 | - |
| | | | | | c PE Cantrell b CJ McDermott | 5 | 22.0 | 2 | 79 | 2 | - |
| 04/11/1988 | Pura | New South Wales | Victoria | Sydney | lbw b SP O'Donnell | 0 | 17.0 | 9 | 21 | 2 | 1 |
| | | | | | c AIC Dodemaide b M Osborne | 24 | 17.0 | 1 | 81 | - | - |
| 11/11/1988 | Tour | New South Wales | West Indians | Sydney | c DL Haynes b IR Bishop | 21 | 10.0 | 2 | 22 | - | 1 |
| 18/11/1988 | Test | Australia | West Indies | Brisbane | lbw b MD Marshall | 4 | 18.0 | 2 | 61 | 2 | - |
| | | | | | c DL Haynes b MD Marshall | 90 | 6.0 | - | 14 | - | - |
| 25/11/1988 | Pura | New South Wales | Tasmania | Devonport | c GA Hughes b PI Faulkner | 39 | 29.0 | 7 | 68 | 2 | 1 |
| | | | | | | - | | | | | |
| 02/12/1988 | Test | Australia | West Indies | Perth | cwk PJL Dujon b CEL Ambrose | 91 | 28.0 | 3 | 90 | - | 1 |
| | | | | | c CL Hooper b BP Patterson | 26 | 23.0 | 1 | 70 | - | - |
| 11/12/1988 | ODI | Australia | Pakistan | Adelaide | | - | 7.4 | - | 27 | 1 | - |
| 13/12/1988 | ODI | Australia | West Indies | Sydney | run out | 40 | 4.0 | - | 15 | - | - |
| 15/12/1988 | ODI | Australia | West Indies | Melbourne | run out | 54 | 10.0 | - | 57 | 3 | - |
| 24/12/1988 | Test | Australia | West Indies | Melbourne | c CG Greenidge b CEL Ambrose | 42 | 21.0 | 3 | 77 | 3 | - |
| | | | | | c (sub)RA Harper b CEL Ambrose | 3 | 24.0 | 5 | 92 | 5 | 1 |
| 02/01/1989 | ODI | Australia | Pakistan | Perth | b Aaqib Javed | 12 | 9.0 | - | 48 | 2 | - |
| 05/01/1989 | ODI | Australia | West Indies | Melbourne | b CEL Ambrose | 34 | 10.0 | - | 36 | - | 1 |
| 08/01/1989 | ODI | Australia | Pakistan | Brisbane | not out | 22* | 9.0 | - | 35 | - | - |
| 10/01/1989 | ODI | Australia | Pakistan | Melbourne | lbw b Tauseef Ahmed | 0 | 4.0 | - | 27 | - | 1 |
| 12/01/1989 | ODI | Australia | West Indies | Sydney | not out | 40* | 3.0 | - | 13 | 1 | - |
| 14/01/1989 | ODI | Australia | West Indies | Melbourne | c and b CEL Ambrose | 33 | 10.0 | - | 43 | - | - |
| 16/01/1989 | ODI | Australia | West Indies | Sydney | st PJL Dujon b CL Hooper | 8 | 8.0 | - | 45 | 1 | 1 |
| 18/01/1989 | ODI | Australia | West Indies | Sydney | not out | 27* | 3.2 | - | 27 | - | 1 |
| 20/01/1989 | Pura | New South Wales | Victoria | Melbourne | b SP O'Donnell | 15 | 6.0 | 1 | 21 | - | - |
| | | | | | b MG Hughes | 10 | 11.0 | 4 | 17 | 1 | 1 |
| 26/01/1989 | Test | Australia | West Indies | Sydney | not out | 55* | 4.0 | - | 18 | - | 1 |
| | | | | | | - | 3.0 | - | 10 | - | - |
| 03/02/1989 | Test | Australia | West Indies | Adelaide | cwk PJL Dujon b CA Walsh | 12 | 3.0 | - | 17 | - | - |
| | | | | | run out | 8 | 9.0 | 3 | 23 | - | - |
| 09/02/1989 | Pura | New South Wales | South Australia | Sydney | c GA Bishop b AK Zesers | 16 | 21.0 | 5 | 54 | 1 | 1 |
| | | | | | | - | | | | | - |
| 15/02/1989 | Pura | New South Wales | Western Australia | Perth | cwk TJ Zoehrer b KH MacLeay | 4 | 13.0 | - | 49 | 3 | 1 |
| | | | | | c WS Andrews b KE Lilly | 45 | 16.0 | 1 | 68 | 3 | 1 |
| 19/02/1989 | ING | New South Wales | Western Australia | Perth | b KH MacLeay | 1 | 9.0 | 2 | 29 | 3 | - |
| 22/02/1989 | Pura | New South Wales | Tasmania | Sydney | b GD Campbell | 14 | 6.0 | 1 | 21 | - | - |
| | | | | | run out | 21 | 14.0 | 7 | 21 | 3 | 1 |
| 26/02/1989 | ING | New South Wales | Tasmania | Sydney | not out | 81* | 6.0 | - | 37 | 2 | - |
| 04/03/1989 | ING | New South Wales | Victoria | Melbourne | lbw b DW Fleming | 0 | 5.0 | - | 31 | - | 1 |
| 10/03/1989 | Pura | New South Wales | Queensland | Sydney | cwk IA Healy b CG Rackemann | 4 | 12.0 | 4 | 21 | - | - |
| | | | | | run out | 44 | 10.0 | - | 51 | 6 | - |
| 13/05/1989 | Tour | Australian XI | Worcestershire | Worcester | cwk SJ Rhodes b PJ Newport | 0 | 6.0 | 1 | 23 | 2 | - |
| | | | | | lbw b IT Botham | 63 | 6.0 | - | 25 | 2 | - |
| 25/05/1989 | ODI | Australia | England | Manchester | c RA Smith b PAJ DeFreitas | 35 | 11.0 | 1 | 45 | 2 | - |
| 27/05/1989 | ODI | Australia | England | Nottingham | run out | 43 | 11.0 | 1 | 47 | 1 | - |
| 29/05/1989 | ODI | Australia | England | Lord's | c GA Gooch b NA Foster | 35 | 11.0 | - | 70 | - | - |
| 03/06/1989 | Tour | Australian XI | Derbyshire | Derby | c BJM Maher b OH Mortensen | 14 | 11.2 | 2 | 35 | 2 | - |
| | | | | | c IR Bishop b SJ Base | 9 | 13.0 | 5 | 18 | - | - |
| 08/06/1989 | Test | Australia | England | Leeds | not out | 177* | 6.0 | 2 | 27 | - | - |
| | | | | | | - | | | | | |

| Start Date | Grade | Team | Opponent | Venue | How Out | Runs | O | M | R | W | Ct |
|---|---|---|---|---|---|---|---|---|---|---|---|
| 14/06/1989 | Tour | Australian XI | Lancashire | Manchester | c JD Fitton b I Folley | 42 | 9.0 | 2 | 28 | 2 | - |
| | | | | | | - | 5.0 | 1 | 13 | 1 | - |
| 17/06/1989 | Tour | Australian XI | Northamptonshire | Northampton | lbw b NGB Cook | 13 | 11.0 | 1 | 40 | 2 | |
| | | | | | b WW Davis | 2 | 4.5 | 1 | 10 | 3 | - |
| 22/06/1989 | Test | Australia | England | Lord's | not out | 152* | 9.0 | 3 | 49 | 1 | |
| | | | | | not out | 21* | 7.0 | 2 | 20 | - | - |
| 01/07/1989 | Tour | Australian XI | Glamorgan | Neath | not out | 34* | 21.0 | 3 | 61 | 1 | |
| | | | | | | - | 10.0 | 2 | 32 | 3 | - |
| 06/07/1989 | Test | Australia | England | Birmingham | b ARC Fraser | 43 | 11.0 | 3 | 38 | 1 | - |
| | | | | | | - | | | | | - |
| 19/07/1989 | Tour | Australian XI | Hampshire | Southampton | c and b SJW Andrew | 112 | 7.0 | 1 | 28 | 2 | - |
| | | | | | lbw b RJ Maru | 67 | 3.0 | 2 | 8 | - | - |
| 27/07/1989 | Test | Australia | England | Manchester | c TS Curtis b ARC Fraser | 92 | 6.0 | 1 | 23 | - | - |
| | | | | | | - | 4.0 | - | 17 | - | - |
| 02/08/1989 | Tour | Australian XI | Nottinghamshire | Nottingham | not out | 46* | 5.0 | 2 | 13 | - | |
| | | | | | not out | 13* | | | | | - |
| 05/08/1989 | Tour | Australian XI | Leicestershire | Leicester | b JP Agnew | 7 | | | | | - |
| 10/08/1989 | Test | Australia | England | Nottingham | c DI Gower b DE Malcolm | 0 | 11.0 | 4 | 23 | - | 2 |
| | | | | | | - | | | | | - |
| 16/08/1989 | Tour | Australian XI | Kent | Canterbury | b DJM Kelleher | 1 | 7.0 | 1 | 29 | 1 | - |
| 19/08/1989 | Tour | Australian XI | Essex | Chelmsford | lbw b JH Childs | 1 | | | | | - |
| | | | | | not out | 100* | | | | | - |
| 24/08/1989 | Test | Australia | England | The Oval | b AP Igglesden | 14 | 3.0 | - | 11 | - | 1 |
| | | | | | not out | 7* | | | | | 1 |
| 19/10/1989 | ODI | Australia | England | Hyderabad | | - | | | | | - |
| 21/10/1989 | ODI | Australia | West Indies | Chennai | not out | 53* | | | | | - |
| 23/10/1989 | ODI | Australia | Pakistan | Mumbai | b Imran Khan | 0 | | | | | 1 |
| 25/10/1989 | ODI | Australia | Sri Lanka | Margoa | run out | 2 | | | | | 1 |
| 27/10/1989 | ODI | Australia | India | Bangalore | c AK Sharma b Kapil Dev | 28 | | | | | 1 |
| 10/11/1989 | Pura | New South Wales | South Australia | Adelaide | c PC Nobes b PJS Alley | 22 | | | | | - |
| | | | | | | - | | | | | - |
| 17/11/1989 | Tour | New South Wales | Sri Lankans | Canberra | c AP Gurusinha b GF Labrooy | 57 | | | | | - |
| | | | | | not out | 11* | | | | | 1 |
| 24/11/1989 | Test | Australia | New Zealand | Perth | c MJ Greatbatch b MC Snedden | 17 | | | | | - |
| | | | | | | - | | | | | - |
| 01/12/1989 | Pura | New South Wales | Queensland | Newcastle | lbw b CJ McDermott | 2 | | | | | - |
| | | | | | cwk IA Healy b CG Rackemann | 13 | | | | | 1 |
| 08/12/1989 | Test | Australia | Sri Lanka | Brisbane | c A Ranatunga b CPH Ramanayake | 60 | | | | | 1 |
| | | | | | b AP Gurusinha | 57 | | | | | - |
| 16/12/1989 | Test | Australia | Sri Lanka | Hobart | cwk HP Tillakaratne b GF Labrooy | 16 | 6.0 | 3 | 6 | - | - |
| | | | | | not out | 134* | | | | | 1 |
| 26/12/1989 | ODI | Australia | Sri Lanka | Melbourne | cwk HP Tillakaratne b A Ranatunga | 5 | 6.0 | - | 26 | 1 | - |
| 30/12/1989 | ODI | Australia | Sri Lanka | Perth | | - | 9.0 | - | 45 | 1 | 1 |
| 03/01/1990 | ODI | Australia | Pakistan | Melbourne | not out | 31* | 1.0 | - | 6 | - | - |
| 04/01/1990 | ODI | Australia | Sri Lanka | Melbourne | cwk HP Tillakaratne b RJ Ratnayake | 0 | | | | | - |
| 06/01/1990 | Pura | New South Wales | Western Australia | Sydney | b TG Hogan | 33 | | | | | - |
| | | | | | | - | | | | | - |
| 12/01/1990 | Test | Australia | Pakistan | Melbourne | cwk Salim Yousuf b Aaqib Javed | 20 | | | | | - |
| | | | | | cwk Salim Yousuf b Wasim Akram | 3 | 3.0 | - | 13 | 1 | - |
| 19/01/1990 | Test | Australia | Pakistan | Adelaide | lbw b Wasim Akram | 17 | | | | | - |
| | | | | | b Tauseef Ahmed | 4 | | | | | 1 |
| 26/01/1990 | Pura | New South Wales | Tasmania | Hobart | cwk RE Soule b GR Robertson | 196 | | | | | - |
| | | | | | not out | 26* | | | | | - |
| 03/02/1990 | Test | Australia | Pakistan | Sydney | | - | | | | | - |
| 11/02/1990 | ODI | Australia | Pakistan | Brisbane | c Salim Malik b Mushtaq Ahmed | 13 | | | | | 1 |
| 13/02/1990 | ODI | Australia | Pakistan | Sydney | c J Miandad b Shoaib Mohammad | 28 | | | | | - |
| 18/02/1990 | ODI | Australia | Sri Lanka | Adelaide | not out | 11* | | | | | - |

| Start Date | Grade | Team | Opponent | Venue | How Out | Runs | O | M | R | W | Ct |
|---|---|---|---|---|---|---|---|---|---|---|---|
| 20/02/1990 | ODI | Australia | Pakistan | Sydney | st Salim Yousuf b Mushtaq Ahmed | 3 | | | | | 2 |
| 23/02/1990 | ODI | Australia | Pakistan | Melbourne | b Wasim Akram | 13 | | | | | - |
| 25/02/1990 | ODI | Australia | Pakistan | Sydney | | - | | | | | - |
| 03/03/1990 | ODI | Australia | India | Christchurch | c SV Manjrekar b Kapil Dev | 10 | | | | | 2 |
| 04/03/1990 | ODI | Australia | New Zealand | Christchurch | run out | 3 | | | | | 1 |
| 08/03/1990 | ODI | Australia | India | Hamilton | c M Prabhakar b ND Hirwani | 23 | | | | | - |
| 10/03/1990 | ODI | Australia | New Zealand | Auckland | cwk IDS Smith b MC Snedden | 36 | | | | | - |
| 11/03/1990 | ODI | Australia | New Zealand | Auckland | | | | | | | - |
| 15/03/1990 | Test | Australia | New Zealand | Wellington | b RJ Hadlee | 25 | | | | | |
| | | | | | c MJ Greatbatch b RJ Hadlee | 25 | | | | | - |
| 23/03/1990 | Pura | New South Wales | Queensland | Sydney | cwk IA Healy b CJ McDermott | 6 | | | | | - |
| | | | | | cwk IA Healy b CG Rackemann | 10 | | | | | - |
| 26/04/1990 | ODI | Australia | New Zealand | Sharjah | run out | 34 | 7.0 | - | 32 | - | - |
| 30/04/1990 | ODI | Australia | Bangladesh | Sharjah | | - | 10.0 | 2 | 22 | 2 | - |
| 02/05/1990 | ODI | Australia | Sri Lanka | Sharjah | | - | 7.0 | - | 36 | 1 | 1 |
| 04/05/1990 | ODI | Australia | Pakistan | Sharjah | c Aaqib Javed b Mushtaq Ahmed | 64 | 5.0 | - | 22 | 1 | |
| 14/10/1990 | ING | New South Wales | Queensland | Brisbane | c AR Border b CJ McDermott | 2 | 5.0 | 1 | 22 | 1 | |
| 16/10/1990 | ING | New South Wales | Tasmania | Sydney | not out | 66* | 7.0 | - | 24 | - | 1 |
| 20/10/1990 | ING | New South Wales | Victoria | Sydney | not out | 9* | 8.2 | 1 | 32 | 4 | - |
| 27/10/1990 | ING | New South Wales | Western Australia | Perth | c PA Capes b BA Reid | 11 | 8.0 | - | 38 | - | - |
| 02/11/1990 | Pura | New South Wales | Tasmania | Sydney | cwk TC Coyle b RJ Tucker | 83 | 10.0 | 1 | 33 | 1 | - |
| | | | | | | - | | | | | |
| 16/11/1990 | Pura | New South Wales | Victoria | St Kilda | c JD Siddons b PR Reiffel | 42 | 23.0 | 4 | 70 | - | 1 |
| | | | | | c GM Watts b DW Fleming | 53 | | | | | - |
| 23/11/1990 | Test | Australia | England | Brisbane | c RA Smith b GC Small | 1 | 7.0 | 2 | 20 | - | 1 |
| | | | | | | - | 4.0 | 2 | 7 | 1 | - |
| 29/11/1990 | ODI | Australia | New Zealand | Sydney | c W Watson b RG Petrie | 7 | 8.0 | 1 | 49 | - | - |
| 02/12/1990 | ODI | Australia | New Zealand | Adelaide | not out | 4* | 10.0 | - | 49 | 1 | - |
| 09/12/1990 | ODI | Australia | England | Perth | not out | 12* | 10.0 | 1 | 52 | 1 | - |
| 11/12/1990 | ODI | Australia | New Zealand | Melbourne | c MD Crowe b DK Morrison | 4 | 10.0 | - | 39 | 2 | - |
| 16/12/1990 | ODI | Australia | England | Brisbane | not out | 14* | 4.0 | - | 20 | - | 1 |
| 18/12/1990 | ODI | Australia | New Zealand | Hobart | cwk BA Young b DK Morrison | 16 | 5.0 | 1 | 18 | 1 | 1 |
| 20/12/1990 | Pura | New South Wales | Western Australia | Perth | not out | 216* | 5.0 | 1 | 18 | - | 1 |
| | | | | | | - | 10.0 | 1 | 43 | 1 | - |
| 26/12/1990 | Test | Australia | England | Melbourne | b ARC Fraser | 19 | 6.0 | 2 | 19 | - | - |
| | | | | | | - | 7.0 | 6 | 4 | - | - |
| 01/01/1991 | ODI | Australia | England | Sydney | cwk AJ Stewart b PCR Tufnell | 3 | 6.0 | - | 25 | 1 | 1 |
| 04/01/1991 | Test | Australia | England | Sydney | c AJ Stewart b DE Malcolm | 48 | 14.0 | 3 | 40 | - | - |
| | | | | | cwk RC Russell b EE Hemmings | 14 | | | | | - |
| 10/01/1991 | ODI | Australia | England | Melbourne | not out | 65* | 7.0 | 1 | 25 | 1 | - |
| 13/01/1991 | ODI | Australia | New Zealand | Sydney | not out | 16* | 7.0 | - | 32 | - | 1 |
| 15/01/1991 | ODI | Australia | New Zealand | Melbourne | | - | 9.0 | 1 | 37 | - | - |
| 19/01/1991 | Pura | New South Wales | South Australia | Sydney | cwk TJ Nielsen b CR Miller | 60 | 15.0 | 3 | 43 | 1 | - |
| | | | | | c AMJ Hilditch b CR Miller | 1 | | | | | |
| 31/01/1991 | Pura | New South Wales | Western Australia | Sydney | b WS Andrews | 61 | | | | | - |
| | | | | | | - | 6.0 | 1 | 22 | - | - |
| 16/02/1991 | Tour | Australian XI | WI Board XI | Basseterre | not out | 96* | 8.0 | 3 | 23 | - | - |
| | | | | | c AH Gray b RC Haynes | 15 | | | | | - |
| 26/02/1991 | ODI | Australia | West Indies | Kingston | not out | 6* | 7.0 | 1 | 32 | 2 | 1 |
| 09/03/1991 | ODI | Australia | West Indies | Port-of-Spain | b AH Gray | 26 | 8.0 | - | 24 | - | 1 |
| 10/03/1991 | ODI | Australia | West Indies | Port-of-Spain | b CEL Ambrose | 23 | 7.0 | - | 39 | 1 | - |
| 13/03/1991 | ODI | Australia | West Indies | Bridgetown | lbw b CEL Ambrose | 5 | 7.0 | - | 25 | 2 | 1 |
| 15/03/1991 | Tour | Australian XI | Trinidad & Tobago | Pointe-a-Pierre | | - | 1.0 | 1 | 0 | - | - |
| 20/03/1991 | ODI | Australia | West Indies | Georgetown | not out | 26* | 3.0 | - | 33 | - | - |
| 23/03/1991 | Test | Australia | West Indies | Georgetown | | - | | | | | - |
| 30/03/1991 | Tour | Australian XI | West Indies U-23s | Kingstown | c BC Lara b HAG Anthony | 85 | 4.0 | - | 16 | - | - |

| Start Date | Grade | Team | Opponent | Venue | How Out | Runs | O | M | R | W | Ct |
|---|---|---|---|---|---|---|---|---|---|---|---|
| 05/04/1991 | Test | Australia | West Indies | Port-of-Spain | cwk PJL Dujon b CA Walsh | 26 | 5.0 | - | 10 | - | 1 |
| | | | | | | | - | | | | - |
| 13/04/1991 | Tour | Australian XI | WI Board XI | Bridgetown | c D Williams b IBA Allen | 1 | 21.0 | 4 | 76 | 3 | - |
| | | | | | - | | 9.0 | 2 | 29 | - | - |
| 19/04/1991 | Test | Australia | West Indies | Bridgetown | cwk PJL Dujon b BP Patterson | 2 | 2.0 | - | 3 | - | - |
| | | | | | not out | 4* | 28.0 | 6 | 77 | - | - |
| 27/04/1991 | Test | Australia | West Indies | St John's | | - | | | | | - |
| 16/09/1991 | Tour | Australian XI | Zimbabweans | Bulawayo | b AH Shah | 119 | 8.0 | 6 | 2 | 2 | 1 |
| | | | | | | - | 6.0 | 4 | 2 | - | - |
| 21/09/1991 | Tour | Australian XI | Zimbabweans | Harare | b EA Brandes | 11 | 6.0 | 2 | 7 | - | 2 |
| | | | | | | - | 7.0 | 2 | 10 | - | - |
| 13/10/1991 | ING | New South Wales | Queensland | Brisbane | c and b AR Border | 74 | 9.0 | 2 | 25 | 3 | - |
| 15/10/1991 | ING | New South Wales | Victoria | North Sydney | b MG Hughes | 126 | 6.0 | 1 | 30 | 2 | - |
| 20/10/1991 | ING | New South Wales | Tasmania | North Sydney | b RJ Tucker | 22 | 10.0 | - | 47 | 2 | - |
| 26/10/1991 | ING | New South Wales | Western Australia | Perth | cwk TJ Zoehrer b KH MacLeay | 17 | 4.0 | - | 25 | - | - |
| 01/11/1991 | Pura | New South Wales | Western Australia | Perth | lbw b TM Alderman | 115 | 12.0 | 5 | 33 | - | 1 |
| | | | | | | - | 13.0 | 4 | 26 | 2 | 1 |
| 08/11/1991 | Pura | New South Wales | Victoria | Sydney | cwk DS Berry b PR Reiffel | 88 | 7.0 | 2 | 15 | 1 | 1 |
| | | | | | | - | 1.0 | - | 6 | - | 1 |
| 15/11/1991 | Pura | New South Wales | Queensland | Brisbane | c DM Wellham b CJ McDermott | 10 | 17.0 | 4 | 51 | 1 | - |
| | | | | | b CJ McDermott | 2 | | | | | - |
| 23/11/1991 | Tour | New South Wales | Indians | Lismore | b ST Banerjee | 13 | 13.0 | 6 | 24 | 2 | - |
| | | | | | | - | 6.0 | 1 | 20 | - | 1 |
| 08/12/1991 | ODI | Australia | India | Perth | c and b RJ Shastri | 5 | 10.0 | 1 | 46 | 3 | - |
| 10/12/1991 | ODI | Australia | India | Hobart | | - | 7.0 | - | 31 | - | 1 |
| 12/12/1991 | ODI | Australia | West Indies | Melbourne | cwk D Williams b AC Cummins | 8 | 6.0 | - | 16 | 2 | 2 |
| 15/12/1991 | ODI | Australia | India | Adelaide | not out | 0* | 10.0 | 1 | 27 | 1 | - |
| 18/12/1991 | ODI | Australia | West Indies | Sydney | b CEL Ambrose | 34 | 6.5 | - | 33 | 2 | 2 |
| 20/12/1991 | Tour | Australian XI | West Indians | Hobart | c CA Best b BP Patterson | 11 | 12.0 | 3 | 37 | 1 | 1 |
| 09/01/1992 | ODI | Australia | West Indies | Melbourne | | - | 8.0 | - | 19 | - | 2 |
| 12/01/1992 | ODI | Australia | West Indies | Brisbane | b BP Patterson | 3 | 10.0 | 2 | 31 | 3 | 1 |
| 14/01/1992 | ODI | Australia | India | Sydney | | - | 5.4 | - | 29 | 2 | - |
| 18/01/1992 | ODI | Australia | India | Melbourne | not out | 5* | 7.0 | - | 32 | 2 | 1 |
| 20/01/1992 | ODI | Australia | India | Sydney | b M Prabhakar | 5 | 10.0 | 1 | 40 | 1 | - |
| 31/01/1992 | Pura | New South Wales | South Australia | Sydney | cwk TJ Nielsen b CJ Owen | 41 | 9.0 | 1 | 29 | 1 | - |
| | | | | | | - | 4.0 | 1 | 16 | - | 2 |
| 13/02/1992 | Pura | New South Wales | Victoria | Melbourne | cwk DS Berry b PR Reiffel | 5 | 11.0 | 2 | 23 | 3 | 1 |
| | | | | | c WG Ayres b AIC Dodemaide | 6 | | | | | - |
| 22/02/1992 | ODI | Australia | New Zealand | Auckland | c and b GR Larsen | 38 | 10.0 | - | 60 | - | - |
| 26/02/1992 | ODI | Australia | South Africa | Sydney | c WJ Cronje b BM McMillan | 27 | 4.0 | 1 | 16 | - | - |
| 01/03/1992 | ODI | Australia | India | Brisbane | b J Srinath | 29 | 10.0 | - | 50 | 1 | 2 |
| 05/03/1992 | ODI | Australia | England | Sydney | run out | 27 | 6.0 | - | 29 | 1 | - |
| 07/03/1992 | ODI | Australia | Sri Lanka | Adelaide | | - | 7.0 | - | 34 | - | - |
| 11/03/1992 | ODI | Australia | Pakistan | Perth | cwk Moin Khan b Imran Khan | 5 | 10.0 | - | 36 | 3 | - |
| 14/03/1992 | ODI | Australia | Zimbabwe | Hobart | b EA Brandes | 55 | 7.0 | - | 28 | 2 | - |
| 18/03/1992 | ODI | Australia | West Indies | Melbourne | b AC Cummins | 6 | 6.4 | - | 24 | 1 | - |
| 28/03/1992 | Pura | New South Wales | Western Australia | Perth | c WS Andrews b BA Reid | 113 | 16.0 | 6 | 36 | 1 | - |
| | | | | | cwk MRJ Veletta b BA Reid | 68 | 4.0 | - | 26 | - | - |
| 11/10/1992 | ING | New South Wales | Western Australia | Perth | cwk TJ Zoehrer b BA Reid | 5 | 8.0 | - | 42 | - | - |
| 18/10/1992 | ING | New South Wales | South Australia | Adelaide | not out | 85* | 6.0 | - | 18 | 2 | 1 |
| 01/11/1992 | ING | New South Wales | Queensland | Brisbane | c SG Law b MS Kasprowicz | 131 | 7.0 | - | 50 | 3 | - |
| 04/11/1992 | ING | New South Wales | Victoria | Sydney | c PC Nobes b JA Sutherland | 48 | 2.0 | - | 12 | - | - |
| 06/11/1992 | Pura | New South Wales | Victoria | Sydney | c PC Nobes b MG Hughes | 0 | 27.0 | 7 | 90 | 3 | - |
| | | | | | run out | 36 | | | | | - |
| 14/11/1992 | Tour | Australian XI | West Indians | Hobart | cwk JR Murray b IR Bishop | 95 | 8.0 | 3 | 31 | 1 | 2 |
| | | | | | not out | 100* | 7.0 | 2 | 22 | - | - |

| Start Date | Grade | Team | Opponent | Venue | How Out | Runs | O | M | R | W | Ct |
|---|---|---|---|---|---|---|---|---|---|---|---|
| 20/11/1992 | Tour | New South Wales | West Indians | Sydney | c JC Adams b CA Walsh | 22 | | | | | - |
| | | | | | | - | 16.0 | 3 | 43 | - | 2 |
| 27/11/1992 | Test | Australia | West Indies | Brisbane | cwk D Williams b CEL Ambrose | 10 | 14.0 | 2 | 46 | 1 | - |
| | | | | | cwk D Williams b CEL Ambrose | 20 | 5.0 | 2 | 6 | - | |
| 06/12/1992 | ODI | Australia | West Indies | Perth | c CL Hooper b PV Simmons | 4 | 8.0 | 2 | 31 | - | - |
| 08/12/1992 | ODI | Australia | West Indies | Sydney | cwk JR Murray b PV Simmons | 1 | 5.3 | - | 25 | 2 | 1 |
| 10/12/1992 | ODI | Australia | Pakistan | Hobart | run out | 26 | 10.0 | - | 56 | 1 | 1 |
| 13/12/1992 | ODI | Australia | Pakistan | Adelaide | not out | 15* | 9.0 | - | 50 | 1 | - |
| 15/12/1992 | ODI | Australia | West Indies | Melbourne | run out | 34 | 10.0 | - | 38 | 1 | - |
| 18/12/1992 | Pura | New South Wales | South Australia | Adelaide | c NR Fielke b TBA May | 38 | 6.0 | 2 | 11 | - | 2 |
| | | | | | lbw b TBA May | 4 | 8.0 | 3 | 30 | - | - |
| 26/12/1992 | Test | Australia | West Indies | Melbourne | c BC Lara b CEL Ambrose | 38 | 4.0 | 1 | 14 | 1 | 1 |
| | | | | | c PV Simmons b IR Bishop | 1 | | | | | - |
| 02/01/1993 | Test | Australia | West Indies | Sydney | c PV Simmons b CEL Ambrose | 100 | 11.0 | 1 | 43 | | - |
| | | | | | | - | | | | | - |
| 10/01/1993 | ODI | Australia | West Indies | Brisbane | c AL Logie b CA Walsh | 24 | 7.0 | 1 | 30 | 1 | 2 |
| 12/01/1993 | ODI | Australia | Pakistan | Melbourne | c and b Asif Mujtaba | 5 | 8.0 | - | 22 | 1 | - |
| 14/01/1993 | ODI | Australia | Pakistan | Sydney | c Asif Mujtaba b Waqar Younis | 64 | 5.0 | - | 26 | - | - |
| 16/01/1993 | ODI | Australia | West Indies | Sydney | c and b CL Hooper | 15 | 10.0 | - | 45 | 2 | - |
| 18/01/1993 | ODI | Australia | West Indies | Melbourne | run out | 25 | 10.0 | 1 | 30 | - | - |
| 23/01/1993 | Test | Australia | West Indies | Adelaide | cwk JR Murray b CEL Ambrose | 42 | 13.0 | 4 | 37 | 1 | 1 |
| | | | | | c KLT Arthurton b CEL Ambrose | 4 | 5.0 | 1 | 8 | - | 1 |
| 30/01/1993 | Test | Australia | West Indies | Perth | cwk JR Murray b IR Bishop | 13 | 6.0 | 3 | 8 | - | 2 |
| | | | | | c (sub)AL Logie b IR Bishop | 0 | | | | | |
| 16/02/1993 | Tour | Australian XI | NZ Board XI | New Plymouth | c (sub)PG Kennedy b DJ Nash | 41 | 8.0 | 2 | 21 | 2 | - |
| | | | | | not out | 31* | 6.0 | 1 | 16 | 1 | 1 |
| 25/02/1993 | Test | Australia | New Zealand | Christchurch | lbw b MB Owens | 62 | 4.0 | 2 | 9 | - | - |
| | | | | | | - | 2.0 | 2 | 0 | - | - |
| 04/03/1993 | Test | Australia | New Zealand | Wellington | cwk TE Blain b DK Morrison | 75 | 15.0 | 7 | 28 | - | - |
| | | | | | | - | | | | | - |
| 12/03/1993 | Test | Australia | New Zealand | Auckland | c AH Jones b W Watson | 41 | 14.0 | 6 | 19 | 1 | 1 |
| | | | | | lbw b DN Patel | 0 | 6.0 | 1 | 15 | 1 | - |
| 19/03/1993 | ODI | Australia | New Zealand | Dunedin | not out | 23* | 7.0 | - | 15 | - | - |
| 21/03/1993 | ODI | Australia | New Zealand | Christchurch | b DK Morrison | 30 | 6.0 | - | 35 | 1 | 1 |
| 24/03/1993 | ODI | Australia | New Zealand | Wellington | b CZ Harris | 9 | 7.0 | - | 37 | - | 2 |
| 27/03/1993 | ODI | Australia | New Zealand | Hamilton | b C Pringle | 19 | 7.4 | - | 59 | - | - |
| 28/03/1993 | ODI | Australia | New Zealand | Auckland | b RT Latham | 39 | 8.0 | - | 27 | 2 | - |
| 05/05/1993 | Tour | Australian XI | Worcestershire | Worcester | not out | 49* | | | | | - |
| | | | | | not out | 12* | | | | | - |
| 08/05/1993 | Tour | Australian XI | Somerset | Taunton | cwk ND Burns b AR Caddick | 38 | | | | | - |
| 13/05/1993 | Tour | Australian XI | Sussex | Hove | st PA Moores b CM Wells | 124 | 2.1 | - | 16 | 1 | - |
| 19/05/1993 | ODI | Australia | England | Manchester | c and b CC Lewis | 27 | 10.0 | - | 53 | 3 | - |
| 21/05/1993 | ODI | Australia | England | Birmingham | not out | 6* | 8.0 | - | 55 | 1 | - |
| 23/05/1993 | ODI | Australia | England | Lord's | c GA Gooch b AR Caddick | 8 | 11.0 | - | 43 | 1 | - |
| 29/05/1993 | Tour | Australian XI | Leicestershire | Leicester | not out | 44* | | | | | - |
| 03/06/1993 | Test | Australia | England | Manchester | b PM Such | 3 | | | | | - |
| | | | | | not out | 78* | | | | | - |
| 12/06/1993 | Tour | Australian XI | Gloucestershire | Bristol | c GD Hodgson b JM De La Pena | 21 | 5.0 | - | 24 | - | - |
| 17/06/1993 | Test | Australia | England | Lord's | not out | 13* | 4.0 | 1 | 5 | - | - |
| | | | | | | - | 2.0 | - | 13 | - | - |
| 26/06/1993 | Tour | Australian XI | Hampshire | Southampton | c TC Middleton b SD Udal | 6 | 6.0 | 1 | 29 | - | - |
| | | | | | b CA Connor | 0 | | | | | - |
| 01/07/1993 | Test | Australia | England | Nottingham | cwk AJ Stewart b MJ McCague | 13 | 8.0 | 4 | 12 | - | 1 |
| | | | | | not out | 47* | 1.0 | - | 3 | - | - |
| 13/07/1993 | Tour | Australian XI | Derbyshire | Derby | | - | 2.0 | 1 | 1 | - | - |
| 17/07/1993 | Tour | Australian XI | Durham | Durham | cwk CW Scott b GK Brown | 19 | 14.0 | 3 | 50 | 1 | - |
| | | | | | not out | 6* | | | | | |

| Start Date | Grade | Team | Opponent | Venue | How Out | Runs | O | M | R | W | Ct |
|---|---|---|---|---|---|---|---|---|---|---|---|
| 22/07/1993 | Test | Australia | England | Leeds | not out | 157* | | | | | - |
| | | | | | | - | | | | | - |
| 28/07/1993 | Tour | Australian XI | Lancashire | Manchester | | - | | | | | - |
| | | | | | b PJ Martin | 17 | 1.0 | - | 5 | - | - |
| 05/08/1993 | Test | Australia | England | Birmingham | cwk AJ Stewart b MP Bicknell | 59 | 5.0 | 2 | 4 | - | 1 |
| | | | | | | - | | | | | 2 |
| 11/08/1993 | Tour | Australian XI | Kent | Canterbury | b AP Igglesden | 123 | 6.0 | 3 | 13 | 1 | - |
| | | | | | | - | 5.0 | 2 | 9 | 2 | - |
| 19/08/1993 | Test | Australia | England | The Oval | b ARC Fraser | 20 | 12.0 | 2 | 45 | 2 | 1 |
| | | | | | lbw b DE Malcolm | 26 | | | | | - |
| 10/10/1993 | ING | New South Wales | Queensland | Brisbane | c DM Wellham b CG Rackemann | 59 | | | | | - |
| 24/10/1993 | ING | New South Wales | Tasmania | North Sydney | run out (Ponting/Buckingham) | 35 | 5.0 | - | 34 | 1 | 2 |
| 29/10/1993 | Tour | New South Wales | New Zealanders | Newcastle | lbw b DN Patel | 88 | 5.0 | 1 | 6 | - | - |
| | | | | | lbw b DK Morrison | 4 | | | | | - |
| 04/11/1993 | Pura | New South Wales | Queensland | Brisbane | b GJ Rowell | 43 | 4.0 | 1 | 15 | 1 | 1 |
| | | | | | not out | 11* | 15.0 | 5 | 40 | 1 | 1 |
| 12/11/1993 | Test | Australia | New Zealand | Perth | cwk TE Blain b DN Patel | 44 | 4.0 | - | 10 | - | 1 |
| | | | | | | - | 7.0 | 2 | 10 | 1 | - |
| 19/11/1993 | Pura | New South Wales | Victoria | Melbourne | c PR Reiffel b SK Warne | 1 | 3.0 | - | 15 | - | 1 |
| | | | | | b PR Reiffel | 122 | 5.0 | 2 | 5 | - | - |
| 26/11/1993 | Test | Australia | New Zealand | Hobart | not out | 25* | 4.0 | 1 | 8 | - | - |
| | | | | | | - | | | | | - |
| 03/12/1993 | Test | Australia | New Zealand | Brisbane | not out | 147* | 3.0 | - | 13 | - | - |
| | | | | | | - | | | | | - |
| 09/12/1993 | ODI | Australia | South Africa | Melbourne | run out (Rhodes) | 33 | 10.0 | - | 37 | - | - |
| 12/12/1993 | ODI | Australia | New Zealand | Adelaide | | - | 7.0 | - | 16 | - | - |
| 14/12/1993 | ODI | Australia | South Africa | Sydney | cwk DJ Richardson b WJ Cronje | 13 | 6.0 | - | 20 | 2 | 1 |
| 16/12/1993 | ODI | Australia | New Zealand | Melbourne | retired hurt | 25+ | | | | | - |
| 31/12/1993 | Pura | New South Wales | South Australia | Adelaide | c DS Webber b PE McIntyre | 73 | | | | | - |
| | | | | | c DS Webber b PE McIntyre | 46 | | | | | - |
| 07/01/1994 | Pura | New South Wales | Tasmania | Hobart | not out | 190* | 4.0 | - | 26 | - | - |
| | | | | | cwk MN Atkinson b CD Matthews | 17 | 2.0 | - | 12 | - | - |
| 16/01/1994 | ODI | Australia | South Africa | Perth | cwk DJ Richardson b DJ Callaghan | 25 | 6.0 | - | 32 | - | - |
| 19/01/1994 | ODI | Australia | New Zealand | Melbourne | not out | 0* | 10.0 | - | 36 | - | - |
| 21/01/1994 | ODI | Australia | South Africa | Melbourne | c PN Kirsten b RP Snell | 27 | 7.0 | - | 27 | 1 | - |
| 23/01/1994 | ODI | Australia | South Africa | Sydney | b AA Donald | 1 | 5.0 | - | 11 | - | 1 |
| 25/01/1994 | ODI | Australia | South Africa | Sydney | b WJ Cronje | 17 | 10.0 | 2 | 39 | 1 | - |
| 28/01/1994 | Test | Australia | South Africa | Adelaide | cwk DJ Richardson b AA Donald | 164 | 18.0 | 7 | 26 | 4 | - |
| | | | | | cwk DJ Richardson b RP Snell | 1 | 6.0 | 3 | 4 | - | 1 |
| 12/02/1994 | Tour | Australian XI | Northern Transvaal | Centurion | | - | | | | | - |
| 19/02/1994 | ODI | Australia | South Africa | Johannesburg | not out | 46* | 10.0 | - | 54 | - | - |
| 20/02/1994 | ODI | Australia | South Africa | Centurion | b EO Simons | 86 | 5.0 | - | 28 | - | 1 |
| 22/02/1994 | ODI | Australia | South Africa | Port Elizabeth | c CR Matthews b AA Donald | 18 | 4.0 | - | 33 | 1 | - |
| 24/02/1994 | ODI | Australia | South Africa | Durban | lbw b EO Simons | 2 | 4.0 | - | 24 | - | - |
| 26/02/1994 | Tour | Australian XI | Free State | Bloemfontein | c BT Player b HC Bakkes | 102 | | | | | 3 |
| | | | | | | - | 6.0 | - | 21 | 1 | - |
| 04/03/1994 | Test | Australia | South Africa | Johannesburg | not out | 45* | 9.0 | 2 | 14 | 1 | - |
| | | | | | cwk DJ Richardson b CR Matthews | 0 | 10.0 | 3 | 28 | 1 | 1 |
| 12/03/1994 | Tour | Australian XI | Boland | Stellenbosch | run out | 32 | 4.0 | 1 | 3 | - | 1 |
| | | | | | lbw b CW Henderson | 71 | 2.0 | 1 | 3 | - | - |
| 17/03/1994 | Test | Australia | South Africa | Cape Town | b CR Matthews | 86 | 9.0 | 3 | 20 | - | - |
| | | | | | | - | 22.3 | 9 | 28 | 5 | 1 |
| 25/03/1994 | Test | Australia | South Africa | Durban | c KC Wessels b CR Matthews | 64 | 27.2 | 12 | 40 | 3 | 1 |
| | | | | | | - | | | | | - |
| 02/04/1994 | ODI | Australia | South Africa | East London | not out | 67* | 9.0 | 1 | 25 | 1 | - |
| 04/04/1994 | ODI | Australia | South Africa | Port Elizabeth | lbw b BM McMillan | 7 | 10.0 | 1 | 48 | 1 | - |
| 06/04/1994 | ODI | Australia | South Africa | Cape Town | b EO Simons | 23 | 4.0 | - | 22 | - | - |

| Start Date | Grade | Team | Opponent | Venue | How Out | Runs | O | M | R | W | Ct |
|---|---|---|---|---|---|---|---|---|---|---|---|
| 08/04/1994 | ODI | Australia | South Africa | Bloemfontein | c BM McMillan b PS De Villiers | 42 | 10.0 | - | 48 | 2 | 1 |
| 14/04/1994 | ODI | Australia | Sri Lanka | Sharjah | | - | 6.0 | - | 17 | 2 | - |
| 16/04/1994 | ODI | Australia | New Zealand | Sharjah | | - | 10.0 | 1 | 48 | - | - |
| 19/04/1994 | ODI | Australia | India | Sharjah | cwk NR Mongia b J Srinath | 53 | 8.0 | - | 52 | - | - |
| 07/09/1994 | ODI | Australia | Pakistan | Colombo | cwk Rashid Latif b Mushtaq Ahmed | 1 | 10.0 | 1 | 16 | 3 | - |
| 09/09/1994 | ODI | Australia | India | Colombo | b M Prabhakar | 22 | 8.0 | - | 33 | 1 | - |
| 13/09/1994 | ODI | Australia | Sri Lanka | Colombo | cwk PB Dassanayake b ST Jayasuriya | 30 | 6.0 | - | 32 | 1 | - |
| 23/09/1994 | Tour | Australian XI | BCCP President's XI | Rawalpindi | not out | 53* | 4.0 | 2 | 2 | - | 1 |
| | | | | | | - | 4.0 | 1 | 10 | - | 1 |
| 28/09/1994 | Test | Australia | Pakistan | Karachi | b Waqar Younis | 73 | 2.0 | - | 9 | - | - |
| | | | | | lbw b Wasim Akram | 0 | 15.0 | 3 | 28 | 1 | - |
| 05/10/1994 | Test | Australia | Pakistan | Rawalpindi | b Waqar Younis | 98 | | | | | 1 |
| | | | | | | - | 13.0 | 2 | 41 | - | 1 |
| 12/10/1994 | ODI | Australia | South Africa | Lahore | c G Kirsten b CR Matthews | 56 | 10.0 | - | 35 | 2 | - |
| 14/10/1994 | ODI | Australia | Pakistan | Multan | not out | 59* | 10.0 | 1 | 37 | - | - |
| 18/10/1994 | ODI | Australia | South Africa | Faisalabad | b EO Simons | 23 | 10.0 | 1 | 40 | - | 1 |
| 22/10/1994 | ODI | Australia | Pakistan | Rawalpindi | lbw b Salim Malik | 14 | 5.0 | - | 26 | - | - |
| 24/10/1994 | ODI | Australia | South Africa | Peshawar | | - | | | | | - |
| 30/10/1994 | ODI | Australia | Pakistan | Lahore | b Aamir Sohail | 1 | 2.0 | - | 6 | - | 1 |
| 18/11/1994 | Pura | New South Wales | Queensland | Sydney | b GJ Rowell | 64 | | | | | - |
| | | | | | | - | | | | | - |
| 25/11/1994 | Test | Australia | England | Brisbane | c GA Hick b PAJ DeFreitas | 19 | | | | | - |
| | | | | | c (sub)C White b PCR Tufnell | 7 | | | | | - |
| 09/12/1994 | Pura | New South Wales | Tasmania | Sydney | c and b S Young | 29 | | | | | 1 |
| | | | | | c MJ Di Venuto b CD Matthews | 52 | | | | | 1 |
| 16/12/1994 | Pura | New South Wales | South Australia | Adelaide | c DS Lehmann b GS Blewett | 43 | | | | | 1 |
| | | | | | run out (Wigney/Siddons) | 42 | | | | | 1 |
| 24/12/1994 | Test | Australia | England | Melbourne | not out | 94* | | | | | 1 |
| | | | | | not out | 26* | | | | | - |
| 01/01/1995 | Test | Australia | England | Sydney | b D Gough | 1 | | | | | - |
| | | | | | cwk SJ Rhodes b ARC Fraser | 0 | | | | | - |
| 10/01/1995 | ODI | Australia | England | Melbourne | cwk SJ Rhodes b ARC Fraser | 0 | | | | | 1 |
| 20/01/1995 | Pura | New South Wales | Tasmania | Hobart | b DJ Millns | 206 | | | | | 1 |
| | | | | | not out | 68* | | | | | 1 |
| 26/01/1995 | Test | Australia | England | Adelaide | c MA Atherton b CC Lewis | 19 | | | | | 1 |
| | | | | | b DE Malcolm | 0 | | | | | - |
| 03/02/1995 | Test | Australia | England | Perth | not out | 99* | | | | | - |
| | | | | | c MR Ramprakash b CC Lewis | 80 | | | | | 1 |
| 15/02/1995 | ODI | Australia | South Africa | Wellington | not out | 44* | | | | | 1 |
| 19/02/1995 | ODI | Australia | New Zealand | Auckland | b C Pringle | 13 | | | | | - |
| 22/02/1995 | ODI | Australia | India | Dunedin | c and b AR Kumble | 23 | | | | | - |
| 26/02/1995 | ODI | Australia | New Zealand | Auckland | c KR Rutherford b SA Thomson | 1 | | | | | - |
| 08/03/1995 | ODI | Australia | West Indies | Bridgetown | b VC Drakes | 26 | | | | | - |
| 11/03/1995 | ODI | Australia | West Indies | Port-of-Spain | b CA Walsh | 58 | 4.0 | - | 15 | - | - |
| 12/03/1995 | ODI | Australia | West Indies | Port-of-Spain | c CL Hooper b PV Simmons | 44 | 9.3 | 1 | 61 | 2 | - |
| 15/03/1995 | ODI | Australia | West Indies | Kingstown | c KLT Arthurton b PV Simmons | 25 | | | | | - |
| 18/03/1995 | ODI | Australia | West Indies | Georgetown | c WKM Benjamin b CL Hooper | 11 | 9.0 | - | 47 | 1 | - |
| 25/03/1995 | Tour | Australian XI | WI Board XI | Castries | not out | 73* | 4.0 | - | 14 | 1 | 1 |
| 31/03/1995 | Test | Australia | West Indies | Bridgetown | cwk JR Murray b KCG Benjamin | 65 | | | | | 2 |
| | | | | | | - | | | | | 2 |
| 08/04/1995 | Test | Australia | West Indies | St John's | b KCG Benjamin | 15 | 6.0 | 1 | 20 | 2 | 1 |
| | | | | | not out | 65* | | | | | - |
| 15/04/1995 | Tour | Australian XI | WI Board XI | Basseterre | c DRE Joseph b HAG Anthony | 8 | | | | | - |
| | | | | | | - | 9.0 | 1 | 24 | 2 | - |
| 21/04/1995 | Test | Australia | West Indies | Port-of-Spain | not out | 63* | 3.0 | 1 | 19 | 1 | - |
| | | | | | c CL Hooper b KCG Benjamin | 21 | | | | | - |

| Start Date | Grade | Team | Opponent | Venue | How Out | Runs | O | M | R | W | Ct |
|---|---|---|---|---|---|---|---|---|---|---|---|
| 29/04/1995 | Test | Australia | West Indies | Kingston | c BC Lara b KCG Benjamin | 200 | 11.0 | 5 | 14 | 2 | - |
| | | | | | | - | 4.0 | - | 9 | - | 1 |
| 03/10/1995 | Tour | New South Wales | Western Province | Hurstville | c HH Gibbs b A Cilliers | 47 | | | | | - |
| | | | | | c HD Ackerman b CR Matthews | 0 | | | | | 1 |
| 15/10/1995 | ING | New South Wales | Queensland | North Sydney | c SG Law b CJ McDermott | 49 | | | | | - |
| 18/10/1995 | Pura | New South Wales | Western Australia | Perth | cwk AC Gilchrist b BP Julian | 0 | 12.0 | 2 | 41 | 1 | - |
| | | | | | c GB Hogg b BJ Oldroyd | 31 | 6.0 | - | 25 | 2 | |
| 22/10/1995 | ING | New South Wales | Western Australia | Perth | c TM Moody b J Stewart | 90 | 4.0 | - | 19 | - | 2 |
| 26/10/1995 | Pura | New South Wales | Tasmania | Sydney | c RT Ponting b MA Hatton | 107 | | | | | - |
| | | | | | c MJ Di Venuto b MA Hatton | 54 | | | | | - |
| 01/11/1995 | Pura | New South Wales | Victoria | Melbourne | c (sub) IJ Harvey b BA Williams | 80 | 7.0 | 2 | 13 | - | - |
| | | | | | c and b PR Reiffel | 5 | | | | | 2 |
| 05/11/1995 | ING | New South Wales | Victoria | Melbourne | cwk DS Berry b PR Reiffel | 1 | | | | | - |
| 09/11/1995 | Test | Australia | Pakistan | Brisbane | not out | 112* | | | | | 1 |
| | | | | | | - | 2.0 | 1 | 3 | - | |
| 17/11/1995 | Test | Australia | Pakistan | Hobart | cwk Moin Khan b Mushtaq Ahmed | 7 | 6.0 | - | 18 | 1 | - |
| | | | | | cwk Moin Khan b M Akram | 29 | 8.0 | 1 | 19 | - | |
| 30/11/1995 | Test | Australia | Pakistan | Sydney | st Rashid Latif b Mushtaq Ahmed | 38 | | | | | - |
| | | | | | b Mushtaq Ahmed | 14 | | | | | - |
| 26/12/1995 | Test | Australia | Sri Lanka | Melbourne | not out | 131* | | | | | - |
| | | | | | | - | | | | | |
| 12/01/1996 | ODI | Australia | Sri Lanka | Perth | b WPUJC Vaas | 11 | 3.0 | - | 14 | - | - |
| 16/01/1996 | ODI | Australia | Sri Lanka | Melbourne | not out | 102* | | | | | - |
| 18/01/1996 | ODI | Australia | Sri Lanka | Melbourne | c A Gurusinha b G Wickramasinghe | 13 | | | | | 1 |
| 20/01/1996 | ODI | Australia | Sri Lanka | Sydney | c RS Kalpage b HDPK Dharmasena | 2 | 1.0 | - | 14 | - | 1 |
| 25/01/1996 | Test | Australia | Sri Lanka | Adelaide | b KR Pushpakumara | 170 | | | | | 1 |
| | | | | | not out | 61* | 19.0 | 8 | 34 | 4 | - |
| 23/02/1996 | ODI | Australia | Kenya | Visakhapatnam | c and b MA Suji | 82 | 7.0 | - | 43 | - | - |
| 27/02/1996 | ODI | Australia | India | Mumbai | run out (Raju) | 7 | 3.0 | - | 22 | 2 | - |
| 01/03/1996 | ODI | Australia | Zimbabwe | Nagpur | not out | 5* | 7.0 | 2 | 22 | 2 | 2 |
| 04/03/1996 | ODI | Australia | West Indies | Jaipur | b CA Walsh | 57 | | | | | - |
| 11/03/1996 | ODI | Australia | New Zealand | Chennai | not out | 59* | 4.0 | - | 25 | - | 1 |
| 14/03/1996 | ODI | Australia | West Indies | Chandigarh | b IR Bishop | 3 | 7.0 | - | 30 | 1 | - |
| 17/03/1996 | ODI | Australia | Sri Lanka | Lahore | c PA De Silva b HDPK Dharmasena | 13 | 3.0 | - | 15 | - | - |
| 23/03/1996 | Pura | New South Wales | South Australia | Sydney | b JN Gillespie | 25 | 12.0 | 3 | 32 | 1 | - |
| | | | | | lbw b PE McIntyre | 41 | 9.0 | 4 | 15 | 1 | - |
| 26/08/1996 | ODI | Australia | Zimbabwe | Colombo | c ADR Campbell b GJ Whittall | 82 | 7.0 | 2 | 24 | 1 | - |
| 30/08/1996 | ODI | Australia | Sri Lanka | Colombo | b M Muralidaran | 22 | 5.0 | 1 | 36 | 1 | - |
| 06/09/1996 | ODI | Australia | India | Colombo | st NR Mongia b AR Kumble | 55 | 6.0 | - | 20 | 1 | 3 |
| 07/09/1996 | ODI | Australia | Sri Lanka | Colombo | c and b UDU Chandana | 55 | 7.0 | - | 31 | - | - |
| 05/10/1996 | Tour | Australian XI | Indian Board President's XI | Patiala | cwk S Saba Karim b AR Kapoor | 27 | | | | | - |
| | | | | | | - | | | | | - |
| 10/10/1996 | Test | Australia | India | Delhi | cwk NR Mongia b AR Kapoor | 0 | 13.0 | 5 | 25 | 1 | - |
| | | | | | not out | 67* | | | | | - |
| 19/10/1996 | ODI | Australia | South Africa | Indore | st DJ Richardson b PL Symcox | 1 | | | | | - |
| 21/10/1996 | ODI | Australia | India | Bangalore | c SC Ganguly b SB Joshi | 41 | 9.0 | - | 52 | 2 | - |
| 25/10/1996 | ODI | Australia | South Africa | Faridabad | c BM McMillan b N Boje | 40 | | | | | 1 |
| 01/11/1996 | ODI | Australia | South Africa | Guwahati | c BM McMillan b N Boje | 37 | 4.0 | - | 24 | - | - |
| 03/11/1996 | ODI | Australia | India | Chandigarh | st NR Mongia b SB Joshi | 33 | | | | | - |
| 08/11/1996 | Pura | New South Wales | Victoria | Sydney | b IJ Harvey | 38 | | | | | 1 |
| | | | | | cwk DS Berry b PR Reiffel | 1 | 6.0 | 2 | 16 | - | 2 |
| 15/11/1996 | Pura | New South Wales | Queensland | Bankstown | b MS Kasprowicz | 106 | 7.0 | 2 | 16 | - | - |
| | | | | | run out (Jackson/Healy) | 35 | 3.0 | 3 | 0 | - | - |
| 22/11/1996 | Test | Australia | West Indies | Brisbane | c BC Lara b IR Bishop | 66 | 8.1 | 1 | 15 | 1 | - |
| | | | | | | - | | | | | - |
| 15/12/1996 | ODI | Australia | Pakistan | Adelaide | c Mohammad Wasim b Saqlain Mushtaq | 57 | | | | | - |

| Start Date | Grade | Team | Opponent | Venue | How Out | Runs | O | M | R | W | Ct |
|---|---|---|---|---|---|---|---|---|---|---|---|
| 19/12/1996 | Pura | New South Wales | Queensland | Brisbane | c JP Maher b AJ Bichel | 55 | 6.0 | 1 | 21 | - | 3 |
| | | | | | not out | 186* | | | | | - |
| 26/12/1996 | Test | Australia | West Indies | Melbourne | cwk JR Murray b IR Bishop | 58 | 10.0 | 5 | 22 | - | |
| | | | | | b KCG Benjamin | 37 | | | | | - |
| 01/01/1997 | ODI | Australia | Pakistan | Sydney | b Saqlain Mushtaq | 42 | | | | | |
| 05/01/1997 | ODI | Australia | West Indies | Brisbane | run out (Chanderpaul/Hooper) | 6 | 3.0 | - | 24 | - | |
| 07/01/1997 | ODI | Australia | Pakistan | Hobart | b Wasim Akram | 5 | | | | | 2 |
| 12/01/1997 | ODI | Australia | West Indies | Perth | c AFG Griffith b S Chanderpaul | 29 | | | | | 1 |
| 16/01/1997 | ODI | Australia | Pakistan | Melbourne | c Wasim Akram b Saqlain Mushtaq | 20 | | | | | - |
| 25/01/1997 | Test | Australia | West Indies | Adelaide | c CL Hooper b S Chanderpaul | 26 | | | | | - |
| | | | | | | - | | | | | 2 |
| 01/02/1997 | Test | Australia | West Indies | Perth | cwk CO Browne b CEL Ambrose | 1 | 7.0 | 1 | 26 | - | - |
| | | | | | c CL Hooper b CA Walsh | 0 | | | | | - |
| 15/02/1997 | Tour | Australian XI | Western Province | Cape Town | c SG Koenig b MW Pringle | 69 | 13.0 | 1 | 47 | - | 1 |
| | | | | | | - | | | | | - |
| 20/02/1997 | Tour | Australian XI | KwaZulu-Natal | Durban | c NC Johnson b PL Symcox | 22 | 6.0 | 1 | 27 | 1 | 1 |
| | | | | | | - | | | | | - |
| 28/02/1997 | Test | Australia | South Africa | Johannesburg | cwk DJ Richardson b JH Kallis | 160 | | | | | 1 |
| | | | | | | - | 4.0 | 1 | 4 | 1 | - |
| 07/03/1997 | Tour | Australian XI | Border | East London | | - | | | | | - |
| 14/03/1997 | Test | Australia | South Africa | Port Elizabeth | cwk DJ Richardson b BM McMillan | 8 | | | | | 1 |
| | | | | | c WJ Cronje b JH Kallis | 18 | 4.3 | - | 16 | - | - |
| 21/03/1997 | Test | Australia | South Africa | Centurion | cwk DJ Richardson b BN Schultz | 67 | | | | | 1 |
| | | | | | not out | 60* | | | | | - |
| 29/03/1997 | ODI | Australia | South Africa | East London | run out (Gibbs) | 50 | | | | | - |
| 31/03/1997 | ODI | Australia | South Africa | Port Elizabeth | not out | 50* | | | | | - |
| 03/04/1997 | ODI | Australia | South Africa | Cape Town | b RE Bryson | 0 | | | | | - |
| 05/04/1997 | ODI | Australia | South Africa | Durban | c DN Crookes b AA Donald | 1 | 5.0 | - | 25 | - | 1 |
| 08/04/1997 | ODI | Australia | South Africa | Johannesburg | b RE Bryson | 20 | | | | | 2 |
| 10/04/1997 | ODI | Australia | South Africa | Centurion | lbw b SM Pollock | 89 | | | | | - |
| 13/04/1997 | ODI | Australia | South Africa | Bloemfontein | b AA Donald | 91 | | | | | - |
| 22/05/1997 | ODI | Australia | England | Leeds | lbw b MA Ealham | 19 | | | | | - |
| 24/05/1997 | ODI | Australia | England | The Oval | b RDB Croft | 24 | 3.0 | - | 20 | - | 1 |
| 25/05/1997 | ODI | Australia | England | Lord's | c GP Thorpe b D Gough | 17 | 4.0 | - | 22 | - | 1 |
| 27/05/1997 | Tour | Australian XI | Gloucestershire | Bristol | b AM Smith | 92 | | | | | - |
| | | | | | | - | | | | | - |
| 31/05/1997 | Tour | Australian XI | Derbyshire | Derby | c PAJ DeFreitas b ID Blackwell | 43 | | | | | 1 |
| | | | | | | - | 1.0 | - | 8 | - | 1 |
| 05/06/1997 | Test | Australia | England | Birmingham | cwk AJ Stewart b AR Caddick | 12 | 12.0 | 2 | 45 | - | - |
| | | | | | lbw b D Gough | 33 | | | | | - |
| 11/06/1997 | Tour | Australian XI | Nottinghamshire | Nottingham | c U Afzaal b MP Dowman | 115 | | | | | - |
| 19/06/1997 | Test | Australia | England | Lord's | lbw b AR Caddick | 0 | | | | | - |
| | | | | | | - | 4.0 | - | 20 | - | - |
| 28/06/1997 | Tour | Australian XI | Hampshire | Southampton | c SD Udal b SJ Renshaw | 11 | | | | | - |
| | | | | | | - | | | | | - |
| 03/07/1997 | Test | Australia | England | Manchester | b D Gough | 108 | | | | | 1 |
| | | | | | cwk AJ Stewart b DW Headley | 116 | | | | | - |
| 19/07/1997 | Tour | Australian XI | Middlesex | Lord's | c MW Gatting b RL Johnson | 57 | | | | | 1 |
| | | | | | | - | 5.0 | 2 | 13 | 1 | - |
| 24/07/1997 | Test | Australia | England | Leeds | c JP Crawley b DW Headley | 4 | | | | | 1 |
| | | | | | | - | 4.0 | 1 | 11 | - | - |
| 01/08/1997 | Tour | Australian XI | Somerset | Taunton | c MN Lathwell b AR Caddick | 62 | | | | | - |
| | | | | | | - | | | | | - |
| 07/08/1997 | Test | Australia | England | Nottingham | b DE Malcolm | 75 | | | | | - |
| | | | | | c AJ Hollioake b AR Caddick | 14 | | | | | 1 |
| 16/08/1997 | Tour | Australian XI | Kent | Canterbury | cwk SA Marsh b PA Strang | 154 | | | | | 1 |
| | | | | | | - | | | | | 1 |

| Start Date | Grade | Team | Opponent | Venue | How Out | Runs | O | M | R | W | Ct |
|---|---|---|---|---|---|---|---|---|---|---|---|
| 21/08/1997 | Test | Australia | England | The Oval | lbw b AR Caddick | 22 | | | | | - |
| | | | | | c GP Thorpe b AR Caddick | 6 | | | | | 1 |
| 05/10/1997 | ING | New South Wales | South Australia | North Sydney | c SP George b BE Young | 72 | 2.0 | - | 12 | 1 | 2 |
| 12/10/1997 | ING | New South Wales | Queensland | Brisbane | cwk IA Healy b BN Creevey | 19 | | | | | 1 |
| 15/10/1997 | Pura | New South Wales | Queensland | Brisbane | run out (Symonds/Healy) | 11 | 6.0 | - | 35 | - | 1 |
| | | | | | c ML Hayden b MS Kasprowicz | 18 | | | | | - |
| 22/10/1997 | Pura | New South Wales | Victoria | North Sydney | not out | 202* | | | | | 2 |
| | | | | | not out | 60* | | | | | - |
| 26/10/1997 | ING | New South Wales | Victoria | North Sydney | cwk DS Berry b DW Fleming | 5 | | | | | 1 |
| 07/11/1997 | Test | Australia | New Zealand | Brisbane | lbw b CL Cairns | 2 | | | | | 1 |
| | | | | | cwk AC Parore b CL Cairns | 23 | | | | | - |
| 14/11/1997 | Pura | New South Wales | Queensland | Newcastle | b AC Dale | 53 | | | | | - |
| | | | | | not out | 6* | | | | | - |
| 20/11/1997 | Test | Australia | New Zealand | Perth | b SB O'Connor | 96 | | | | | 2 |
| | | | | | | - | | | | | 1 |
| 27/11/1997 | Test | Australia | New Zealand | Hobart | c CD McMillan b SB Doull | 7 | 9.0 | 2 | 20 | 3 | - |
| | | | | | not out | 2* | 6.0 | 4 | 10 | 1 | - |
| 04/12/1997 | ODI | Australia | South Africa | Sydney | lbw b PL Symcox | 1 | | | | | - |
| 07/12/1997 | ODI | Australia | New Zealand | Adelaide | lbw b GR Larsen | 7 | | | | | - |
| 09/12/1997 | ODI | Australia | South Africa | Melbourne | cwk DJ Richardson b L Klusener | 0 | | | | | - |
| 17/12/1997 | ODI | Australia | New Zealand | Melbourne | cwk AC Parore b CL Cairns | 0 | | | | | 1 |
| 19/12/1997 | Pura | New South Wales | South Australia | Adelaide | lbw b BE Young | 2 | 3.0 | 1 | 12 | - | 1 |
| | | | | | | - | | | | | - |
| 26/12/1997 | Test | Australia | South Africa | Melbourne | c DJ Cullinan b AA Donald | 96 | 2.0 | - | 12 | - | - |
| | | | | | cwk DJ Richardson b SM Pollock | 17 | 7.0 | 2 | 12 | 1 | - |
| 02/01/1998 | Test | Australia | South Africa | Sydney | b AA Donald | 85 | 8.0 | 4 | 10 | - | 1 |
| | | | | | | | | | | | - |
| 11/01/1998 | ODI | Australia | South Africa | Brisbane | c PL Symcox b JH Kallis | 4 | 4.0 | - | 14 | 1 | - |
| 18/01/1998 | ODI | Australia | South Africa | Perth | cwk DJ Richardson b AA Donald | 0 | | | | | - |
| 21/01/1998 | ODI | Australia | New Zealand | Melbourne | not out | 45* | | | | | - |
| 23/01/1998 | ODI | Australia | South Africa | Melbourne | cwk DJ Richardson b BM McMillan | 53 | | | | | - |
| 26/01/1998 | ODI | Australia | South Africa | Sydney | | - | | | | | - |
| 27/01/1998 | ODI | Australia | South Africa | Sydney | run out (McMillan/Pollock) | 71 | | | | | 1 |
| 30/01/1998 | Test | Australia | South Africa | Adelaide | cwk DJ Richardson b SM Pollock | 6 | 10.0 | 3 | 27 | 1 | - |
| | | | | | cwk DJ Richardson b L Klusener | 34 | 4.0 | 1 | 13 | - | - |
| 08/02/1998 | ODI | Australia | New Zealand | Christchurch | | - | 10.0 | 1 | 24 | 1 | - |
| 10/02/1998 | ODI | Australia | New Zealand | Wellington | c SP Fleming b SB O'Connor | 47 | 9.3 | - | 46 | 2 | - |
| 12/02/1998 | ODI | Australia | New Zealand | Napier | cwk AC Parore b CL Cairns | 42 | 10.0 | - | 56 | - | - |
| 14/02/1998 | ODI | Australia | New Zealand | Auckland | c (sub)SJ Peterson b MW Priest | 23 | | | | | 1 |
| 01/03/1998 | Tour | Australian XI | Indian Board President's XI | Visakhapatnam | | - | 5.0 | 1 | 6 | - | - |
| 06/03/1998 | Test | Australia | India | Chennai | b AR Kumble | 12 | 4.0 | 1 | 11 | - | 1 |
| | | | | | c RS Dravid b SL Venkatapathy Raju | 27 | 8.0 | - | 27 | - | 1 |
| 13/03/1998 | Tour | Australian XI | India A | Jamshedpur | c V Rathore | 107 | | | | | - |
| | | | | | b KN Ananthapadmanabhan | - | | | | | - |
| 18/03/1998 | Test | Australia | India | Kolkata | run out (Dravid/Kumble) | 80 | | | | | - |
| | | | | | lbw b AR Kumble | 33 | | | | | - |
| 01/04/1998 | ODI | Australia | India | Kochi | c and b SR Tendulkar | 26 | | | | | - |
| 03/04/1998 | ODI | Australia | Zimbabwe | Ahmedabad | b GJ Whittall | 48 | | | | | - |
| 07/04/1998 | ODI | Australia | India | Kanpur | st NR Mongia b HH Kanitkar | 0 | | | | | - |
| 11/04/1998 | ODI | Australia | Zimbabwe | Delhi | | - | 10.0 | - | 55 | 1 | 1 |
| 14/04/1998 | ODI | Australia | India | Delhi | b AR Kumble | 57 | 7.0 | - | 42 | 2 | 1 |
| 18/04/1998 | ODI | Australia | New Zealand | Sharjah | lbw b CD McMillan | 3 | | | | | - |
| 19/04/1998 | ODI | Australia | India | Sharjah | b Harvinder Singh | 8 | 9.0 | - | 40 | 4 | - |
| 21/04/1998 | ODI | Australia | New Zealand | Sharjah | lbw b PJ Wiseman | 32 | 4.0 | - | 38 | - | - |
| 22/04/1998 | ODI | Australia | India | Sharjah | run out (Tendulkar) | 10 | 9.0 | - | 65 | 1 | - |
| 24/04/1998 | ODI | Australia | India | Sharjah | c AB Agarkar b HH Kanitkar | 70 | 6.0 | - | 28 | - | - |

| Start Date | Grade | Team | Opponent | Venue | How Out | Runs | O | M | R | W | Ct |
|---|---|---|---|---|---|---|---|---|---|---|---|
| 20/08/1998 | Tour | Ireland | Australia A | Dublin | cwk RJ Campbell b JN Gillespie | 31 | 6.0 | 1 | 27 | - | - |
| | | | | | cwk RJ Campbell b BP Julian | 45 | | | | | - |
| 25/09/1998 | Tour | Australian XI | Karachi City | Karachi | cwk Atiq-uz-Zaman | 92 | | | | | - |
| | | | Cricket Association | | b Shahid Afridi | - | | | | | |
| 01/10/1998 | Test | Australia | Pakistan | Rawalpindi | c Saqlain Mushtaq b Aamir Sohail | 157 | 2.0 | - | 6 | - | - |
| | | | | | | - | | | | | - |
| 15/10/1998 | Test | Australia | Pakistan | Peshawar | cwk Moin Khan b Shoaib Akhtar | 1 | 8.0 | 1 | 19 | 1 | 1 |
| | | | | | not out | 49* | | | | | - |
| 22/10/1998 | Test | Australia | Pakistan | Karachi | lbw b Shahid Afridi | 0 | 2.0 | - | 6 | - | - |
| | | | | | cwk Moin Khan b Shakeel Ahmed | 28 | 8.0 | 5 | 10 | - | - |
| 28/10/1998 | ODI | Australia | India | Dhaka | c and b SR Tendulkar | 7 | 3.0 | - | 23 | - | - |
| 06/11/1998 | ODI | Australia | Pakistan | Karachi | c Shahid Afridi b Arshad Khan | 10 | 3.2 | - | 22 | 1 | - |
| 08/11/1998 | ODI | Australia | Pakistan | Peshawar | lbw b Saqlain Mushtaq | 0 | 10.0 | - | 44 | - | 1 |
| 10/11/1998 | ODI | Australia | Pakistan | Lahore | b Saqlain Mushtaq | 30 | 6.0 | - | 31 | - | - |
| 20/11/1998 | Test | Australia | England | Brisbane | cwk AJ Stewart b AD Mullally | 112 | 3.0 | - | 17 | - | - |
| | | | | | not out | 16* | | | | | - |
| 28/11/1998 | Test | Australia | England | Perth | b AJ Tudor | 33 | | | | | - |
| | | | | | not out | 15* | | | | | - |
| 06/12/1998 | ING | New South Wales | Tasmania | Hobart | cwk TA Pinnington b GJ Rowell | 29 | | | | | - |
| 11/12/1998 | Test | Australia | England | Adelaide | c GA Hick b D Gough | 59 | | | | | - |
| | | | | | c GA Hick b DW Headley | 7 | 2.0 | 1 | 3 | - | - |
| 19/12/1998 | Pura | New South Wales | Victoria | Sydney | cwk DS Berry b MWH Inness | 116 | | | | | - |
| | | | | | cwk DS Berry b IJ Harvey | 5 | | | | | - |
| 26/12/1998 | Test | Australia | England | Melbourne | not out | 122* | 6.0 | 2 | 8 | 2 | - |
| | | | | | not out | 30* | | | | | - |
| 02/01/1999 | Test | Australia | England | Sydney | b PM Such | 96 | | | | | - |
| | | | | | b DW Headley | 8 | | | | | - |
| 17/01/1999 | ODI | Australia | England | Sydney | c D Gough b AJ Hollioake | 0 | | | | | - |
| 21/01/1999 | ODI | Australia | Sri Lanka | Hobart | c DPM Jayawardene b ST Jayasuriya | 20 | | | | | - |
| 27/02/1999 | Tour | Australian XI | W I Board XI | Pointe-a-Pierre | cwk W Phillip b RD King | 57 | | | | | - |
| | | | | | | - | | | | | 1 |
| 05/03/1999 | Test | Australia | West Indies | Port-of-Spain | cwk RD Jacobs b M Dillon | 14 | | | | | - |
| | | | | | cwk RD Jacobs b PT Collins | 0 | | | | | - |
| 13/03/1999 | Test | Australia | West Indies | Kingston | c DRE Joseph b PT Collins | 100 | | | | | - |
| | | | | | cwk RD Jacobs b NO Perry | 9 | | | | | - |
| 20/03/1999 | Tour | Australian XI | West Indies A | St John's | c SC Williams b CL Hooper | 7 | | | | | - |
| | | | | | c and b NC McGarrell | 10 | | | | | 1 |
| 26/03/1999 | Test | Australia | West Indies | Bridgetown | lbw b NO Perry | 199 | | | | | 1 |
| | | | | | b PT Collins | 11 | 5.0 | - | 19 | - | - |
| 03/04/1999 | Test | Australia | West Indies | St John's | not out | 72* | | | | | - |
| | | | | | cwk RD Jacobs b CEL Ambrose | 4 | | | | | - |
| 11/04/1999 | ODI | Australia | West Indies | Kingstown | b HR Bryan | 10 | | | | | - |
| 14/04/1999 | ODI | Australia | West Indies | St George's | c BC Lara b RD King | 0 | 3.3 | - | 13 | 1 | 1 |
| 17/04/1999 | ODI | Australia | West Indies | Port-of-Spain | b PV Simmons | 2 | | | | | - |
| 18/04/1999 | ODI | Australia | West Indies | Port-of-Spain | lbw b M Dillon | 16 | 5.0 | - | 13 | - | - |
| 21/04/1999 | ODI | Australia | West Indies | Georgetown | not out | 72* | 5.0 | - | 23 | - | 1 |
| 24/04/1999 | ODI | Australia | West Indies | Bridgetown | cwk RD Jacobs b NO Perry | 5 | | | | | - |
| 25/04/1999 | ODI | Australia | West Indies | Bridgetown | cwk RD Jacobs b RD King | 30 | 3.0 | - | 17 | 1 | - |
| 16/05/1999 | ODI | Australia | Scotland | Worcester | not out | 49* | 6.0 | - | 22 | 1 | 1 |
| 20/05/1999 | ODI | Australia | New Zealand | Cardiff | c NJ Astle b CZ Harris | 7 | 4.0 | - | 25 | - | - |
| 23/05/1999 | ODI | Australia | Pakistan | Leeds | b Shoaib Akhtar | 49 | 6.0 | - | 37 | - | 1 |
| 27/05/1999 | ODI | Australia | Bangladesh | Chester-le-Street | | - | | | | | - |
| 30/05/1999 | ODI | Australia | West Indies | Manchester | not out | 19* | | | | | - |
| 04/06/1999 | ODI | Australia | India | The Oval | c AR Kumble b DS Mohanty | 36 | 2.0 | - | 8 | 2 | 1 |
| 09/06/1999 | ODI | Australia | Zimbabwe | Lord's | b GJ Whittall | 62 | | | | | - |
| 13/06/1999 | ODI | Australia | South Africa | Leeds | not out | 120* | | | | | - |
| 17/06/1999 | ODI | Australia | South Africa | Birmingham | cwk MV Boucher b SM Pollock | 56 | | | | | 1 |

| Start Date | Grade | Team | Opponent | Venue | How Out | Runs | O | M | R | W | Ct |
|---|---|---|---|---|---|---|---|---|---|---|---|
| 20/06/1999 | ODI | Australia | Pakistan | Lord's | | - | | | | | 2 |
| 22/08/1999 | ODI | Australia | Sri Lanka | Galle | b ST Jayasuriya | 6 | | | | | 1 |
| 23/08/1999 | ODI | Australia | India | Galle | | - | | | | | - |
| 26/08/1999 | ODI | Australia | Sri Lanka | Colombo | cwk RS Kaluwitharana | 12 | 3.1 | - | 26 | 1 | - |
| | | | | | b UDU Chandana | | | | | | |
| 28/08/1999 | ODI | Australia | India | Colombo | c and b RR Singh | 6 | | | | | - |
| 31/08/1999 | ODI | Australia | Sri Lanka | Colombo | b M Muralidaran | 43 | 3.0 | - | 16 | - | - |
| 03/09/1999 | Tour | Australian XI | Sri Lankan | Colombo | lbw b NRG Perera | 42 | | | | | - |
| | | | Board President's XI | | cwk HAPW Jayawardene | 21 | | | | | - |
| | | | | | b MS Villavarayan | | | | | | |
| 09/09/1999 | Test | Australia | Sri Lanka | Kandy | c PA De Silva b DNT Zoysa | 19 | | | | | - |
| | | | | | | - | | | | | - |
| 22/09/1999 | Test | Australia | Sri Lanka | Galle | cwk RS Kaluwitharana | 19 | | | | | 1 |
| | | | | | b HMRKB Herath | - | | | | | |
| 30/09/1999 | Test | Australia | Sri Lanka | Colombo | cwk RS Kaluwitharana b H Herath | 14 | | | | | - |
| 09/10/1999 | Tour | Australian XI | Zimbabwe | Bulawayo | c and b TR Gripper | 27 | | | | | - |
| | | | President's XI | | c EA Brandes b M Mbangwa | 161 | | | | | - |
| 14/10/1999 | Test | Australia | Zimbabwe | Harare | not out | 151* | 4.0 | 1 | 17 | - | - |
| | | | | | | | | | | | 1 |
| 21/10/1999 | ODI | Australia | Zimbabwe | Bulawayo | c NC Johnson b AR Whittall | 14 | | | | | - |
| 23/10/1999 | ODI | Australia | Zimbabwe | Harare | | - | | | | | - |
| 24/10/1999 | ODI | Australia | Zimbabwe | Harare | | - | | | | | - |
| 05/11/1999 | Test | Australia | Pakistan | Brisbane | cwk Moin Khan b Shoaib Akhtar | 1 | 1.0 | - | 1 | - | - |
| | | | | | | - | | | | | - |
| 18/11/1999 | Test | Australia | Pakistan | Hobart | c Ijaz Ahmed b Wasim Akram | 24 | | | | | - |
| | | | | | c and b Saqlain Mushtaq | 28 | 4.0 | 1 | 19 | - | 1 |
| 26/11/1999 | Test | Australia | Pakistan | Perth | c Yousuf Youhana | 5 | | | | | 1 |
| | | | | | b M Akram | - | | | | | 1 |
| 10/12/1999 | Test | Australia | India | Adelaide | cwk MSK Prasad b AB Agarkar | 150 | | | | | 2 |
| | | | | | cwk MSK Prasad b AB Agarkar | 5 | | | | | 1 |
| 17/12/1999 | Pura | New South Wales | Western Australia | Perth | lbw b J Angel | 9 | | | | | - |
| | | | | | c DR Martyn b J Angel | 128 | | | | | - |
| 26/12/1999 | Test | Australia | India | Melbourne | cwk MSK Prasad | 32 | | | | | - |
| | | | | | b BK Venkatesh Prasad | | | | | | |
| | | | | | lbw b AB Agarkar | 32 | | | | | - |
| 02/01/2000 | Test | Australia | India | Sydney | lbw b J Srinath | 57 | | | | | 1 |
| | | | | | | - | | | | | - |
| 09/01/2000 | ODI | Australia | Pakistan | Brisbane | lbw b Shoaib Akhtar | 0 | | | | | - |
| 12/01/2000 | ODI | Australia | India | Melbourne | run out (Srinath/Tendulkar/Dighe) | 23 | | | | | - |
| 14/01/2000 | ODI | Australia | India | Sydney | lbw b J Srinath | 4 | | | | | - |
| 16/01/2000 | ODI | Australia | Pakistan | Melbourne | not out | 81* | | | | | 1 |
| 19/01/2000 | ODI | Australia | Pakistan | Sydney | b Shoaib Akhtar | 6 | | | | | 1 |
| 23/01/2000 | ODI | Australia | Pakistan | Melbourne | c Wasim Akram b Shoaib Akhtar | 6 | | | | | - |
| 26/01/2000 | ODI | Australia | India | Adelaide | | - | 2.0 | - | 5 | - | - |
| 30/01/2000 | ODI | Australia | India | Perth | b RR Singh | 19 | 4.0 | - | 17 | - | - |
| 02/02/2000 | ODI | Australia | Pakistan | Melbourne | not out | 19* | | | | | 2 |
| 04/02/2000 | ODI | Australia | Pakistan | Sydney | run out (Saqlain Mushtaq) | 37 | | | | | 1 |
| 17/02/2000 | ODI | Australia | New Zealand | Wellington | | - | | | | | - |
| 19/02/2000 | ODI | Australia | New Zealand | Auckland | not out | 4* | | | | | - |
| 23/02/2000 | ODI | Australia | New Zealand | Dunedin | retired hurt | 43+ | | | | | - |
| 26/02/2000 | ODI | Australia | New Zealand | Christchurch | b CZ Harris | 54 | | | | | 1 |
| 01/03/2000 | ODI | Australia | New Zealand | Napier | not out | 43* | | | | | 1 |
| 03/03/2000 | ODI | Australia | New Zealand | Auckland | c SP Fleming b CL Cairns | 1 | | | | | - |
| 11/03/2000 | Test | Australia | New Zealand | Auckland | c CM Spearman b DL Vettori | 17 | | | | | - |
| | | | | | c and b PJ Wiseman | 10 | | | | | 2 |
| 18/03/2000 | Tour | Australian XI | Central Districts | Napier | cwk MA Sigley b LJ Hamilton | 23 | | | | | - |
| | | | | | c CJM Furlong b LJ Hamilton | 6 | | | | | 1 |

| Start Date | Grade | Team | Opponent | Venue | How Out | Runs | O | M | R | W | Ct |
|---|---|---|---|---|---|---|---|---|---|---|---|
| 24/03/2000 | Test | Australia | New Zealand | Wellington | not out | 151* | 4.0 | - | 10 | - | - |
| | | | | | c SP Fleming b SB O'Connor | 15 | | | | | 2 |
| 31/03/2000 | Test | Australia | New Zealand | Hamilton | c SP Fleming b CL Cairns | 3 | | | | | - |
| | | | | | retired hurt | 18+ | 3.0 | - | 10 | - | - |
| 12/04/2000 | ODI | Australia | South Africa | Durban | cwk MV Boucher b M Ntini | 2 | 3.0 | - | 18 | - | 1 |
| 14/04/2000 | ODI | Australia | South Africa | Cape Town | | - | | | | | |
| 16/04/2000 | ODI | Australia | South Africa | Johannesburg | b M Hayward | 51 | | | | | - |
| 16/08/2000 | ODI | Australia | South Africa | Melbourne | not out | 114* | | | | | - |
| 18/08/2000 | ODI | Australia | South Africa | Melbourne | b AJ Hall | 30 | | | | | - |
| 20/08/2000 | ODI | Australia | South Africa | Melbourne | c SM Pollock b L Klusener | 17 | | | | | - |
| 07/10/2000 | ODI | Australia | India | Nairobi | b Zaheer Khan | 23 | 4.0 | - | 28 | 1 | - |
| 15/10/2000 | ING | New South Wales | Victoria | North Sydney | not out | 27* | | | | | - |
| 22/10/2000 | ING | New South Wales | Queensland | Bankstown | cwk WA Seccombe b SA Prestwidge | 49 | | | | | 1 |
| 25/10/2000 | Pura | New South Wales | Victoria | Richmond | c BJ Hodge b MWH Inness | 13 | | | | | - |
| | | | | | run out (Craig) | 25 | | | | | 1 |
| 29/10/2000 | ING | New South Wales | Victoria | Richmond | c IJ Harvey b BC Oliver | 36 | | | | | - |
| 07/11/2000 | Pura | New South Wales | Tasmania | Hobart | c and b DJ Marsh | 7 | | | | | - |
| | | | | | | - | 6.0 | 3 | 11 | - | |
| 11/11/2000 | ING | New South Wales | Tasmania | Hobart | not out | 75* | | | | | - |
| 19/11/2000 | ING | New South Wales | South Australia | North Sydney | c DS Lehmann b PC Rofe | 41 | | | | | - |
| 23/11/2000 | Test | Australia | West Indies | Brisbane | c SL Campbell b M Dillon | 41 | | | | | - |
| | | | | | | - | | | | | |
| 01/12/2000 | Test | Australia | West Indies | Perth | c SL Campbell b CA Walsh | 26 | | | | | - |
| | | | | | | - | | | | | |
| 26/12/2000 | Test | Australia | West Indies | Melbourne | not out | 121* | | | | | - |
| | | | | | cwk RD Jacobs b CEL Stuart | 20 | | | | | - |
| 02/01/2001 | Test | Australia | West Indies | Sydney | b MV Nagamootoo | 103 | | | | | - |
| | | | | | lbw b MN Samuels | 38 | | | | | - |
| 11/01/2001 | ODI | Australia | West Indies | Melbourne | c MV Nagamootoo b MN Samuels | 29 | | | | | 1 |
| 26/01/2001 | ODI | Australia | West Indies | Adelaide | | - | | | | | - |
| 28/01/2001 | ODI | Australia | Zimbabwe | Sydney | cwk A Flower b DP Viljoen | 36 | | | | | - |
| 30/01/2001 | ODI | Australia | Zimbabwe | Hobart | lbw b BA Murphy | 79 | | | | | - |
| 04/02/2001 | ODI | Australia | Zimbabwe | Perth | | - | | | | | - |
| 07/02/2001 | ODI | Australia | West Indies | Sydney | cwk RD Jacobs b LR Williams | 38 | | | | | - |
| 09/02/2001 | ODI | Australia | West Indies | Melbourne | not out | 10* | | | | | 2 |
| 17/02/2001 | Tour | Australian XI | India A | Nagpur | cwk NR Mongia b AD Nehra | 0 | | | | | 2 |
| | | | | | c SS Das b Rao, WD Balaji | 17 | | | | | |
| 22/02/2001 | Tour | Australian XI | Mumbai | Mumbai | not out | 106* | | | | | - |
| | | | | | not out | 34* | | | | | - |
| 27/02/2001 | Test | Australia | India | Mumbai | c RS Dravid b RL Sanghvi | 15 | | | | | 1 |
| | | | | | | - | | | | | 1 |
| 06/03/2001 | Tour | Australian XI | Indian Board President's XI | Delhi | c Surendra Singh b Sarandeep Singh | 109 | | | | | - |
| | | | | | | - | | | | | |
| 11/03/2001 | Test | Australia | India | Kolkata | lbw b Harbhajan Singh | 110 | | | | | 1 |
| | | | | | c (sub)HK Badani b Harbhajan Singh | 24 | | | | | - |
| 18/03/2001 | Test | Australia | India | Chennai | handled ball | 47 | | | | | - |
| | | | | | c SS Das b Harbhajan Singh | 47 | | | | | 1 |
| 25/03/2001 | ODI | Australia | India | Bangalore | lbw b V Sehwag | 18 | | | | | - |
| 28/03/2001 | ODI | Australia | India | Pune | | - | | | | | - |
| 31/03/2001 | ODI | Australia | India | Indore | c SR Tendulkar b SC Ganguly | 23 | | | | | - |
| 03/04/2001 | ODI | Australia | India | Visakhapatnam | c J Srinath b Zaheer Khan | 35 | 6.0 | - | 29 | 3 | 2 |
| 06/04/2001 | ODI | Australia | India | Margoa | c AB Agarkar b SR Tendulkar | 17 | | | | | 1 |
| 01/06/2001 | Tour | Australian XI | Worcestershire | Worcester | b CG Liptrot | 30 | | | | | - |
| | | | | | b MJ Rawnsley | 32 | | | | | - |
| 09/06/2001 | ODI | Australia | Pakistan | Cardiff | not out | 54* | | | | | - |
| 10/06/2001 | ODI | Australia | England | Bristol | not out | 26* | | | | | - |
| 14/06/2001 | ODI | Australia | England | Manchester | lbw b D Gough | 64 | | | | | - |

| Start Date | Grade | Team | Opponent | Venue | How Out | Runs | O | M | R | W | Ct |
|---|---|---|---|---|---|---|---|---|---|---|---|
| 19/06/2001 | ODI | Australia | Pakistan | Nottingham | c Saqlain Mushtaq b Waqar Younis | 56 | | | | | - |
| 21/06/2001 | ODI | Australia | England | The Oval | | - | | | | | - |
| 23/06/2001 | ODI | Australia | Pakistan | Lord's | | - | | | | | - |
| 25/06/2001 | Tour | Australian XI | MCC | Arundel | b CM Willoughby | 45 | | | | | - |
| | | | | | c Asif Mujtaba b GJ Kruis | 105 | | | | | 1 |
| 05/07/2001 | Test | Australia | England | Birmingham | lbw b D Gough | 105 | | | | | - |
| | | | | | | - | | | | | - |
| 19/07/2001 | Test | Australia | England | Lord's | cwk AJ Stewart b DG Cork | 45 | | | | | - |
| | | | | | | - | | | | | - |
| 28/07/2001 | Tour | Australian XI | Hampshire | Southampton | c NC Johnson b JEK Schofield | 10 | | | | | 2 |
| | | | | | c and b GW White | 40 | | | | | - |
| 02/08/2001 | Test | Australia | England | Nottingham | c MA Atherton b AR Caddick | 13 | | | | | - |
| | | | | | retired hurt | 1+ | | | | | 1 |
| 23/08/2001 | Test | Australia | England | The Oval | not out | 157* | | | | | - |
| | | | | | | - | | | | | 1 |
| 08/11/2001 | Test | Australia | New Zealand | Brisbane | cwk AC Parore b CD McMillan | 3 | | | | | 2 |
| | | | | | | - | | | | | |
| 18/11/2001 | ING | New South Wales | Queensland | Sydney | not out | 101* | | | | | - |
| 22/11/2001 | Test | Australia | New Zealand | Hobart | lbw b SE Bond | 0 | | | | | - |
| 30/11/2001 | Test | Australia | New Zealand | Perth | cwk AC Parore b DL Vettori | 8 | | | | | - |
| | | | | | run out (Vettori) | 67 | | | | | 1 |
| 14/12/2001 | Test | Australia | South Africa | Adelaide | c ND McKenzie b CW Henderson | 8 | | | | | - |
| | | | | | c SM Pollock b CW Henderson | 13 | | | | | - |
| 26/12/2001 | Test | Australia | South Africa | Melbourne | run out (Gibbs) | 90 | | | | | - |
| | | | | | | - | | | | | - |
| 02/01/2002 | Test | Australia | South Africa | Sydney | b SM Pollock | 30 | | | | | - |
| | | | | | | - | | | | | - |
| 11/01/2002 | ODI | Australia | New Zealand | Melbourne | run out (Vincent/Parore) | 15 | | | | | 1 |
| 13/01/2002 | ODI | Australia | South Africa | Melbourne | b JH Kallis | 62 | | | | | - |
| 17/01/2002 | ODI | Australia | New Zealand | Sydney | c CZ Harris b SE Bond | 9 | | | | | 1 |
| 20/01/2002 | ODI | Australia | South Africa | Brisbane | not out | 22* | | | | | - |
| 22/01/2002 | ODI | Australia | South Africa | Sydney | | - | | | | | 1 |
| 26/01/2002 | ODI | Australia | New Zealand | Adelaide | c SP Fleming b DL Vettori | 30 | | | | | - |
| 29/01/2002 | ODI | Australia | New Zealand | Melbourne | cwk AC Parore b DJ Nash | 7 | 6.0 | - | 33 | - | - |
| 03/02/2002 | ODI | Australia | South Africa | Perth | b N Boje | 42 | 4.0 | - | 26 | - | - |
| 10/02/2002 | ING | New South Wales | Tasmania | Devonport | not out | 32* | | | | | - |
| 17/02/2002 | Tour | Australian XI | South Africa A | Potchefstroom | not out | 102* | | | | | - |
| | | | | | | - | | | | | - |
| 22/02/2002 | Test | Australia | South Africa | Johannesburg | c HH Gibbs b JH Kallis | 32 | | | | | 1 |
| | | | | | | - | | | | | - |
| 01/03/2002 | Tour | Australian XI | South Africa A | Port Elizabeth | cwk TL Tsolekile b D Pretorius | 4 | | | | | - |
| | | | | | | - | | | | | 1 |
| 08/03/2002 | Test | Australia | South Africa | Cape Town | b PR Adams | 0 | | | | | - |
| | | | | | b PR Adams | 14 | 3.0 | - | 16 | - | - |
| 15/03/2002 | Test | Australia | South Africa | Durban | cwk MV Boucher b PR Adams | 7 | | | | | - |
| | | | | | c JH Kallis b M Ntini | 42 | | | | | - |
| 22/08/2002 | County | Kent | Leicestershire | Canterbury | c DL Maddy b J Srinath | 16 | | | | | 1 |
| | | | | | | - | | | | | 1 |
| 04/09/2002 | County | Kent | Somerset | Taunton | c PD Bowler b PS Jones | 0 | 3.0 | - | 15 | - | - |
| | | | | | cwk RJ Turner b PS Jones | 37 | | | | | - |
| 11/09/2002 | County | Kent | Lancashire | Canterbury | lbw b G Chapple | 5 | | | | | 1 |
| | | | | | not out | 20* | | | | | - |
| 18/09/2002 | County | Kent | Yorkshire | Leeds | cwk RJ Blakey b RJ Kirby | 146 | | | | | - |
| | | | | | | - | | | | | - |
| 03/10/2002 | Test | Australia | Pakistan | Colombo | c Younis Khan b Saqlain Mushtaq | 31 | | | | | - |
| | | | | | lbw b Shoaib Akhtar | 0 | | | | | 2 |

| Start Date | Grade | Team | Opponent | Venue | How Out | Runs | O | M | R | W | Ct |
|---|---|---|---|---|---|---|---|---|---|---|---|
| 11/10/2002 | Test | Australia | Pakistan | Sharjah | c (sub)Imran Farhat b S Mushtaq | 0 | | | | | - |
| | | | | | | | | | | | 2 |
| 19/10/2002 | Test | Australia | Pakistan | Sharjah | not out | 103* | | | | | - |
| | | | | | | | | | | | - |
| 02/11/2002 | ING | New South Wales | South Australia | Adelaide | c RJ Harris b MA Higgs | 47 | | | | | - |
| 07/11/2002 | Test | Australia | England | Brisbane | c JP Crawley b AR Caddick | 7 | 4.0 | 2 | 5 | - | - |
| | | | | | c ME Trescothick b AR Caddick | 12 | | | | | - |
| 14/11/2002 | Pura | New South Wales | South Australia | Sydney | c DA Fitzgerald b PC Rofe | 135 | | | | | 2 |
| | | | | | lbw b BA Johnson | 7 | | | | | - |
| 21/11/2002 | Test | Australia | England | Adelaide | c MA Butcher b C White | 34 | 5.0 | 1 | 9 | - | - |
| | | | | | | | | | | | - |
| 29/11/2002 | Test | Australia | England | Perth | b AJ Tudor | 53 | | | | | - |
| | | | | | | | | | | | 1 |
| 19/12/2002 | Pura | New South Wales | Victoria | Sydney | c CL White b MWH Inness | 45 | 7.0 | 2 | 15 | 2 | - |
| | | | | | lbw b ML Lewis | 12 | | | | | - |
| 26/12/2002 | Test | Australia | England | Melbourne | cwk JS Foster b C White | 77 | 4.0 | - | 13 | 1 | - |
| | | | | | c MA Butcher b AR Caddick | 14 | 2.0 | - | 9 | - | 1 |
| 02/01/2003 | Test | Australia | England | Sydney | c MA Butcher b MJ Hoggard | 102 | 4.0 | 3 | 2 | 1 | - |
| | | | | | b AR Caddick | 6 | 6.0 | 2 | 5 | - | - |
| 19/01/2003 | ING | New South Wales | Western Australia | Coffs Harbour | cwk RJ Campbell b MW Clark | 12 | | | - | | - |
| 23/01/2003 | Pura | New South Wales | Western Australia | Newcastle | c MEK Hussey b MJ Nicholson | 20 | 4.0 | - | 13 | - | - |
| | | | | | cwk RJ Campbell b MW Clark | 0 | | | | | - |
| 02/02/2003 | ING | New South Wales | Tasmania | Drummoyne | c J Cox b DJ Marsh | 104 | | | | | - |
| 05/02/2003 | Pura | New South Wales | Victoria | Melbourne | b MWH Inness | 211 | | | | | - |
| | | | | | | | | | | | - |
| 09/02/2003 | ING | New South Wales | Victoria | Melbourne | c DJ Hussey b RJ Cassell | 4 | | | | | 1 |
| 12/02/2003 | ING | New South Wales | Western Australia | Perth | cwk RJ Campbell b BA Williams | 17 | | | | | 1 |
| 16/02/2003 | ING | New South Wales | South Australia | Homebush | run out (Blewett) | 71 | | | | | - |
| 23/02/2003 | ING | New South Wales | Western Australia | Perth | cwk RJ Campbell b BA Williams | 88 | | | | | 1 |
| 27/02/2003 | Pura | New South Wales | Western Australia | Perth | cwk RJ Campbell b MJ Nicholson | 24 | | | | | - |
| | | | | | lbw b MJ Nicholson | 2 | | | | | 2 |
| 06/03/2003 | Pura | New South Wales | Queensland | Sydney | b AA Noffke | 0 | | | | | 2 |
| | | | | | b AA Noffke | 138 | | | | | 1 |
| 14/03/2003 | Pura | New South Wales | Queensland | Brisbane | lbw b JH Dawes | 9 | | | | | 1 |
| | | | | | lbw b MS Kasprowicz | 56 | | | | | - |
| 05/04/2003 | Tour | Australian XI | Carib Beer XI | Georgetown | not out | 106* | | | | | - |
| | | | | | c and b OAC Banks | 2 | | | | | - |
| 10/04/2003 | Test | Australia | West Indies | Georgetown | lbw b M Dillon | 25 | | | | | - |
| | | | | | | - | 8.0 | 1 | 29 | - | - |
| 19/04/2003 | Test | Australia | West Indies | Port-of-Spain | | - | 7.0 | 2 | 16 | - | - |
| 26/04/2003 | Tour | Australian XI | Uni. of W.Indies | Bridgetown | cwk MG Sinclair b CD Collymore | 46 | | | | | 1 |
| | | | Vice Chancellor's XI | | cwk MG Sinclair b CH Gayle | 1 | | | | | - |
| 01/05/2003 | Test | Australia | West Indies | Bridgetown | b JJC Lawson | 115 | | | | | - |
| | | | | | | - | 4.0 | 1 | 6 | - | - |
| 09/05/2003 | Test | Australia | West Indies | St John's | c RD Jacobs b M Dillon | 41 | | | | | - |
| | | | | | not out | 45* | 5.0 | - | 25 | - | 1 |
| 18/07/2003 | Test | Australia | Bangladesh | Darwin | not out | 100* | | | | | - |
| | | | | | | - | | | | | - |
| 25/07/2003 | Test | Australia | Bangladesh | Cairns | not out | 156* | 5.0 | 3 | 4 | - | - |
| | | | | | | - | | | | | - |
| 09/10/2003 | Test | Australia | Zimbabwe | Perth | c and b SM Ervine | 78 | 5.0 | 1 | 10 | - | 1 |
| | | | | | | - | 8.0 | 2 | 26 | - | 1 |
| 17/10/2003 | Test | Australia | Zimbabwe | Sydney | c SV Carlisle b RW Price | 61 | 4.0 | - | 7 | - | - |
| | | | | | | | | | | | 1 |
| 26/10/2003 | ING | New South Wales | Victoria | Bowral | c AB McDonald b DJ Hussey | 38 | | | | | - |
| 02/11/2003 | ING | New South Wales | Western Australia | North Sydney | not out | 101* | | | | | - |

| Start Date | Grade | Team | Opponent | Venue | How Out | Runs | O | M | R | W | Ct |
|---|---|---|---|---|---|---|---|---|---|---|---|
| 04/11/2003 | Pura | New South Wales | Western Australia | Sydney | lbw b B Casson | 0 | | | | | - |
| | | | | | not out | 117* | 7.0 | - | 23 | 1 | - |
| 12/11/2003 | Pura | New South Wales | Tasmania | Hobart | c MJ Di Venuto b DG Wright | 157 | | | | | - |
| | | | | | lbw b DG Wright | 0 | 4.0 | - | 7 | - | - |
| 18/11/2003 | Pura | New South Wales | South Australia | Adelaide | c MJ Cosgrove b PC Rofe | 0 | 3.0 | - | 14 | - | - |
| | | | | | c JN Gillespie b MF Cleary | 31 | | | | | - |
| 23/11/2003 | ING | New South Wales | South Australia | Adelaide | c JM Davison b PC Rofe | 55 | 2.0 | - | 8 | - | 1 |
| 29/11/2003 | ING | New South Wales | Tasmania | Hobart | c (sub)GJ Denton b DJ Marsh | 14 | | | | | - |
| 04/12/2003 | Test | Australia | India | Brisbane | hit wicket b Zaheer Khan | 0 | 7.0 | 3 | 16 | - | - |
| | | | | | not out | 56* | | | | | - |
| 12/12/2003 | Test | Australia | India | Adelaide | b A Nehra | 30 | 9.0 | 2 | 15 | - | - |
| | | | | | c RS Dravid b SR Tendulkar | 42 | 4.0 | - | 10 | - | - |
| 26/12/2003 | Test | Australia | India | Melbourne | lbw b AR Kumble | 19 | 9.0 | - | 35 | 1 | - |
| | | | | | | - | | | | | - |
| 02/01/2004 | Test | Australia | India | Sydney | cwk PA Patel b IK Pathan | 40 | 2.0 | - | 6 | - | - |
| | | | | | c SR Tendulkar b AR Kumble | 80 | | | | | - |
| 09/01/2004 | Pura | New South Wales | Victoria | Newcastle | cwk PJ Roach b ML Lewis | 7 | | | | | - |
| | | | | | run out (Hussey) | 31 | | | | | - |
| 17/01/2004 | ING | New South Wales | Queensland | Homebush | c ML Love b JR Hopes | 48 | | | | | - |
| 21/01/2004 | ING | New South Wales | Western Australia | Perth | cwk RJ Campbell b MEK Hussey | 42 | | | | | - |
| 23/01/2004 | Pura | New South Wales | Western Australia | Perth | cwk MEK Hussey b BM Edmondson | 51 | | | | | - |
| | | | | | cwk MEK Hussey b KM Harvey | 21 | | | | | - |
| 30/01/2004 | ING | New South Wales | Queensland | Brisbane | cwk WA Seccombe b JR Hopes | 16 | | | | | - |
| 01/02/2004 | Pura | New South Wales | Queensland | Brisbane | c JP Maher b JH Dawes | 8 | | | | | - |
| | | | | | lbw b JH Dawes | 28 | | | | | - |
| 15/02/2004 | ING | New South Wales | South Australia | Drummoyne | c RJ Harris b MF Cleary | 14 | | | | | 1 |
| 17/02/2004 | Pura | New South Wales | South Australia | Sydney | lbw b SW Tait | 35 | | | | | 1 |
| | | | | | | - | | | | | 2 |
| 22/02/2004 | ING | New South Wales | Tasmania | Sydney | not out | 50* | | | | | - |
| 04/03/2004 | Pura | New South Wales | Queensland | Sydney | cwk CD Hartley b NM Hauritz | 65 | 1.0 | - | 8 | - | - |
| | | | | | c ML Love b JH Dawes | 9 | 1.0 | - | 13 | - | - |

# STEVE WAUGH'S FACTS AND FIGURES

## TEST CRICKET

(Statistics are at the end of Steve Waugh's final Test)

### Calendar Years

| Year | M | Inn | NO | Runs | H.S | 0 | 50 | 100 | Avrge | Ct | Overs | Mdns | Runs | Wkts | Avrge | Best |
|---|---|---|---|---|---|---|---|---|---|---|---|---|---|---|---|---|
| 1985 | 1 | 2 | - | 18 | 13 | - | - | - | 9.00 | - | 11.0 | 5 | 36 | 2 | 18.00 | 2/36 |
| 1986 | 11 | 17 | 4 | 391 | 79* | 3 | 3 | - | 30.08 | 10 | 174.3 | 34 | 563 | 16 | 35.19 | 5/69 |
| 1987 | 4 | 6 | - | 220 | 73 | 1 | 3 | - | 36.67 | 5 | 87.0 | 32 | 188 | 3 | 62.67 | 1/2 |
| 1988 | 8 | 13 | - | 395 | 91 | 1 | 3 | - | 30.38 | 7 | 248.5 | 47 | 718 | 19 | 37.79 | 5/92 |
| 1989 | 11 | 16 | 6 | 865 | 177* | 1 | 4 | 3 | 86.50 | 7 | 82.0 | 21 | 282 | 2 | 141.00 | 1/38 |
| 1990 | 6 | 8 | - | 114 | 25 | - | - | - | 14.25 | 2 | 27.0 | 12 | 63 | 2 | 31.50 | 1/7 |
| 1991 | 3 | 5 | 1 | 94 | 48 | - | - | - | 23.50 | 1 | 49.0 | 9 | 130 | 0 | - | - |
| 1992 | 2 | 4 | - | 69 | 38 | - | - | - | 17.25 | 1 | 23.0 | 5 | 66 | 2 | 33.00 | 1/14 |
| 1993 | 15 | 21 | 6 | 969 | 157* | 2 | 4 | 3 | 64.60 | 11 | 126.0 | 39 | 290 | 6 | 48.33 | 2/45 |
| 1994 | 8 | 13 | 3 | 677 | 164 | 2 | 5 | 1 | 67.70 | 7 | 131.5 | 44 | 238 | 15 | 15.87 | 5/28 |
| 1995 | 11 | 18 | 5 | 959 | 200 | 2 | 5 | 3 | 73.77 | 9 | 40.0 | 9 | 102 | 6 | 17.00 | 2/14 |
| 1996 | 4 | 7 | 2 | 459 | 170 | 1 | 4 | 1 | 91.80 | 1 | 50.1 | 19 | 96 | 6 | 16.00 | 4/34 |
| 1997 | 15 | 25 | 2 | 973 | 160 | 2 | 5 | 3 | 42.30 | 13 | 59.3 | 13 | 176 | 6 | 29.33 | 3/20 |
| 1998 | 11 | 20 | 5 | 906 | 157 | 1 | 3 | 3 | 60.40 | 4 | 65.0 | 18 | 157 | 4 | 39.25 | 2/8 |
| 1999 | 14 | 22 | 2 | 993 | 199 | 1 | 2 | 4 | 49.65 | 9 | 14.0 | 2 | 56 | 0 | - | - |
| 2000 | 7 | 11 | 3 | 479 | 151* | - | 1 | 2 | 59.88 | 5 | 7.0 | - | 20 | 0 | - | - |

| Year | M | Inn | NO | Runs | H.S | 0 | 50 | 100 | Avrge | Ct | Overs | Mdns | Runs | Wkts | Avrge | Best |
|---|---|---|---|---|---|---|---|---|---|---|---|---|---|---|---|---|
| 2001 | 13 | 19 | 2 | 894 | 157* | 1 | 2 | 4 | 52.59 | 9 | - | - | - | - | - | - |
| 2002 | 11 | 16 | 1 | 456 | 103* | 3 | 2 | 1 | 30.40 | 7 | 18.0 | 3 | 52 | 1 | 52.00 | 1/13 |
| 2003 | 12 | 15 | 4 | 876 | 156* | 1 | 3 | 4 | 79.63 | 4 | 85.0 | 20 | 206 | 2 | 103.00 | 1/2 |
| 2004 | 1 | 2 | - | 120 | 60 | - | 1 | - | 60.00 | - | 2.0 | - | 6 | 0 | - | - |

## Home and Away

| Tests | M | Inn | NO | Runs | H.S | 0s | 50 | 100 | Avrge |
|---|---|---|---|---|---|---|---|---|---|
| Home Tests | 89 | 140 | 20 | 5710 | 170 | 9 | 30 | 15 | 47.58 |
| Away Tests | 79 | 120 | 26 | 5217 | 200 | 13 | 20 | 17 | 55.50 |

## Captain

| Tests Best | M | Inn | NO | Runs | H.S | 0s | 50 | 100 | Avrge | Ct | Overs | Mdns | Runs | Wkts | Avrge |
|---|---|---|---|---|---|---|---|---|---|---|---|---|---|---|---|
| As Captain 1/2 | 57 | 83 | 12 | 3714 | 199 | 6 | 10 | 15 | 52.31 | 34 | 126.0 | 25 | 340 | 3 | 113.33 |
| As Non Captain 5/28 | 111 | 177 | 34 | 7213 | 200 | 16 | 40 | 17 | 50.44 | 78 | 1174.5 | 307 | 3105 | 89 | 34.89 |

| Test Opponents | Tests | Won | Lost | Draw | Tie | Won |
|---|---|---|---|---|---|---|
| Bangladesh | 2 | 2 | - | - | - | 100.00 |
| England | 9 | 8 | 1 | - | - | 88.89 |
| India | 10 | 5 | 3 | 1 | - | 50.00 |
| New Zealand | 6 | 3 | - | 3 | - | 50.00 |
| Pakistan | 6 | 6 | - | - | - | 100.00 |
| Sri Lanka | 3 | - | 1 | 2 | - | 0.00 |
| South Africa | 6 | 5 | 1 | - | - | 83.33 |
| West Indies | 12 | 9 | 3 | - | - | 75.00 |
| Zimbabwe | 3 | 3 | - | - | - | 100.00 |
| | | | | | | |
| Home Tests | 29 | 22 | 2 | 4 | - | 75.86 |
| Away Tests | 28 | 19 | 7 | 2 | - | 67.86 |
| **Total** | **57** | **41** | **10** | **6** | **-** | **71.92** |

## Most Successful Captains

| Captain | Captain | Won | Lost | Draw | Won |
|---|---|---|---|---|---|
| SR Waugh (Aus) | 57 | 41 | 10 | 6 | 71.92 |
| DG Bradman (Aus) | 24 | 15 | 3 | 6 | 62.50 |
| DR Jardine (Eng) | 15 | 9 | 1 | 5 | 60.00 |
| FMM Worrell (WI) | 15 | 9 | 3 | 2 | 60.00 |
| Waqar Younis (Pak) | 17 | 10 | 7 | 0 | 58.82 |
| LA Hassett (Aus) | 24 | 14 | 4 | 6 | 58.33 |
| MJ Brearley (Eng) | 31 | 18 | 4 | 9 | 58.06 |
| WM Woodfull (Aus) | 25 | 14 | 7 | 4 | 56.00 |
| IVA Richards (WI) | 50 | 27 | 8 | 15 | 54.00 |
| SM Pollock (SAf) | 26 | 14 | 5 | 7 | 53.85 |
| (Minimum 15 Tests) | | | | | |

## Australian Team Mates (70)

ME Waugh 108, IA Healy 101, SK Warne 96, GD McGrath 89, MA Taylor 85, DC Boon 79, RT Ponting 70, JL Langer 69, MJ Slater 67, AR Border 65, AC Gilchrist 49, ML Hayden 48, JN Gillespie 46, GS Blewett 44, CJ McDermott 43, MG Hughes 42, GR Marsh 40, DM Jones 37, B Lee 36, DR Martyn 35, PR Reiffel 33, SCG MacGill 29, BA Reid 23, TBA May 21, DW Fleming 20, AJ Bichel 19, MTG Elliott 19, TM Alderman 17, GRJ Matthews 17, CR Miller 17, MG Bevan 16, MS Kasprowicz 15, DS Lehmann 14, GM Ritchie 11, GF Lawson 10, PR Sleep 10, PL Taylor 10, TJ Zoehrer 10, AIC Dodemaide 8, MRJ Veletta 8, RJ Bright 7, TV Hohns 7, CG Rackemann 7, GC Dyer 6, BP Julian 6, GM Wood 6, DR Gilbert 5, ML Love 5, WB Phillips 5, SM Katich 5, J Angel 4, GD Campbell 4, GB Hogg 4, TM Moody 4, CD Matthews 3, GR Robertson 3, MR Whitney 3, BA Williams 3, NW Bracken 3, SH Cook 2, PE McIntyre 2, SA Muller 2, AC Dale 1, SP Davis 1, RG Holland 1, DW Hookes 1, MJ Nicholson 1, DM Wellham 1, P Wilson 1, S Young 1.

## Most Appearances as an Opponent

30 MA Atherton (Eng), AJ Stewart, (Eng); 28 CA Walsh (WI); 25 BC Lara (WI); 23 CEL Ambrose (WI); 22 N Hussain (Eng); 21 CL Hooper (WI); 19 JC Adams (WI), MA Butcher (Eng); 18 GA Gooch (Eng); 17 AR Caddick (Eng); 16 D Gough (Eng), G Kirsten (SAF), RB Richardson (WI), GP Thorpe (Eng); 14 CL Cairns (NZ), JP Crawley (Eng), MW Gatting (Eng), DI Gower (Eng); 13 SL Cambpell (WI), Ijaz Ahmed (Pak), DE Malcolm (Eng), RA Smith (Eng), Wasim Akram (Pak), RS Dravid (Ind), SC Ganguly (Ind), SR Tendulkar (Ind); 12 AA Donald (SAf), DL Haynes (WI), JH Kallis (SAf), Waqar Younis (Pak); 11 MD Crowe (NZ), PAJ De Freitas (Eng), ARC Fraser (Eng), Inzamam-ul-Haq (Pak), VVS Laxman (Ind), DK Morrison (NZ), MR Ramprakash (Eng), KR Rutherford (NZ), Salim Malik (Pak); 10 WJ Cronje (SAf), JE Emburey (Eng), GA Hick (Eng), RD Jacobs (WI), AH Jones (NZ), AC Parore (NZ), DN Patel (NZ), DJ Richardson (SAf), PCR Tufnell (Eng), JG Wright (NZ).

## Bowlers who Dismissed Steve Waugh

11 CEL Ambrose (WI).

10 AR Caddick (Eng).

5 KCG Benjamin (WI), IR Bishop (WI), ARC Fraser (Eng), D Gough (Eng), DE Malcolm (Eng).

4 JG Bracewell (NZ), M Dillon (WI), DW Headley (Eng), AR Kumble (Ind), CA Walsh (WI), Wasim Akram (Pak).

3 PR Adams (SAF), AB Agarkar (Ind), CL Cairns (NZ), PT Collins (WI), AA Donald (SAF), JE Emburey (Eng), RJ Hadlee (NZ), HarbhajanSingh (Ind), Iqbal Qasim (Pak), JH Kallis (SAF), CR Matthews (SAF), Mushtaq Ahmed (Pak), SM Pollock (SAF), Saqlain Mushtaq (Pak), Shoaib Akhtar (Pak), GC Small (Eng).

2 GR Dilley (Eng), CW Henderson (SAF), R Herath (SL), CC Lewis (Eng), MD Marshall (WI), Mohammad Akram (Pak), DK Morrison (NZ), SB O'Connor (NZ), DN Patel (NZ), BP Patterson (WI), NO Perry (WI), RJ Shastri (Ind), MC Snedden (NZ), PM Such (Eng), Tauseef Ahmed (Pak), AJ Tudor (Eng), DL Vettori (NZ), Waqar Younis (Pak), C White (Eng), NS Yadav (Ind).

1 Aamir Sohail (Pak, Aaqib Javed (Pak), KN Amalean (SL), MP Bicknell (Eng), SE Bond (NZ), S Chanderpaul (WI), EJ Chatfield (NZ), JV Coney (NZ), DG Cork (Eng), PAJ DeFreitas (Eng), SB Doull (NZ), PH Edmonds (Eng), SM Ervine (Zim), AP Gurusingha (SL), EE Hemmings (Eng), MJ Hoggard (Eng), AP Igglesden (Eng), AR Kapoor (Ind), L Klusener (SAF), GF Labrooy (SL), JJC Lawson (WI), MJ McCague (Eng), BM McMillan (SAF), CD McMillan (NZ), AD Mullally (Eng), MV Nagamootoo (WI), A Nehra (Ind), M Ntini (SAF), IK Pathan (Ind), MB Owens (NZ), RW Price (Zim), KR Pushpukamara (SL), CPH Ramanayake (SL), MN Samuels (WI), RL Sanghvi (Ind), BN Schultz (SAF), Shahid Afridi (Pak), Shakeel Ahmed (Pak), Shoaib Mohammad (Pak), L Sivaramakrishnan (Ind), RP Snell (SAF), J Srinath (Ind), CEL Stuart (WI), SR Tendulkar (Ind), PCR Tufnell (Eng), SLV Raju (Ind), BKV Prakash (Ind), W Watson (NZ), PJ Wiseman (NZ), Zaheer Khan (Ind), DNT Zoysa (SL).

## Batsmen Dismissed by Steve Waugh

6 CL Hooper (WI).

4 WJ Cronje (SAF).

3 BC Broad (Eng), MW Gatting (Eng), BM McMillan (SAF), JN Rhodes (SAF).

2 PAJ DeFreitas (Eng), GR Dilley (Eng), RS Dravid (Ind), GA Gooch (Eng), AC Hudson (SA), Inzamam-ul-Haq (Pak), MD Marshall (WI), IVA Richards (WI), IDS Smith (NZ), CA Walsh (WI).

1 MA Atherton (Eng), M Azharuddin (Ind), KJ Barnett (Eng), WKM Benjamin (WI), IT Botham (Eng), JV Coney (NZ), JJ Crowe (NZ), MD Crowe (NZ), DJ Cullinan (SAF), RG De Alwis (SL), PA De Silva (SL), PS De Villiers (SAF), HDPK Dharmasena (SL), AA Donald (SAF), PJL Dujon (WI), SP Fleming (NZ), JS Foster (Eng), DI Gower (Eng), CZ Harris (NZ), DL Haynes (WI), WK Hegg (Eng), Javed Miandad (Pak), ST Jayasuriya (SL), RS Kaluwitharana (SL), RWT Key (Eng), SMH Kirmani (Ind), PN Kirsten (SAF), BC Lara (WI), AL Logie (WI), CD McMillan (NZ), KS More (Ind), DK Morrison (NZ), AC Parore (NZ), CPH Ramanayake (SL), Rameez Raja (Pak), MR Ramprakash (Eng), A Ranatunga (SL), S Ranatunga (S), Rahid Latif (Pak), JF Reid (NZ), CJ Richards (Eng), RB Richardson (WI), RC Russell (Eng), KR Rutherford (NZ), RJ Shastri (Ind), Shoaib Mohammad (Pak), PV Simmons (WI), PL Symcox (SAF), GB Troup (NZ), DL Vettori (NZ).

## Century Partnerships

| Total | Wicket | Partner | Opponent | Venue | Series |
|---|---|---|---|---|---|
| 385 | (5th) | GS Blewett | South Africa | Johannesburg | 1996-97 |
| 332* | (5th) | AR Border | England | Leeds | 1993 |
| 281 | (5th) | RT Ponting | West Indies | Bridgetown | 1998-99 |
| 260* | (6th) | DM Jones | Sri Lanka | Hobart | 1989-90 |
| 250 | (4th) | DS Lehmann | Bangladesh | Cairns | 2003 |
| 239 | (5th) | RT Ponting | India | Adelaide | 1999-00 |
| 231 | (4th) | ME Waugh | West Indies | Kingston | 1994-95 |
| 208 | (5th) | AR Border | South Africa | Adelaide | 1993-94 |
| 207 | (4th) | ML Hayden | Zimbabwe | Perth | 2003-04 |
| 203 | (6th) | GS Blewett | England | Perth | 1994-95 |
| 200 | (5th) | GM Wood | West Indies | Perth | 1988-89 |
| 199 | (5th) | MJ Slater | New Zealand | Wellington | 1999-00 |
| 198 | (4th) | MJ Slater | Pakistan | Rawalpindi | 1998-99 |
| 197 | (3rd) | ME Waugh | England | The Oval | 2001 |
| 190 | (4th) | ME Waugh | England | Sydney | 1998-99 |
| 187 | (6th) | IA Healy | England | Brisbane | 1998-99 |

| Total | Wicket | Partner | Opponent | Venue | Series |
|---|---|---|---|---|---|
| 180* | (6th) | IA Healy | England | Manchester | 1993 |
| 177 | (6th) | AR Border | New Zealand | Christchurch | 1985-86 |
| 174* | (5th) | ML Love | Bangladesh | Cairns | 2003 |
| 159 | (5th) | AR Border | New Zealand | Brisbane | 1993-94 |
| 153 | (5th) | ME Waugh | England | Birmingham | 1993 |
| 153 | (4th) | ME Waugh | New Zealand | Perth | 1997-98 |
| 149 | (4th) | MA Taylor | Sri Lanka | Brisbane | 1989-90 |
| 147 | (7th) | MG Hughes | England | Leeds | 1989 |
| 146* | (6th) | GRJ Matthews | England | Adelaide | 1986-87 |
| 145 | (5th) | RT Ponting | South Africa | Melbourne | 1997-98 |
| 142* | (7th) | SK Warne | New Zealand | Brisbane | 1993-94 |
| 142 | (6th) | IA Healy | West Indies | Brisbane | 1996-97 |
| 142 | (5th) | SM Katich | India | Sydney | 2003-04 |
| 138 | (5th) | DM Jones | England | Leeds | 1989 |
| 135 | (5th) | GS Blewett | Pakistan | Brisbane | 1995-96 |
| 135 | (4th) | RT Ponting | Zimbabwe | Sydney | 2003-04 |
| 133 | (9th) | JN Gillespie | India | Kolkata | 2000-01 |
| 133 | (4th) | ME Waugh | England | Birmingham | 2001 |
| 132 | (5th) | RT Ponting | West Indies | Sydney | 2000-01 |
| 130 | (9th) | GF Lawson | England | Lord's | 1989 |
| 130 | (6th) | IA Healy | Sri Lanka | Adelaide | 1995-96 |
| 129 | (4th) | JL Langer | England | Melbourne | 2002-03 |
| 128* | (4th) | DR Martyn | India | Brisbane | 2003-04 |
| 126 | (5th) | DS Lehmann | Pakistan | Rawalpindi | 1998-99 |
| 124 | (6th) | AJ Bichel | West Indies | Bridgetown | 2002-03 |
| 123 | (4th) | ML Hayden | India | Chennai | 2000-01 |
| 121 | (5th) | MG Bevan | Pakistan | Karachi | 1994-95 |
| 121 | (4th) | JL Langer | India | Sydney | 1999-00 |
| 118 | (2nd) | DC Boon | West Indies | Sydney | 1992-93 |
| 117 | (7th) | PR Reiffel | Sri Lanka | Adelaide | 1995-96 |
| 116 | (4th) | ME Waugh | South Africa | Sydney | 1997-98 |
| 116 | (4th) | AR Border | New Zealand | Adelaide | 1987-88 |
| 115 | (5th) | RT Ponting | Sri Lanka | Melbourne | 1995-96 |
| 114 | (8th) | DW Fleming | Zimbabwe | Harare | 1999-00 |
| 114 | (6th) | DR Martyn | New Zealand | Wellington | 1999-00 |
| 113 | (5th) | AC Gilchrist | West Indies | Bridgetown | 2002-03 |
| 113 | (5th) | GS Blewett | West Indies | Kingston | 1994-95 |
| 112 | (5th) | RT Ponting | India | Calcutta | 1997-98 |
| 112 | (4th) | ME Waugh | West Indies | Kingston | 1998-99 |
| 109 | (6th) | IA Healy | Pakistan | Rawalpindi | 1994-95 |
| 108 | (7th) | SK Warne | India | Adelaide | 1999-00 |
| 108 | (6th) | IA Healy | South Africa | Cape Town | 1993-94 |
| 108 | (4th) | JL Langer | West Indies | Bridgetown | 1998-99 |
| 108 | (4th) | JL Langer | England | Adelaide | 1998-99 |
| 107* | (5th) | DR Martyn | England | The Oval | 2001 |
| 107 | (4th) | ME Waugh | England | Lord's | 2001 |
| 102 | (5th) | GS Blewett | West Indies | Melbourne | 1996-97 |
| 102 | (4th) | MJ Slater | West Indies | Sydney | 2000-01 |

## Most Appearances

| Player | Tests |
|---|---|
| SR Waugh (Aus) | 168 |
| AR Border (Aus) | 156 |
| CA Walsh (WI) | 132 |
| Kapil Dev (Ind) | 131 |
| AJ Stewart (Eng) | 130 |
| ME Waugh (Aus) | 128 |
| SM Gavaskar (Ind) | 125 |
| Javed Miandad (Pak) | 124 |
| IVA Richards (WI) | 121 |
| IA Healy (Aus) | 119 |

## Most Runs

| Batsman | Runs |
|---|---|
| AR Border (Aus) | 11174 |
| SR Waugh (Aus) | 10927 |
| SM Gavaskar (Ind) | 10122 |
| SR Tendulkar (Ind) | 8964 |
| BC Lara (WI) | 8916 |
| GA Gooch (Eng) | 8900 |
| Javed Miandad (Pak) | 8832 |
| IVA Richards (WI) | 8540 |
| AJ Stewart (Eng) | 8326 |
| DI Gower (Eng) | 8231 |

## Most Runs in Australia

| Batsman | Runs |
|---|---|
| AR Border (Aus) | 5743 |
| SR Waugh (Aus) | 5710 |
| DC Boon (Aus) | 4541 |
| GS Chappell (Aus) | 4515 |
| DG Bradman (Aus) | 4322 |
| ME Waugh (Aus) | 4019 |
| MA Taylor (Aus) | 3993 |
| RT Ponting (Aus) | 3348 |
| KD Walters (Aus) | 3065 |
| JL Langer (Aus) | 2960 |

## Most Runs by No. 5 Batsman

| Batsman | Runs |
|---|---|
| SR Waugh (Aus) | 5517 |
| M Azharuddin (Ind) | 3578 |
| A Flower (Zim) | 2488 |
| Yousuf Youhana (Pak) | 2258 |
| AR Border (Aus) | 2253 |
| CL Hooper (WI) | 2188 |
| IVA Richards (Ind) | 1917 |
| CH Lloyd (WI) | 1907 |
| Zaheer Abbas (Pak) | 1877 |
| A Ranatunga (SL) | 1689 |

## Most Runs by No. 6 Batsman

| Batsman | Runs |
|---|---|
| SR Waugh (Aus) | 2460 |
| HP Tillakaratne (SL) | 2087 |
| IT Botham (Eng) | 2029 |
| AW Greig (Eng) | 1760 |
| CH Lloyd (WI) | 1726 |
| RT Ponting (Aus) | 1713 |
| GS Sobers (WI) | 1609 |
| AR Border (Aus) | 1520 |
| CD McMillan (NZ) | 1411 |
| KD Walters (Aus) | 1404 |

## Most Centuries

| Batsman | 100s |
|---|---|
| SM Gavaskar (Ind) | 34 |
| SR Waugh (Aus) | 32 |
| SR Tendulkar (Ind) | 31 |
| DG Bradman (Aus) | 29 |
| AR Border (Aus) | 27 |
| GS Sobers (WI) | 26 |
| GS Chappell (Aus) | 24 |
| IVA Richards (WI) | 24 |
| Javed Miandad (Pak) | 23 |
| BC Lara (WI) | 23 |

## Most Half Centuries

| Batsman | 50s |
|---|---|
| AR Border (Aus) | 63 |
| SR Waugh (Aus) | 50 |
| ME Waugh (Aus) | 47 |
| GC Gooch (Eng) | 46 |
| MA Atherton (Eng) | 46 |
| SM Gavaskar (Ind) | 45 |
| IVA Richards (WI) | 45 |
| AJ Stewart (Eng) | 45 |
| Javed Miandad (Pak) | 43 |
| G Boycott (Eng) | 42 |
| BC Lara (WI) | 42 |

## Most Innings

| Batsman | Innings |
|---|---|
| AR Border (Aus) | 265 |
| SR Waugh (Aus) | 260 |
| AJ Stewart (Eng) | 235 |
| GC Gooch (Eng) | 215 |
| SM Gavaskar (Ind) | 214 |
| MA Atherton (Eng) | 212 |
| ME Waugh (Aus) | 209 |
| DI Gower (Eng) | 204 |
| DL Haynes (WI) | 202 |
| G Boycott (Eng) | 193 |

## Most Times Dismissed Bowled

| Batsman | Bowled |
|---|---|
| AR Border (Aus) | 53 |
| JR Reid (NZ) | 44 |
| GR Viswanath (Ind) | 41 |
| AJ Stewart (Eng) | 40 |
| SR Waugh (Aus) | 39 |
| WR Hammond (Eng) | 38 |
| TG Evans (Eng) | 37 |
| CA Walsh (WI) | 37 |
| GC Gooch (Eng) | 36 |
| IVA Richards (WI) | 36 |

## Most Ducks

| Batsman | 0s |
|---|---|
| CA Walsh (WI) | 43 |
| SK Warne (Aus) | 27 |
| CEL Ambrose (WI) | 26 |
| GD McGrath (Aus) | 26 |
| M Dillon (WI) | 25 |
| DK Morrison (NZ) | 24 |
| BS Chandrasekar (Ind) | 23 |
| SR Waugh (Aus) | 22 |
| M Muralidaran (SL) | 22 |
| Waqar Younis (Pak) | 21 |

## Most Scores in the 90s

| Batsman | 90s |
|---|---|
| SR Waugh (Aus) | 10 |
| MJ Slater (Aus) | 9 |
| AI Kallicharan (WI) | 8 |
| C Hill (Aus) | 6 |
| RB Kanhai (WI) | 6 |
| G Boycott (Eng) | 6 |
| CG Greenidge (WI) | 6 |
| Inzamam-ul-Haq (Pak) | 6 |

## Longest Career by an Australian

| Player | Days |
|---|---|
| ES Gregory | 8062 |
| RB Simpson | 7431 |
| DG Bradman | 7197 |
| WW Armstrong | 7162 |
| CG Macartney | 6818 |
| SR Waugh | 6582 |
| C Kellaway | 6567 |
| WW Blackham | 6485 |
| WW Bardsley | 6288 |
| WAS Oldfield | 5916 |

## Youngest to Play a 100 Tests

| Player | Years | Days |
|---|---|---|
| SR Tendulkar (Ind) | 29 | 134 |
| Kapil Dev (Ind) | 30 | 313 |
| DI Gower (Eng) | 31 | 111 |
| MA Atherton (Eng) | 32 | 133 |
| Javed Miandad (Pak) | 32 | 172 |
| SK Warne (Aus) | 32 | 176 |
| SR Waugh (Aus) | 32 | 214 |
| DB Vengsarkar (Ind) | 32 | 232 |
| AR Border (Aus) | 33 | 150 |
| IA Healy (Aus) | 33 | 275 |

## Most Man of the Match Awards

| Players | Awards |
|---|---|
| Wasim Akram (Pak) | 16 |
| CEL Ambrose (WI) | 14 |
| SR Waugh (Aus) | 14 |
| SK Warne (Aus) | 14 |
| M Muralidaran (SL) | 13 |
| BC Lara (WI) | 11 |
| SR Tendulkar (Ind) | 11 |
| JH Kallis (SAf) | 11 |
| PA De Silva (SL) | 10 |
| GD McGrath (Aus) | 10 |

## Mosts on Australian Venues

| Venue | Games | (Rank) | Runs | (Rank) |
|---|---|---|---|---|
| Adelaide Oval | 15 | ( 2nd) | 1056 | (2nd) |
| Bellerive Oval | 6 | ( 1st) | 272 | (5th) |
| Cairns | 1 | (=1st) | 156 | (2nd) |
| Darwin | 1 | (=1st) | 100 | (2nd) |
| Gabba | 17 | ( 1st) | 915 | (2nd) |
| M.C.G. | 17 | (=2nd) | 1284 | (2nd) |
| S.C.G. | 17 | (=1st) | 1084 | (4th) |
| W.A.C.A. | 15 | ( 2nd) | 843 | (3rd) |

# Australian First-Class Records

## Most Runs

| Batsman | Career | M | Inn | NO | Runs | H.S | 50 | 100 | Avrge |
|---|---|---|---|---|---|---|---|---|---|
| DG Bradman | 1927-28 - 1948-49 | 234 | 338 | 43 | 28067 | 452* | 69 | 117 | 95.14 |
| AR Border | 1976-77 - 1995-96 | 385 | 625 | 97 | 27131 | 205 | 142 | 70 | 51.38 |
| ME Waugh | 1985-86 - 2003-04 | 368 | 591 | 75 | 26855 | 229* | 133 | 81 | 52.04 |
| GS Chappell | 1966-67 - 1983-84 | 322 | 542 | 72 | 24535 | 247* | 111 | 74 | 52.20 |
| SR Waugh | 1984-85 - 2003-04 | 356 | 551 | 88 | 24051 | 216* | 97 | 79 | 51.95 |
| DC Boon | 1978-79 - 1999 | 350 | 585 | 53 | 23413 | 227 | 114 | 68 | 44.01 |
| KJ Greives | 1945-46 - 1964 | 490 | 746 | 79 | 22454 | 224 | 136 | 29 | 33.66 |
| SG Law | 1988-89 - 2003-04 | 294 | 487 | 55 | 22134 | 263 | 105 | 65 | 51.24 |
| RN Harvey | 1946-47 - 1962-63 | 306 | 461 | 35 | 21699 | 231* | 94 | 67 | 50.93 |
| RB Simpson | 1952-53 - 1977-78 | 257 | 436 | 62 | 21029 | 359 | 100 | 60 | 56.22 |
| TM Moody | 1985-86 - 2000-01 | 300 | 501 | 47 | 21001 | 272 | 94 | 64 | 46.26 |
| DS Lehmann | 1987-88 - 2003-04 | 229 | 389 | 27 | 20647 | 255 | 90 | 67 | 57.04 |

## MOST CENTURIES

| Batsman | Career | M | Inn | 100 | Inn/100 |
|---|---|---|---|---|---|
| DG Bradman | 1927-28 - 1948-49 | 234 | 338 | 117 | 2.89 |
| ME Waugh | 1985-86 - 2003-04 | 368 | 591 | 81 | 7.29 |
| SR Waugh | 1984-85 - 2003-04 | 356 | 551 | 79 | 6.97 |
| GS Chappell | 1966-67 - 1983-84 | 322 | 542 | 74 | 7.32 |
| AR Border | 1976-77 - 1995-96 | 385 | 625 | 70 | 8.92 |
| DC Boon | 1978-79 - 1999 | 350 | 585 | 68 | 8.60 |
| RN Harvey | 1946-47 - 1962-63 | 306 | 461 | 67 | 6.88 |
| DS Lehmann | 1987-88 - 2003-04 | 229 | 389 | 67 | 5.80 |
| ML Hayden | 1991-92 - 2003-04 | 233 | 402 | 66 | 6.09 |
| SG Law | 1988-89 - 2003-04 | 294 | 487 | 65 | 7.49 |
| TM Moody | 1985-86 - 2000-01 | 300 | 501 | 64 | 7.82 |
| JL Langer | 1991-92 - 2003-04 | 250 | 436 | 62 | 7.03 |
| RB Simpson | 1952-53 - 1977-78 | 257 | 436 | 60 | 7.27 |
| IM Chappell | 1961-62 - 1979-80 | 263 | 448 | 59 | 7.59 |
| AL Hassett | 1932-33 - 1953-54 | 216 | 322 | 59 | 5.46 |
| MG Bevan | 1989-90 - 2003-04 | 214 | 357 | 59 | 6.05 |
| DM Jones | 1981-82 - 1997-98 | 245 | 415 | 55 | 7.55 |
| W Bardsley | 1903-04 - 1926-27 | 250 | 376 | 53 | 7.09 |
| WM Lawry | 1955-56 - 1971-72 | 250 | 417 | 50 | 8.34 |
| RT Ponting | 1992-93 - 2003-04 | 166 | 277 | 50 | 5.54 |

## HIGHEST FIRST-CLASS PARTNERSHIPS

| 4th | 462* | DW Hookes & WB Phillips | South Australia v Tasmania, Adelaide, 1986-87 |
|---|---|---|---|
| 5th | 464* | ME Waugh & SR Waugh | New South Wales v Western Australia, Perth, 1990-91 |
| 1st | 456 | WH Ponsford & RE Mayne | Victoria v Queensland, Melbourne, 1923-24 |
| 2nd | 451 | WH Ponsford & DG Bradman | Australia v England, The Oval, 1934 |
| 8th | 433 | VT Trumper & A Sims | Australians v Canterbury, Christchurch, 1913-14 |
| 1st | 431 | MRJ Veletta & GR Marsh | Western Australia v South Australia, Perth, 1989-90 |
| 6th | 428 | MA Noble & WW Armstrong | Australians v Sussex, Hove, 1902 |
| 4th | 424 | IS Lee & SO Quin | Victoria v Tasmania, Melbourne, 1933-34 |
| 5th | 405 | SG Barnes & DG Bradman | Australia v England, Sydney, 1946-47 |

## MOST FIRST-CLASS APPEARANCES FOR NEW SOUTH WALES

| Player | Career | Games | | Player | Career | Games |
|---|---|---|---|---|---|---|
| GRJ Matthews | 1982-83 - 1997-98 | 135 | | KD Walters | 1962-63 - 1980-81 | 103 |
| PA Emery | 1987-88 - 1998-99 | 120 | | MA Taylor | 1985-86 - 1998-99 | 100 |
| GF Lawson | 1977-78 - 1991-92 | 115 | | J Dyson | 1975-76 - 1988-89 | 94 |
| ME Waugh | 1985-86 - 2003-04 | 108 | | MR Whitney | 1980-81 - 1993-94 | 94 |
| SJ Rixon | 1974-75 - 1987-88 | 107 | | SR Waugh | 1984-85 - 2003-04 | 93 |
| MG Bevan | 1990-91 - 2003-04 | 105 | | | | |

## MOST FIRST-CLASS RUNS FOR NEW SOUTH WALES

| Batsman | M | Inn | NO | Runs | H.S | 50 | 100 | Avrge |
|---|---|---|---|---|---|---|---|---|
| MG Bevan | 105 | 183 | 36 | 9309 | 216 | 35 | 37 | 63.33 |
| ME Waugh | 108 | 182 | 24 | 8416 | 229* | 39 | 25 | 53.27 |
| AF Kippax | 87 | 135 | 16 | 8005 | 315* | 18 | 32 | 67.27 |
| MA Taylor | 100 | 172 | 3 | 6997 | 199 | 38 | 17 | 41.40 |
| SR Waugh | 93 | 159 | 15 | 6946 | 216* | 26 | 22 | 48.24 |
| J Dyson | 94 | 170 | 17 | 6773 | 241 | 37 | 14 | 44.27 |
| KD Walters | 103 | 179 | 21 | 6612 | 253 | 30 | 19 | 41.84 |
| W Bardsley | 83 | 132 | 11 | 6419 | 235 | 27 | 20 | 53.04 |
| GRJ Matthews | 135 | 200 | 35 | 6266 | 184 | 32 | 9 | 37.98 |
| RB McCosker | 79 | 140 | 17 | 5998 | 168 | 30 | 19 | 48.76 |

# Bibliography

Geoff Armstrong, *A Century of Summers: 100 Years of Sheffield Shield Cricket*, Ironbark Press, Sydney, 1992.

Geoff Armstrong and Mark Gately, *The People's Game: Australia in International One-Day Cricket*, Ironbark Press, Sydney, 1994.

Richie Benaud, *The Appeal of Cricket: The Modern Game*, Hodder and Stoughton, London, 1995.

David Boon, *Under the Southern Cross: The Autobiography of David Boon*, HarperSports, Sydney, 1996.

David Boon and A. Mark Thomas, *Boon In the Firing Line: An Autobiography*, Pan Macmillan, Sydney, 1993.

Mike Coward and Michael Rayner, *Caribbean Odyssey: Australia and Cricket in the West Indies*, Simon and Schuster, Roseville, 1991.

Marc Dawson, *The Bumper Book of Cricket Extras*, Kangaroo Press, Kenthurst, 1993.

Philip Derriman (compiled), *Ashes From Ashes: How the 1989 Australians Recaptured Cricket's Greatest Prize*, ABC Books, Sydney, 1989.

Roland Fishman, *Calypso Cricket. The inside story of the 1991 Windies Tour*, Margaret Gee Publishing, Sydney, 1991.

Adam Gilchrist, *Walking to Victory: A Personal Story of the Ashes and World Cup Campaigns 2002-03*, Macmillan Australia, Sydney, 2003.

Adam Gilchrist with John Townsend, *One-Day Cricket: Playing the One-Day Game*, HarperSports, Sydney, 1999.

Edward Griffiths, *Kepler: The Biography*, Pelham Books, London, 1994.

Ian Healy, *Hands & Heals: The Autobiography*, HarperSports, Sydney, 2000.

David Hookes with Alan Shiell, *Hookesy*, ABC Books, Sydney, 1993.

Garrie Hutchinson (ed.), *Test Team of the Century: An Anthology of the Greatest Australian Test Players of the Twentieth Century*, HarperSports, Sydney, 2000.

Patrick Keane with Merv Hughes, *Merv, the Full Story*, HarperSports, Sydney, 1997.

Bill Lawry, *Bill Lawry's Great Cricket Joke Book*, Information Australia, Melbourne, 1998.

Geoff Lawson, *Henry: The Geoff Lawson Story*, Ironbark Press, Sydney, 1993.

Geoff Lawson and Mark Ray, *Geoff Lawson's Diary of the Ashes*, Collins/Angus & Robertson Publishers Australia, North Ryde, 1990.

Craig McDermott, *Strike Bowler*, ABC Books, Sydney, 1992.

Glenn McGrath with Daniel Lane, *Pacemaker: The inner thoughts of Glenn McGrath*, Ironbark Press, Sydney, 1998.

Kersi Meher-Homji, *Heroes of 100 Tests*, Rosenberg Publishing, Dural, 2003.

Rod Nicholson, *Border's Heroes: Return of the Ashes*, Magenta Press, Scoresby, 1989.

Roland Perry, *Captain Australia: A History of the Celebrated Captains of Australian Cricket*, Random House, Sydney, 2000.

Ken Piesse, *Warne: Sultan of Spin*, Modern Publishing Group, Melbourne, 1995.

Ricky Ponting and Brian Murgatroyd, *Ricky Ponting's World Cup Diary*, HarperSports, Sydney, 2003.

Mark Ray, *Border & Beyond*, ABC Books, Sydney, 1995.

Paul Reiffel, *Inside Out*, HarperSports, Sydney, 1998.

Paul Reiffel with Greg Baum, *The Dominators*, Hodder, Sydney, 2000.

Peter Roebuck, *Tangled Up in White: Peter Roebuck on Cricket*, William Heinemann Australia, Port Melbourne, 1990.

Bob Simpson, *The Reasons Why: A Decade of Coaching, a Lifetime of Cricket*, HarperSports, Sydney, 1996.

Michael Slater, *Slats Opens Up: Inside the World of Michael Slater*, HarperCollins, Sydney, 1997.

Mick Stephenson, *Bankstown Cricket Club 50 Not Out*, Bookworks Pty Ltd, Sydney, 2001.

Mark Taylor, *Taylor Made: A Year in the Life of Australia's Cricket Captain*, Pan Macmillan, Sydney, 1995.

Shane Warne with Richard Hobson, *My Autobiography*, Hodder & Stoughton, Sydney, 2001.

Steve Waugh, *Never Say Die: The Inspiration Behind an Epic Hundred*, HarperSports, Sydney, 2003.

Steve Waugh, *Captain's Diary 2002*, HarperSports, Sydney, 2002.

Steve Waugh, *Ashes Diary 2001*, HarperSports, Sydney, 2001.

Peter West and Wendy Wimbush, *The Battle For the Ashes '87*, London Daily Telegraph, London, 1987.

Mike Whitney, *Whiticism: Confessions of a Left Arm Quick*, Ironbark Press, Sydney, 1995.

Mike Whitney, *Quick Whit: The Mike Whitney Story*, Ironbark Press, Sydney, 1993.

*Tales from the Locker Room: Classic Stories of Australian Sport*, Ironbark Press, Sydney, 1993.

# Picture Credits

# Acknowledgments

To write this book I have drawn both on my own writings on Steve Waugh over the years — I was first published in the *Sydney Morning Herald* just after he wore the baggy green for the first time, and have followed his career since — and the writings of many others.

All of the books I used are listed in the Bibliography, but I am especially indebted to the wonderful work of such journalists as Greg Baum, Peter Roebuck, Robert Craddock, Martin Blake, Gideon Haigh, Kersi Meher-Homji, Malcolm Conn, Mark Ray, Daniel Williams and Malcolm Knox.

Beyond that I thank those Test cricketers of Steve Waugh's era who I spoke to, and both James Knight and Gregor Salmon for their valued work in helping with my research. I also thank Gregor for editing this book, and my valued colleague at the *Sydney Morning Herald*, Harriet Veitch, for straightening out my twisted sentences and giving valuable advice on the structure of the book as a whole.

The team at HarperCollins — especially Jenny Grigg, Tracey Gibson, Sophie Hamley, Ali Orman, Toby Forage, Natalie Winter, Anthony Vandenberg, Alison Urquhart and Shona Martyn were wonderful to work with.

Finally, I warmly thank Steve Waugh himself for the letter he wrote for the beginning of this book, and note what a useful source his own writings have been over the years.

Acknowledgments

SAFE SPEEDING. THERE'S NO SUCH THING.
BRADMAN STAND
AUS 3-170
KUMBLE 2/69
Commonwealth
video call
sport
LG

**HarperCollins*Publishers***

First published in Australia in 2004
by HarperCollins*Publishers* Pty Limited
ABN 36 009 913 517
A member of the HarperCollins*Publishers* (Australia) Pty Limited Group
www.harpercollins.com.au

Text copyright © Peter FitzSimons 2004

**HarperCollins*Publishers***
25 Ryde Road, Pymble, Sydney, NSW 2073, Australia
31 View Road, Glenfield, Auckland 10, New Zealand
77–85 Fulham Palace Road, London, W6 8JB, United Kingdom
2 Bloor Street East, 20th floor, Toronto, Ontario M4W 1A8, Canada
10 East 53rd Street, New York NY 10022, USA

FitzSimons, Peter.
  Steve Waugh
  Bibliography.
  ISBN 0 7322 7647 0.
  1. Waugh, Steve, 1965- . 2. Cricket captains - Australia -
  Biography. 3. Cricket players - Australia - Biography. 4.
  Cricket - Australia. I. Title.
796.358092

Creative direction by Jenny Grigg
Cover design by Jenny Grigg
Internal design by Anthony Vandenberg and Natalie Winter
Front cover photograph: AAP Image/Tony McDonough
Back cover photograph by Mark Baker © Picture Media/Reuters/Mark Baker
Photo research by Toby Forage (reporter/producer for NEWS.com.au),
  Tracey Gibson, Sophie Hamley and the HarperCollins Design Studio
Statistics prepared by Ross Dundas (Cricket Solutions)
Timeline prepared by Gregor Salmon (who, at the age of 11, was bowled
  out by Steve Waugh at Ingleburn Oval)
Typeset in Charter 10/13
Printed in China through Phoenix Offset on 128g matt art

5 4 3 2 1    04 05 06